in the best

in the best possible taste

THE CRAZY LIFE OF KENNY EVERETT

DAVID LISTER

BLOOMSBURY

For my Mother and Father

First published in Great Britain 1996

This paperback edition published 1997

Bloomsbury Publishing Plc, 38 Soho Square, London W1V 5DF

PICTURE SOURCES

BBC: pages 2 *bottom*, 5
Chris Harris/Rex Features: page 8 *bottom*
PA News Ltd.: page 6 *top left*
Rex Features: page 6 *top right*
Sun/Rex Features: page 10 *bottom*
Syndication International: page 8 *top*

A CIP catalogue record for this book
is available from the British Library

ISBN 0 7475 3083 1

10 9 8 7 6 5 4 3 2 1

Typeset by Hewer Text Composition Services, Edinburgh
Printed in Great Britain by Clays Ltd, St Ives plc

CONTENTS

ACKNOWLEDGEMENTS

I received invaluable co-operation from Kenny Everett's sister, Kate Horgan, and her husband, Conor, and from Kenny Everett's parents, Tom and Elizabeth Cole. All agreed to speak about him for the first time and not very long after his death, which cannot have been easy for them. I am also exceedingly grateful to Lee Everett Alkin, who went in detail over events which are still painful to her, and to her husband, John Alkin. I have quoted from, and am grateful to, the following four works: *Kinds of Loving* by Lee Everett Alkin; *The Custard Stops at Hatfield* by Kenny Everett and Simon Booker; *Pop Went the Pirates*, the exhaustive study of pirate radio by Keith Skues; and Brian Long's equally exhaustive unpublished research on Radio London. My considerable thanks to my two researchers, Nanci Lister and Sean Smith; to my agent, Simon Trewin at Sheil Land, for his encouragement; to Richard Dawes and Penny Phillips at Bloomsbury; and to the many people, famous and not so famous, who helped me, notably: Angela Bond, Dave Cash, Johnny Beerling, Barry Cryer, Tim Blackmore, Peter Brown, Derek Taylor, Aidan Day, Jonathan Morrish, Tony Olivestone, Ed Stewart, Eric and Jane Gear, Father William Hofton, Jo Gurnett, and many others, from Liverpool to the Sudan, who played a part.

PREFACE

On 30 January 1996 Paul McCartney opened the Liverpool Institute for the Performing Arts, a fame school for would-be musicians and technicians. Within the school is the radio studio of Kenny Everett, donated by his family to his home city: a symbol of how music, technical brilliance and inspired creativity can come together to delight millions. On the wall is the Sony Gold Award for lifetime achievement in broadcasting, and next to it a citation for excellence in television comedy from the Golden Rose of Montreux panel.

Not long afterwards I travelled to Western Australia, to where Everett's sister and parents had emigrated, to discover more about their talented but unpredictable and often outrageous relative. They were kind enough to see me and, for the first time ever, to speak about him on the record. This experience offered numerous insights into a man whose influence on music radio broadcasting was unrivalled, just as my conversations with his ex-wife and close friends illuminated a private life that was a helter-skelter of emotions and activity.

Kenny Everett was one of the funniest and most inventive broadcasters that Britain has produced. Yet he was also an angst-ridden depressive who tried to take his own life. Kenny Everett was a rebel who defied the establishment at every turn, his irreverence more than once earning him the sack. Yet he was also deemed a Thatcherite when he appeared notoriously at a Conservative election rally. Kenny Everett was a glittering socialite who hung out with some of pop music's most dazzling icons: the Beatles in the sixties, Elton John in the seventies, Freddie Mercury in the eighties. Yet he suffered continual crises of confidence over his appearance, his ability and his popularity.

He was a man who for fourteen years was married to an attractive sixties swinger. With her at his side he publicly extolled the bliss of matrimony. Yet this marriage swung from passionate romance to bitter vitriol and culminated in his 'coming out' as a homosexual and a bitter estrangement which resulted in husband and wife never speaking again. He wrote and spoke often about growing up in a Liverpool 'slum' and being unable to communicate with his parents. Yet, as we shall see, this was nonsense. He had a normal childhood, wanted for nothing and was as devoted to his family as they were to him.

The contradictions in the life of Kenny Everett are as bewildering as the innovative and precocious talent which at times single-handedly transformed the fledgeling art of music radio. These same skills made him a household name when they were transferred to television, where his zany shows won massive audiences with their array of original and outlandish characters, sexually provocative dancers and surreal scripts which harked back to the best traditions of music hall yet broke new ground in the use of the medium. His television audience included the heir to the throne. The Princess of Wales was to tell Everett that her husband used to shut himself in his study to watch the programmes, and she would hear roars of laughter.

At the time of writing, the television station UK Gold has for some time been transmitting sketches from Everett's TV shows every night of the week. A year after his death, and eight years after his last television shows, he is the only comedian of any nationality whose work is being broadcast every single night of the week to British audiences.

When he died, on 4 April 1995, the sincere and deeply affectionate tributes to him demonstrated the high regard in which this innovation and this talent were held. 'Kenny Everett was quite simply a genius . . . and he was the major force in completely changing radio,' said one of the first claimants to his mantle of radio lunacy, Noel Edmonds. 'He was the most original figure who ever performed on British radio,' said a later pupil, Chris Tarrant. 'He was a brilliant man and comic genius,' said his long-time friend, Elton John. Everett's last employer, Richard Park, director of programmes at London's Capital Radio, summed up all the column inches by concluding simply: 'Kenny Everett was the best DJ this country has ever produced.'

It's hard to recall that there was once a time when radio disc jockeys were 'presenters', merely there to introduce the records they played, or that to do this they read from a script and, by Jove, read it in their best, starched BBC English. Or if they worked for Radio Luxembourg they spoke in made-to-measure transatlantic accents. To be just an enthusiastic Liverpool kid who loved music and had a great sense of humour and be a radio disc jockey was unheard of before Everett.

It's also hard to recall that, before him, disc jockeys in Britain had never used jingles or dreamt up comic characters with daft voices. Everett changed all that, composing, mixing and usually singing the now all-pervasive jingle. But then it's hard to recall that there was a time when the BBC was only ever called the BBC and not the 'Beeb', the word which Everett also invented and has now passed into the language.

Actually, it's not quite accurate to say that Everett always wrote his own jingles. On one occasion the Beatles composed and sang a jingle for his radio show. Such was his pre-eminence in his profession.

The outpouring of affection for Everett after his death was not solely because his manic voice, mischievous face and cult television series evoked happy memories of more innocent, innovative and hopeful times. His life itself was an embodiment of some of the social changes that occurred over a long and eventful era; punctuation marks, if you like, in the lives of his listeners and viewers.

His was one of the prime voices associated with pop and rock music at a time when pop was *the* most vital and influential cultural force. He was, superficially at least, a rebel in the decade when all youth heroes had to be rebels. He was a comic, yet his humour was innocent, never hostile, malicious or snide. Rather it was 'cuddly', to use the description he always liked to apply to himself.

But later in life Cuddly Ken was to go a step further than nearly any of his contemporaries from the sixties youth explosion. He came out as gay, at the same time becoming something of a role model for gay young people in his insistence that his desire was not to proselytize, lobby or campaign, but to live the life of a normal, everyday, Radio Ga Ga music nut who just happened to fancy men rather than women – though, as it happens, beyond the glare of publicity he was to live his new life to dangerous, indeed fatal, excess.

His final public declaration found him embodying the last tragic curse of that era: Aids, the unholy revenge of some malignant force against the permissive society.

It is as an extraordinary broadcaster that Kenny Everett should and will be remembered. But the contradictions in his life cannot be divorced from his achievement. He was far from being the first funny man to suffer from loneliness, depression and suicidal impulses. But perhaps he was the first to find release from those dark, brooding spirits and cloying neuroses in the claustrophobic isolation of a radio studio, a place he turned into a magic kingdom of fantasy and comic invention, perhaps the only place where he could be truly happy.

His early heroes, the Goons, had depended on a group dynamic in the studio for their comic inspiration. But Everett plucked his fantasies from inside his own head and found in that most curious communion — the communion between disembodied voice and millions of unseen and unknown listeners — a source of pleasure, happiness and fun that banished his depressive demons — at least until the end of the show.

The story of Kenny Everett is, in part, the story of repression and its results. His denial of his homosexuality over many years, coupled with his sense of guilt about it after a religious upbringing, meant that he channelled much of his pent-up energy into his art. Indeed, his talent and output were undoubtedly at their peak when he was privately in the depths of despair. The ending of years of repression resulted in a hedonistic lifestyle and a deliberate choice of relationships that brought pleasure and pain, both mental and physical.

Years earlier he had sought a much deeper, infinitely more spiritual fulfilment. It was in a world so far divorced from the instant gratification of pop music and Radio 1, that even to imagine the young Everett as part of it demands a supreme effort of will. When he was twelve he enrolled in a seminary to train as a Roman Catholic missionary to the poor and starving in Africa. The head of that school, whom I traced to the Sudan, where he is a priest, still remembers the young prankster from Liverpool who wanted to be a missionary.

For Kenny Everett, it was an episode in his life which afterwards he only referred to in passing, and then simply to ridicule and dismiss it. It had not, he assured anyone who asked – and few did – affected him in any way. When he left the missionary school, he also left behind any pretence of practising the Catholic faith of his parents; and, like many of his generation, he mocked and rejected organized religion.

Aids is a cruel illness. And it struck Everett cruelly. He contracted TB and pneumonia. He was constantly being sick and, towards the very end, walking and talking were debilitating efforts. But shortly before his death he found serenity in a manner that would have startled his friends and fans. The madcap entertainer who for thirty years had castigated religion asked to see a priest.

1

SKIPPING TO STARDOM

'I spent so much time talking to myself in Liverpool that I probably developed a line of patter.'

Everett on Radio 4's *Desert Island Discs*,
23 October 1993

The midwife who delivered the future Kenny Everett would have been obliged to have a name that could belong in a *Goon Show* sketch. And so she did. Florence Nightingale Robinson officiated at the home of her next-door neighbours, Tom and Lily Cole, at 14 Hereford Road in the Liverpool suburb of Seaforth, and little Maurice (both the adjective and the name were to be sources of annoyance to him throughout his childhood) emerged at three a.m. on Christmas Day 1944.

Apparently he didn't like what he saw. Years later he said he hated Liverpool 'from the moment I came out – of my mum'. He remembered it as 'cruddy'; it was grey, it was bleak, it was industrial, it was full of yobs and bullies who challenged you with: 'Oy, what the bluddy 'ell er yooo lookin' at?' 'Before you knew it,' he said, 'your face was all over the floor.' People wanted to thump you if you so much as ventured out into the street. And when your parents name you Maurice after your grandfather and spell it in the French way, and you're painfully thin and notably short to boot, what chance have you got?

Had he been born fifty years later there might have been something in that view. Hereford Road now is a characterless thoroughfare at the edge of a dual carriageway in an area full of the symptoms of the ill-thought-out urban regeneration which turns into urban blight. High-rise blocks, vandalism, petty crime, few recreational facilities and a lack of community spirit characterize such areas, and like so many other urban sprawls, it is not a place where parents allow their children to play in the street.

But as the Second World War neared its conclusion, and in the decade that followed before the insultingly named slum clearance, which actually created slums from well-tended, crime-free neighbourhoods, Hereford Road was completely different: a neat, suburban street of terraced houses, with back and front gardens, tiny but well cared for. All the residents knew each other; the children played together in the street and local park and best of all on the 'beach': the sandhills beside the Mersey that were just across the road.

A new baby in the street was a special event; and neighbours took it in turn to take Maurice in his pram to the park. Florence Nightingale Robinson's daughter Bunty, who, half a century later, still lives at number sixteen, did exactly that. 'I remember that Christmas Day my mum went next door to help Mrs Cole. Maurice became the new baby in the road. I used to take him in his pram to the park across the road called Potters Barn. If there was a new baby in the road, you would take them out for a walk.'

Hereford Road always knew there was a war going on. Since 1941 German warplanes had made the Liverpool docks a prime target, and bomb damage was everywhere. All the houses in the street had suffered some damage, and number thirteen, opposite the Coles, had had its roof blown off. The railings from every house in Hereford Road had been taken for the war effort. And at the end of the street was the large Seaforth barracks, which served as a home for American servicemen.

Maurice's parents were a popular couple. Tom was a tugboat mate on the Mersey. Elizabeth, known as Lily, later ran a sweetshop. Two nights a week they joined the locals at the Doric, a pub at the end of their street where a primitive form of karaoke took place. A microphone was brought round to each customer, who performed the song of their choice. The couple mixed in well and were well liked, but their real focus was their children: Maurice and his sister Cathy, just two years older. For until their arrival a family was something that Mrs Cole had never properly known in her life, a life blighted by tragedy that few outside the Cole family circle ever knew.

When Lily Cole, born Elizabeth Haugh, was herself two years old, her sister Jane, a year older, died in nightmarish circumstances. Jane was all but worshipped by her father, James, an engineer. He adored his first child and could not see enough of her. One afternoon Jane's mother was pushing her on a swing when her father came into view. Jane waved as soon as she saw him, and as she did so, fell from the swing, smashing her head against the concrete. The toddler contracted meningitis and quickly died. The whole family was devastated, but no grief could equal that of her father. For the next six months James Haugh carried his dead daughter's tiny shoes in his breast pocket. At the end of those six months, he was dead himself. Even the doctors said they could cite no reason for his death but a broken heart.

When Elizabeth was fourteen her mother died of heart failure. She had lost all her immediate relatives and went to live with her aunt. What she did not lose was a phobia of funerals. She would never attend another in her life, she pledged to herself. Had her own son's funeral more than half a century later been in the same city, rather than on the other side of the world, it is unlikely that she could have brought herself to go.

As well as tragedy there was some exoticism in Maurice's ancestry. His mother's grandfather had been an interpreter to the Earl of Sligo in Ireland. And his paternal grandfather, Maurice, was a Liverpool character. Tall and dapper, he always dressed in a three-piece suit and grey Homburg, and carried a walking cane with an ivory top. He was actually from Devon, where he ran a farm and abattoir which supplied Dartmoor prison with meat. He went to Liverpool to catch the steamship to emigrate to Australia, but his mother, who was with him, became ill and during her illness he gambled away most of his inheritance, and stayed. Seaforth, all parkland and beach, took his fancy.

And parkland and beach it still was when Maurice and Cathy grew up. Ged Ormesher, a friend who lived across the road, recalls: 'When we were children it was all sandhills. That's where you spent your summer holidays: on the sandhills. A bottle of pop and some butties.' Like most childhoods in the late forties and early fifties, theirs was quiet, innocent and strictly controlled. Maurice and Cathy never went out in the evenings, and during the day they played with their friends in the street or the park or on the beach, lost in games that now resonate with a nostalgic innocence, games that have long disappeared from the daily round of a generation reared on multimedia entertainments.

Sharon Ormesher, who was later to sit next to Maurice at school, recalls those street games. 'We used to play Farmer Farmer. One person would stand alone on one side of the street and be the farmer. The other children would all be on the opposite side. Then we used to say: "Farmer, farmer can we cross your waters?" And he used to say: "Not unless you've got the colour blue or Not unless you're wearing a ribbon in your hair." And we used to play Queeny-I: "Queeny-I, Queeny-I, who's got the ball? I haven't got it, it isn't in my pocket. Queeny-I, Queeny-I, who's got the ball?" Then you used to throw it behind you and whoever caught the ball would put it behind them. Then the thrower had to guess who had the ball.'

The more sporty games didn't really appeal to Maurice. He seemed to be smaller than everyone else, and a slower runner. He was certainly much quieter. Ged Ormesher, Sharon's older brother, who, like Bunty Robinson, also stayed put in Hereford Road, says: 'Maurice took after his father, Tommy, who was a very quiet man. Maurice was such a quiet boy, he just blended into the background. You didn't know he was there until you actually saw him. He didn't strike you as being a happy boy because he was so quiet. You never heard him laugh a lot. He used to smile, did Maurice. You could get a smile out of him but never a hearty laugh.'

Maurice may not have looked happy to the boys in the street; but then even at a very young age he didn't much like socializing. He was happiest at home with his parents and with his sister, who unreservedly doted on him. 'We were very close as kids,' she says, looking back now, 'incredibly close. I was mad about him. He was gorgeous. He was like my doll. He had lovely, curly blond hair. We had bicycles and skates and a tent we used to put up in Potters Barn. We always went round together. Sometimes other friends came with us on their skates and we made these great big long snakes.'

They were innocent times with innocent entertainment. Maurice and Cathy used to go on walks with their father every Sunday to a park in the Waterloo district of Liverpool, where there was a lake, or another park where there was a duck pond, because Maurice had a little boat with sails. Sometimes his father took them on the old overhead railway, now demolished, which ran from the docks to Bootle. That was particularly exciting. There were fourteen miles of docks then, and the children could watch the *Mauretania* and other grand liners departing. Their father also took them on the ferry across the Mersey, and with a special pride they all shared, on to his tugboat with its polished brass.

There were other treats. An annual carnival lit up the local streets. And every summer a circus would set up at Potters Barn. The children would watch it being assembled and talk to the performers. Maurice's family knew for certain he was a happy boy. They only had to hear him singing in the bath or, to Cathy's embarrassment, full-throated on the top of the bus when they went to Bootle to visit his aunt. 'He was a very happy child,' she says. 'He used to sing his head off.'

At home, Maurice and Cathy had what might now be called a strict upbringing, but was in fact little different from that of most households at the time. Their parents were keen to see they were 'well brought up', and politeness was expected at all times. Tommy Cole was full of adages such as 'Do as you would be done by' or 'Children should be seen and not heard', and stories like that of Robert the Bruce and the spider were trotted out with regularity to illustrate the need for perseverance. But all this was viewed with great affection by the children, who knew their father to be an extremely gentle and stoical man.

As the then Cathy Cole remembers: 'Maurice was very happy within the family unit. He didn't have many friends and loved being around the house. We were a very close, very loving family. It actually used to annoy us that our parents never argued. Perhaps it was too overprotective. Perhaps we were too cloistered, too sheltered. When we finally left home we were very innocent.'

Every Sunday the Coles went to Mass at the nearby church of St Thomas of Canterbury, and the parish priest took tea with them at least once a week, just as he or one of his fellow-priests would visit the other households in the predominantly Catholic suburb. But it was not, despite Maurice's protestations in later years, a strictly religious household. There were no prayers at night, no visits to confession.

Most of the religious instruction came from school. When Maurice was five, he was enrolled at St Edmund's Primary School. The headmistress was a Miss Pierce, prim and ferocious. Like a moment in a Dickens novel, at the start of every week the partitions that divided the classrooms would be drawn back, and Miss Pierce would rise like a galleon and freeze the children with a look that promised divine retribution for any sinner, before quizzing her charges on the sacraments. It was a moment both Cathy and Maurice dreaded. This was the weekly Mass register; and the whole school went to Mass each week. They didn't have far to go: church and school were in the same building.

Maurice went to school each day with Cathy. A fellow-pupil was Mike Ahern, later to become a Capital Radio DJ. He still bears the scars. Maurice was playing with a brick one morning (that's all there was to play with in Liverpool, he later observed) and threw it over a wall, hitting the unfortunate Ahern.

For Maurice, school just filled in the hours till he and Cathy could be back home. He was still the baby of the family, and his mother would dress him up at home in little dicky bows and gleaming white trousers and white shirt which became less gleaming the time Maurice went on a hunt for Father Christmas up the chimney. That little escapade resulted in a wallop.

Cathy had a close friend, Margaret Terry, whose younger brother, Peter, became Maurice's best pal. Peter Terry was a prankster and certainly encouraged Maurice to be the same. The four played together all the time, and soon some of the best pranks were originating from Maurice's brain. The local parish priest, Father McKiernan, was a regular visitor and had a habit of pulling Margaret's plaits when he saw her. When Margaret had her hair cut, Maurice persuaded her to keep the plaits. He fastened them on to her head lightly, and when the priest gave them his usual irritating tug at the end of his visit, they came off in his hand. Margaret let rip with a well-rehearsed scream, Maurice and Cathy looked horrified and the priest left in consternation as the children burst into hysterics.

It was by no means Maurice's only practical joke. On one occasion he, Ged Ormesher and another boy, Sidney Abbot, decided to tie a piece of string round the toe of Ged's younger brother, Mick, and take the string right across the road and into Sidney's house, then diagonally across the road again to Maurice's toe. The idea was that whichever of the boys woke up first would yank the string, which would pull the big toe of the others and wake them up too. It was the ultimate Heath Robinson alarm clock, or would have been if Mrs Ormesher hadn't discovered the string in the night and taken her scissors to it.

Generally, though, Maurice was happier listening and watching than taking centre stage. His favourite outing was the weekly visit with Cathy to Saturday-morning pictures at the local Odeon for sixpence a week, half of Maurice's pocket money. The cinema ran a competition before the film and both Cathy and Maurice won it: Cathy sang 'Old Father Thames' and Maurice won a skipping contest. It is hard in the age of multiplexes to imagine the packed Odeon having to wait patiently for Zorro while this little boy skipped the rope 280 times on stage. But, though presumably bored out of their minds, they applauded politely.

They applauded rather more enthusiastically when Maurice, who was a member of the local scout troop, had a part as a woman in the annual scout show. He borrowed a red corduroy pinafore dress from his sister, wore white ankle socks and black patent-leather shoes, and appeared beneath a long blonde wig with two bunches and red bows. Some of the audience were completely taken in, thinking he was a girl. One parent gasped when Maurice took off his wig at the end. 'It was the first intimation I ever got that he was actually brilliant,' says his sister. 'He had such stage presence. The whole show seemed to revolve around him.'

If Saturday-morning pictures was the one adventure away from home that Maurice looked forward to, his favourite activity was being at home listening to the radio or playing records. He began to buy 78s, mostly classical, at threepence a time from Rosie's junk shop next door to St Edmund's, and played them on his Kiddygram, a plastic toy record player, often spinning them round with his finger until they reached approximately the required number of revolutions per minute. George Butterworth's sweet melody *The Banks of Green Willow* was the first record he bought. After that he would sometimes buy them at the rate of one a day.

The undisputed highlight of the week was when the whole family gathered around the Marconiphone wireless in the living room, listening to either tales of Dick Barton the private investigator or Maurice's absolute favourite, *The Goon Show*. The off-the-wall humour of Spike Milligan, Peter Sellers, Harry Secombe and Michael Bentine was a revelation to him.

At night he would be in his bedroom listening to his own radio, usually to the Home Service. The announcers, with their plummy but cosy BBC accents, seemed so remarkably reassuring somehow, especially last thing at night. His later, probably inaccurate, memory had the announcers talking him into a serene sleep as they said the gas lamps were flickering and it was time to go to bed. As he grew older and changed from the Home Service to tune in instead to Radio Luxembourg on the latest technology – his red plastic Philips transistor, which had just come out – he still drifted off to sleep with a piece of cosy, quaint Englishness in his ears. The broadcasts closed with the nostalgic, lilting lullaby 'At the End of the Day' by Steve Conway. It was, thought Maurice, like Ovaltine for your ears.

At the age of eleven Maurice, who failed his eleven–plus examinations, moved on to St Bede's, an austere-looking secondary modern. His sister can't recall him ever being seriously bullied, but agrees that 'maybe he felt intimidated. He wasn't a big chap, and he wasn't all that sporty. He was always a bit of a moocher.' And Maurice quickly learned that the way to fend off bullies himself was to make them laugh. He began to keep a repertoire of jokes in his head.

Sharon Ormesher, who sat next to him at St Bede's, and stood opposite him in the regular country-dancing sessions at school, for all the world like a scene from *Seven Brides for Seven Brothers*, remembers being continually amused by her neighbour and dancing partner. 'He was able to blow all different sorts of raspberries. He called them Tudor and Elizabethan and Jacobean.' She loved sitting next to Maurice (who years later gave her a few name-checks on the radio) because, despite his own doubts about his intelligence, he was one of the brightest boys in the A stream. He was clever and quick-witted, and the teachers always enjoyed teaching him.

'I'll tell you what he was really good at,' says Sharon now. 'You know in the Holy Bibles you get all that inscription. He was absolutely brilliant at that. His handwriting was beautiful.'

By the age of twelve Maurice was an altar boy and, thanks to having perfect pitch, a choirboy at church. He and Cathy still went to Mass every week: the stern religious reminders of Miss Pierce had merely been superseded by the curates from St Peter and St Paul Church, who came in to teach at St Bede's; and both children belonged to Catholic youth groups. Cathy was in the Children of Mary, where she would do shopping for the elderly. Maurice was in a male equivalent.

One afternoon the two of them, and most of their friends, were booked on a coach to go to a monastery in the countryside where there was a vocational exposition – a recruitment drive for religious orders. The various orders had stalls selling their missions. Brother and sister looked but did not buy. But Peter Terry did. He signed on with the Verona Fathers and announced to his wide-eyed friends on the coach that he would be joining their school in Yorkshire to be educated to become a missionary in darkest Africa. There was considerable excitement in the community at Peter's decision, though for Maurice it meant above all the loss of one of his few close friends at St Bede's.

When Peter came back to Liverpool for his first end-of-term break, he regaled Maurice, Cathy and Margaret with stories about the St Peter Clavier junior missionary school at Stillington Hall, the school that the Verona Fathers ran. It was a grand stately home in beautiful countryside. The boys had the run of the house, and spent their free time catching moles and hedgehogs and pilfering apples from a nearby orchard. Even the God stuff wasn't so bad, he said.

For Maurice, contemplating another term dodging bullies, enduring lessons and skiving off sport at his bleak secondary modern, the thought of joining Peter in scrumping apples in the country was too great a temptation to resist. And, while religion came a low third to radio and music in his life, he was interested enough to give it a go. He begged his parents to write a letter to the Verona Fathers asking if he could enrol.

There would be a uniform to buy and termly fees to pay. It would be difficult, but Lily and Tom Cole had been careful with their money and were only too happy to spend what they had on the school fees if that was what Maurice wanted. Tom had been promoted from tugboat mate to captain, and Lily now owned a sweetshop which also had a repository selling religious artefacts. So they found the money to fund Maurice's sudden new enthusiasm, which they were secretly rather delighted about anyway. But first he had to be vetted. The Verona Fathers checked him out with the local parish priest, who swallowed his pride over the incident of the pulled-off plaits and gave the whole family a glowing report.

The next term Maurice set off for Yorkshire and a life in holy orders.

2

WHERE CHRIST'S PIONEERS ARE MADE

'I remember the first summer evening I had a peep at the grounds, a strong pleasant scent of lilies greeted me on entering the garden; there were hundreds of them, all beautiful white Yorkshire lilies. I soon thought that also Stillington Hall aims at producing other and better lilies – the pure white souls of boys for the missionary priesthood.'

An old boy of Stillington Hall writing
in the *African Missions* magazine

The eyes of twelve-year-old Maurice Cole from Liverpool must have nearly popped out of his head when he arrived at Stillington Hall. The picturesque lawns of the former stately home in its wooded park afforded an uninterrupted view across the Yorkshire landscape to the towers of York Minster, ten miles to the south.

At the main entrance was the house's coat of arms with the motto *Esse Quam Videri* – To be rather than to seem. The Palladian brick mansion could be traced back to the Lord Mayor of York, who bought it in 1649. The adjoining parish of Stillington, on the banks of the River Foss, once had as its vicar the great Irish writer Laurence Sterne, best known for the novel *Tristram Shandy*, who baptized his daughter Lydia in the church.

The Verona Fathers, who bought the house after the Second World War to use as a seminary for training missionaries to Africa, were, and still are, a thriving Roman Catholic order following the spiritual teachings of Bishop Daniel Comboni, who was born in 1831 in northern Italy. Comboni dedicated his life to bringing the gospel to the people of central Africa and training Africans to become priests. Consecrated bishop of Central Africa in 1877, he died four years later of tropical fever in Khartoum, the capital of Sudan.

Today there are 4000 Comboni missionaries working in thirty-six countries. The organization no longer has a school in Britain, and no longer uses adverts of the sort it ran when young Maurice Cole joined them; adverts such as 'Bring A Pagan Child To God. With 5 shillings you may be a sponsor in the baptism of a black boy or girl, and give him or her the name you like. The new Christian will be told to pray for you and your intentions.'

The seminary was run by the Sons of the Sacred Heart, the educational wing of the Verona Fathers. Its journals during the 1950s carried on their inside front cover a picture of clean-cut Stillington pupils on the lawn with the request: 'Please Help These Boys who are preparing to be the Apostles of tomorrow, at Stillington Hall. Not all can afford to pay the full fee . . . Send in your donations: 3 shillings towards the upkeep of a student for 1 day, £1 for 1 week, £200 for a Foundation of a Scholarship. The boy benefitting from your donation will be notified and offer up his prayers and sacrifices for you. Why not make a donation to remember any deceased person dear to you?'

Writing in one of these mission magazines in the early fifties, under the heading 'Where Christ's Pioneers Are Made', a past pupil, Master F. Sheen, pictured brandishing a hockey stick, waxed lyrical about the institution young Maurice was shortly to attend: 'The boys come from all parts of the British Isles, and have the Fathers, Lay Brothers and Sisters of our Society to look after them. You may wonder what they do at Stillington Hall. Well, they pray and they work, which means that they study, they have gardening, they play and (believe me) they eat too. They have cycling or hiking every week. A brass band leaves no room for sadness; and a great spirit of fun keeps them in a perpetual serene and joyful atmosphere.

'When I look back on the years I spent there in preparation for my great missionary adventure, the happiest memories crowd to my mind – those feast days and church functions, those choir and brass band practices, those holiday excursions to the nearby vale of Pickering, the Abbeys of Fountains, Ripon and Rievaulx . . . The parks with walks and the pond fringed with weeping willows give the boys every possibility to enjoy themselves without causing trouble to the neighbouring farmers.'

As it happens, causing trouble to the neighbouring farmers is the one thing that Maurice Cole is vividly remembered for. The head of Stillington Hall in 1957–8, when Maurice was there, was Father Luigi Cocci. I tracked him down in 1995 in the Sudan, where, at the age of seventy-three, he was still a missionary. Even forty years on, Fr Cocci could recall Maurice Cole and Peter Terry, describing them affectionately as 'a pair of rascals'. Maurice he remembers as 'the rather lively, pleasant young boy' from Liverpool, but only for one incident, and one that still made him chuckle.

'There was an orchard, and some of the boys were given to throwing balls up to knock off the apples; and of course we would tell them not to do this, not to steal. And then, one evening, during prayers, I saw these two little boys and their pockets were bulging, stuffed. I said: "I thought we had told you about this, that you are not to steal apples." And quick as anything came back the answer: "Father, we are not stealing apples – these are pears."'

It was the first example of a Maurice Cole verbal joke, and in the circumstances not a bad one. The lad rapidly had his first fan in his new headmaster. Fr Cocci says now: 'He was a good boy. I used to laugh just to see him.'

And Maurice was indeed very happy. His parents and sister certainly found him so when they came to visit him. They were seemingly, against all expectations, going to have a priest in the family. Ged Ormesher, back in Liverpool, remembers the Coles were delighted with the way things had turned out. 'With a Catholic household everyone wanted to have a priest in the family. And lots of boys would think they wanted to be priests in those days.'

Maurice Cole did. Yet nearly thirty years later he wrote in his own oddball memoir with a gratuitous swipe at the mother and father who paid for him to go at his own request: 'Isn't it odd that parents can be happy for their child to become a priest which means never having a family or getting married to the one you love?'

None of this scepticism was evident to his family at the time. He may not have enjoyed the regular football, in which he became adept at skulking on the wing as far from the ball as possible; there was little attraction in the brass band; and he wasn't wild about sleeping in a large dormitory, getting up at six a.m. or having to take showers with no doors or curtains, and even worse, no hot water. But once ablutions were over, he loved to wander round the house. It was, he recalled years later, 'just like a movie set, staircases, balustrades and minstrel galleries, all made from mahogany and populated by priests gliding about like ghosts on roller skates'.

And he seemed to enjoy the remarkably disciplined and spiritual aspects of the daily round. The day began at seven with forty-five minutes of morning prayers and daily Mass followed by a spiritual talk from one of the Fathers. Having thus worked up an appetite, the boys had breakfast, followed by lessons, lunch and then more lessons or perhaps games. In the late afternoon and early evening they would have time for private prayer. On Sundays there was benediction, followed by the Rosary, a group of prayers which included fifty Hail Marys before the evening meal. Even on weekday nights they had up to thirty minutes of prayer before supper. Bedtime, preceded by five minutes' more prayer, was always at nine o clock.

The school was officially known as St Peter Clavier Juniorate, a Jesuit term, which tended to result in letters being addressed to 'St Peter Clavier Junior 8'. The man who set up the school in 1948 and was its first director and Latin teacher was twenty-nine-year-old Father Centis, who handed over the directorship to Fr Cocci in 1953. In 1995 the seventy-seven year old Fr Centis was serving as a priest in Italy after fifty-four years in missionary work. He told me that while he and Fr Cocci and one other priest (all then in their twenties) started the school with the best of intentions, and it was a happy and spiritual place, he could now see it did not give a fully rounded education.

'We advertised for boys,' Fr Centis remembers. 'We approached parish priests and schools and told boys about our work in the missions. Most of the boys were full of good will to serve God. They had pride in their vocation. They came at the age of eleven or twelve. Some of them came with only a very faint idea of being priests, but we tried to accept only those who wanted to become priests and missionaries. We tested the boys throughout their time at Stillington. Many left because they discovered it was only a fancy they had to become missionaries because they had heard stories about Africa.

'Before accepting a boy we would go to the parish priest and say, "What do you think of the family? Is it a good Catholic family? Is he a good Catholic boy?" We would always get a report from the parish priest.

'But looking back, I feel we were not prepared for this enterprise. My English was very poor. I was Italian and had spent less than one year in England. It was a grammar school with only four classes, a very small school, about forty boys, and only about twenty per cent became missionaries. We could not claim to be a very good grammar school. We were all Italians and we did not claim to be well versed in the English language or English customs. Only after three years did we introduce cricket. But you must remember the whole atmosphere was leading to a religious and spiritual life. We had our own spiritual practices. We were like a family among ourselves. And we were working for God. If we made mistakes we knew we were forgiven, for the good intention was there, and most of the boys kept in touch after they left.'

By the time Fr Cocci became head of the school he was more than pleased with the way things were going. 'It was very happy. We had an ice-cream man come out from York. The boys would play football on a Sunday, there were lovely bonfire nights. We put on pantomimes at Christmas and all the local people would come from the villages all around.'

The school was in one way, at least, ahead of its time. A composer on the staff, Fr Poalto, had set the singing parts of the Mass in English, making Stillington the first Catholic establishment to use English in the Mass. 'Our Sunday Mass was sung very beautifully,' says Fr Cocci, 'and the parents were always very happy when they came. Government inspectors spent some days with us and were especially pleased with the church activities, the way we aimed to foster community spirit.'

Fr Cocci himself gave many of the spiritual talks to the boys. He was not unaware that with dozens of adolescent boys in his charge, the air was thick with sex drive. But there was an answer for that – go and play rugger when such thoughts came to you. One of the subjects covered in his talks would have been homosexuality. Fr Cocci recalls forty years on what his views have always been. And one can imagine the tenor of the talk that Maurice and his classmates would have heard quite frequently. Fr Cocci describes his views, and the views of the Verona Fathers, thus: 'On the question of homosexuality, we refuse the sin, the fault, the wrong, but we have great understanding of the sinner. It's against nature. We cannot accept homosexuality, but we have compassion for the sinner.'

Once a week there was confession for the boys, though Maurice realized pretty quickly that it might be best not to unburden yourself of your sins too wholeheartedly. After all, you were confessing to the people who ran the school, and a sin too far could result in expulsion. Which is exactly what happened.

One night Maurice, Peter Terry and a few others raided the vestry and ate the hosts, the wafers used in the Communion service. Thus emboldened, they decided a few nights later to break into the church, try on the vestments, drink the wine they found in the cellars and hold a mock Mass. For once, Maurice's skinny frame came in useful. He was able to squeeze through the bars of the metal gates into the cellars and pass bottles of wine out to his fellow trainee missionaries, who happily guzzled it down.

'We didn't see why the priests should have all the fun,' he told Cathy during the next holidays. 'We didn't understand why we couldn't see what it was like to be a priest.' It was Maurice's sense of the theatrical being given full vent – in flowing robes at midnight in the dark church under the black sky of rural Yorkshire.

The breaking and entering was skilfully accomplished, and the miscreants might well have got away with it, were it not for Maurice's respect for the confessional. The next night he told all, and he and his fellow-conspirators received a sharp reprimand. Maurice went back to Liverpool at the end of that term still happy – doubly happy, in fact, for he had pulled off a major theatrical coup and cleansed his soul of any guilt in the sanctity of the confessional. Unfortunately, there was clearly a moment when the Verona Fathers left behind the confessional and transmuted from priests into teachers.

In the middle of the holidays came a letter from Stillington saying Maurice was not proving to be missionary material and need not return for the next term. Peter Terry seemed to have been forgiven for his part in the escapade and went back without his friend, going on to become a priest, although he later left the priesthood to run a baby-care shop in Ireland with his wife.

Fr Cocci says now that it was a common occurrence for boys to drop out on finding they did not have the necessary vocation. But the Cole family thought a letter in the middle of the holidays was a cruel way to end the aspirations of a lad who, to them at least, had shown no sign at all of being discontented with his chosen path. To add to the unfortunate set of circumstances, it was much later learned that the school had sent a letter to Maurice's parish priest asking his opinion on the boy's staying on at the school; but the priest was seriously ill and did not attend to the letter.

And so Maurice faced up wearily to the prospect of going back to St Bede's and forgetting Stillington Hall and the life of a missionary. 'He was certainly sad,' remembers Cathy. 'There was gloom about the place. He was very upset about it.' Mrs Cole, as ever, safeguarded the family's privacy and did not proffer any explanations to the neighbours. Ged Ormesher just recalls her saying: 'Maurice has been taken bad.'

Whether it was the seeming injustice of his enforced departure from the school, or his discomfort with some of the spiritual guidance he received there, Maurice began to drift away from his religion after he had returned home, convincing himself, and telling anyone who would listen in later years, of his extremely negative feelings about Catholicism. He began to think about it obsessively. Why should he be in such a state of fright? As he was to say on radio nearly forty years later: 'I was brought up a Catholic in the true sense. If you do something slightly naughty, you go to purgatory for an awfully long time and it's really awful. But if you commit one of these list of sins and you don't get to confession in time, you go to hell for ever and hell is unimaginable agony for EVER. Fancy telling that to a kid. It's outrageous. It made me terrified, of course. It also made me behave for a while.'

Back home again, fourteen-year-old Maurice decided to put one of these threats to the test. Masturbation, he had been told again and again, was a mortal sin. And God would strike you dead if you indulged in it. In the safety of his bedroom one night, he did indulge in it. Nothing happened. He was not struck dead. No punishment followed at all. Years later he vividly recalled that moment to his wife. It had been terribly important to him. In fact, he was completely shattered by it. If that threat was not true, then maybe none of the other ones was either. Why should he believe anything he had been told? To all intents and purposes, Maurice lapsed on that first night of his adolescence.

But if he lapsed, he did not forget. Fr Cocci maintains that it would be impossible for any pupil to forget the school and its teachings. 'Everyone would remember those days as a precious time. They came as small boys with only a faint idea that they might become priests. Only a few do. We just tried to give them a solid basis of faith and community spirit.'

That last term at Stillington Hall was the last visible involvement of Maurice with Catholicism until the last few days of his life. But inside he would never go very long without thinking about religion, and about the lessons of Fr Cocci and the other teachers. Nor would he go very long without experiencing torment as he tried to reconcile that imbibed guilt with his natural inclinations. For years this torment would manifest itself in diatribes against organized religion, particularly Catholicism, which he would dismiss as 'a business and a very clever business'. In better moods he just made jokes about it. But no one who got close to him would be able to avoid discussion of God for very long.

It proved to be the supreme irony. The rest of the family, whom Maurice would label 'strict Catholics', were to live quite contentedly, with religion playing only a part in their lives. For Maurice, the vehement non-believer, it was to be an obsession he would agonize over for much of his existence.

The lessons he had learned from school, from his local church and, not least, from Fr Cocci's nightly talks would never leave him altogether. God was all-powerful and saw everything. And certain activities, certain feelings, were unlawful, unnatural and beyond the pale. Even to think about them was a sin. Indulge yourself in them and punishment would surely follow.

A couple of years after Maurice departed, the Verona Fathers gave up running the school at Stillington Hall. In 1966 the grand old building was demolished and the land gave way to a housing estate. No records of the school are kept by the Fathers. Fr Cocci in Khartoum may remember the lad whom he had to turn away from the priesthood. But none of the Verona Fathers at any of their British offices claims any knowledge of him – except, for a second or two, one Father at the head office in Britain. When I asked him if it was true that Maurice had left them after a short while, he replied unguardedly and rather curiously: 'Yes, thanks be to God.'

This reaction suggested that for the followers of Bishop Daniel Comboni the spiritual instruction of Maurice Cole was a chapter that they, like Maurice, had affected to forget.

3

RADIO GA GA

'Are your parents connected with show business?'
'Oh, no, they're quite boring really.'
Everett's first on-air *faux pas*, in
his very first broadcast, 1964

The last year at St Bede's passed, though probably not quickly enough for Maurice. School was now a necessary evil which filled up the hours before getting home and enjoying himself with his two rediscovered loves: music and the radio. One or the other was always on, preferably the two combined. The exception to this routine was Saturday-morning pictures, the scene of the famous skipping triumph. He still had few friends – fewer than before Stillington Hall – as he had lost both Peter Terry and two years in which he could have got to know schoolmates at St Bede's. But he still had his sister and, more than ever before, he had the radio.

As Mrs Cole was now finding to her cost, Maurice was becoming as interested in the technical side of how the equipment worked as he was in the programmes. Anything that didn't move he was likely to take to pieces to discover its secrets. First a clock was dismantled, then the keys were taken off the piano – every single one of them – to see how they made music; then, to his mum's audibly expressed horror, the washing machine was found pulled apart. 'Can I have a tape recorder, Dad?' Maurice began to plead with his father. 'Not likely,' Tom replied. 'You'll only take it to pieces.'

But he relented and bought his son a Grundig reel-to-reel, only to discover to his consternation that the ecstatic Maurice then used money he earned from a paper round to buy another one. Maurice rushed round to his neighbour, Tony Ormesher, who was training to become a jazz guitarist and was the first person in Hereford Road to own a tape recorder. He asked Tony to show him how to use it. But Tom Cole could still not puzzle out why Maurice needed two. The answer was that his teenage son was already experimenting with sound on sound. His bedroom became a sound laboratory.

As soon as he rushed in from school – and later from work – Maurice would go upstairs and play with his equipment. 'Practise' may be a more appropriate word, for these were embryonic jingles and sketches that were echoing round the house. His bedroom became his world for the next few years, the equipment it contained being of far greater interest to him than the lure of friends or parties or pubs or going to see Liverpool or Everton play. He even missed out on taking the short bus ride to the Cavern Club in Matthew Street to see the local beat groups, Gerry and the Pacemakers and the Beatles. He was not part of any set, and he would have felt uncomfortable going on his own.

In fact, he went out as little as possible. He was too busy refining his editing techniques, putting voice on voice, cutting and splicing tapes and sticking them on windows and walls, labelled for further use. 'Do not clean this window' was an instruction his mother got used to seeing written in her son's bedroom beside the strips of tape stuck across the pane. 'I couldn't get in to dust,' she remembers. 'There were bits of tape and wire everywhere. And then one day he wrote on the mirror: "BBC HERE I COME." I think he used one of my lipsticks to write it. It didn't come off for ages.'

Like every self-respecting teenager of the time, Maurice curled up in bed with Radio Luxembourg coming out of the transistor radio he had under the pillow. But his favourite show was actually on the BBC's Light Programme, and it even vied with *The Goon Show* for his affections. It was Jack Jackson's *Record Roundabout*. Jackson may have had the traditional BBC accent, but his show broke the mould and influenced a new generation of DJs. Between records he would splice in tapes featuring snatches of dialogue from current comedy shows. And he would in turn interject his comments and questions into the conversation. So, Tony Hancock or Harold Steptoe seemed to be giving his view on the latest record by Johnny Mathis or the Searchers. There were no jingles or invented characters on Jackson's programme. But he showed what could be done to a basic record show with a love of comedy and some judicious mixing. Maurice was enthralled.

He fixed up loudspeakers in the house and gave his mother the shock of his life by announcing in a perfect BBC accent that Catherine Cole of Hereford Road, Liverpool, had just won a star prize. It took Cathy, who was in on the joke, some time to convince her mother that the voice belonged to Maurice upstairs.

His hobby was all-consuming. He made his own tapes. Inspired by Jackson, he combined some contemporary pop with a classical fanfare, jokes and sound effects, but went further, doing a few daft voices of his own and taking a burst of a speech from President Kennedy, edited so that it still sounded suitably presidential but actually made no sense at all. He started corresponding with the editor of *Tape Recording Magazine*, sending him his tapes and swapping ideas – 'tapesponding', as it was called. His sister remembers how excited he would become when he received letters from his new correspondent.

But the school-leaving age then was fifteen and Maurice had to get a job. There was a family conference, and he said how much he was interested in cooking. He would train to be a chef. If it wasn't going to be Maurice in a priest's vestments, it looked like it might be Maurice in a chef's hat and apron. He was extremely enthusiastic when his parents found him a job training at the now defunct Cooper's Bakery in Liverpool. Unfortunately, this was to be training on the job rather than any structured course. And the job consisted at first of scraping the fat off trays of sausage rolls in the company of loutish workmates. This was not at all what he had had in mind.

'He had a vivid imagination,' his sister remembers. 'He envisaged himself in a tall, white hat cooking exotic foods. My parents were delighted. But the company gave him the dogsbody jobs and he was miserable.' This fairly minor episode of bad luck became embedded in his psyche. Twenty years later, when a producer complained of having a rotten day, that producer was told sharply: 'You think that was bad? You should try scraping the fat off a tray of sausage rolls.'

The fantasy of becoming Maurice Cole, Master Chef was short-lived. Cathy, recognizing he was artistic, tried to persuade him to be a hairdresser. But he chose instead to be a copy boy with Douglass and Company, an advertising agency on Chapel Street in the city centre. He stayed for four years and did well there, rising to Assistant Production Manager and enjoying the company of more refined people than he had known either at secondary school or at the bakery. And yet he claimed later that he took fright when the firm threatened to promote him.

'He came away with fabulous references,' his sister noted. 'He was a perfectionist, very neat and thorough.' The managing director of Douglass and Co Ltd, Registered Practitioners in Advertising, a Mr H. Stansfield, wrote in his reference for Maurice: 'Mr Maurice Cole has been in our employment for the past four years. Starting as a junior in the organisation, he has made steady progress and has achieved the position of Assistant Production Manager. At all times he worked intelligently and conscientiously, and is to be congratulated on his courteous manner and neat appearance. We have no hesitation in giving him every recommendation and wish him every success in the future.'

Douglass and Company passed the time, the months, the years, until he was nineteen.

A short film that Maurice had seen called *This is the BBC*, with pictures of the sun setting over Broadcasting House and the transmitters helping nation to speak unto nation, served only to increase his undying passion to work for the British Broadcasting Corporation. But how could such a dream ever come to pass? The summer of 1964 found him still spending quality time in his bedroom with his radio and tape recorder, and swapping ideas with Alan Edward Beeby, the editor of *Tape Recording Magazine*. He made a short tape, *The Maurice Cole Quarter of an Hour*, actually lasting about twelve minutes, complete with jokes, music and that deliberately jumbled excerpt from Kennedy's speech, and sent it to Beeby. It's good, Beeby wrote back. But why send it to me? Send it to the BBC. So Maurice sent it to a programme called *Midweek*, and to his amazement received not a letter but a telegram from the producer, Wilfred De'Ath, telling him to come immediately. They would play his tape and interview him about it.

He rang Cathy, who was working for a Catholic fund–raising agency in London. 'He said: "I'm going to be on the radio,"' she recalls. 'There was great excitement. So I hired a radio for two shillings and sixpence. We listened to it during my lunch hour. It was announced as *The Maurice Cole Quarter of an Hour*. It had sound effects, records and jokes.'

Paying his first visit to London was thrill enough, but when Maurice walked through the stately portals of Broadcasting House in Portland Place, he was entranced by what he saw. The carpets, he noted, went right to the edge. And the people were so polite and spoke so well, and offered him cups of tea. He was shown into the office of Wilfred De'Ath, who told him he was a 'find' and could even become a star. Maurice's head was spinning. It would soon be spinning even more. De'Ath took him home and in BBC style fed him on gin and tonics before dinner. He then showed Maurice to the hotel where a room had been booked for him. The next morning, still pinching himself, Maurice was back at Broadcasting House, to be interviewed by Ronald Fletcher, with De'Ath producing. They played the whole of *The Maurice Cole Quarter of an Hour*. Nowadays it would be a radical gesture indeed to play the entire tape of an unknown nineteen-year-old on national radio. It was then, too. De'Ath received a ticking-off for his impetuosity. When the tape had finished playing, Maurice was asked a few questions. 'Are your parents connected with show business?' was one. 'Oh, no, they're quite boring really,' came the reply. But Mr and Mrs Cole didn't mind. They and Cathy were glued to the radio, lost in admiration.

Thirty years later Wilfred De'Ath was still bitter at the outcome. 'I took the risk of transmitting *The Maurice Cole Quarter of an Hour* in its entirety, thus bringing the wrath of the entire BBC establishment down on my head. The experience left me with a contempt for BBC authority which has never left me. They agreed, with reluctance, to pay his rail fare, but I was obliged to put him up in a hotel at my own expense.

'Maurice came over to my flat and drank gin and tonic like water and put his bread on the plate and cut it into small pieces. My then wife somewhat snootily observed: "He has never been with middle-class people before." But he was a genius. I loved him.'

When the interview ended Maurice plucked up courage. Having glimpsed Mecca, he was none too keen on returning to Liverpool. He asked De'Ath if there was any chance of a job. De'Ath said he would try to help him. He gave the tape to Chris Peers, an agent and record company promotions man, who was impressed with what he heard and arranged for Maurice to have an audition at the BBC with Derek Chinnery, a senior producer. A couple of weeks later another telegram arrived to amaze the Cole household, and Maurice was again summoned to Broadcasting House. He was to audition as a disc jockey – bring some records, do a little chat and generally sparkle – with the appropriate decorum, of course.

Maurice was even more nervous than before. Having his tape played had been exciting. But this was the chance of a job in London, with the BBC, on that endless sea of carpets. He drowned his nervousness in gin and tonics. After all, that was what real BBC people did. It did not help his interview or his audition. He clearly did not make much of an impression. Though he told later how Derek Chinnery had been unimpressed with him, Chinnery has no memory at all of the session taking place or of meeting Maurice Cole.

The nervy interview with Ronald Fletcher could easily have been Maurice Cole's first and last appearance on national radio, and the nervier and tipsy interview with Derek Chinnery his last visit to Broadcasting House. But as he returned, utterly deflated, to Liverpool, believing that his fledgeling broadcasting career was already over, fate dealt him a good turn. Chris Peers, who had kept his tape, was hired to do a service for a curious outfit with a curious mission.

On 22 October 1964 a ship set sail from Miami. Though her crew didn't know it and her captain was sworn to secrecy, she was bound for England. It was a ghostly, ghastly voyage. All the main shipping lines were avoided, there was no radio contact with another human being, and the weather was tempestuous. Grown men began to cry.

The clandestine voyage was like a modern–day version of *The Rime of the Ancient Mariner*. The crew had no contact with the outside world throughout the whole journey. Had the ship capsized, no one would ever have found them.

'It was a nightmare,' recalls one crew member. 'You couldn't see the mast and flying fish came flying in . . . The weather was really bad. Sometimes if you went on deck the captain ordered you to tie yourself to the ship in case you went in. I believe we took seventeen days crossing, but for fifteen days we didn't even see an aeroplane pass or a bird fly by.'

It would probably have been scant consolation to them to know that the nightmare was for a good cause. In a few weeks that same ship would be broadcasting Brian Poole and the Tremeloes and Freddie and the Dreamers. Pirate radio was on its way.

The ship had been dispatched on the orders of a consortium from Dallas, Texas, which was rumoured to include Lady Bird Johnson, the wife of the American President, Lyndon B. Johnson. It had decided to start a pirate radio station in the North Sea, three miles from the British coast and thus in international waters and outside British jurisdiction. It would cash in on the new boom in pop music among young people, who were ill served by the traditionalist BBC – where a needle-time agreement with the Musicians Union meant that only a proportion of air-time could be devoted to records. The rest was devoted to dance bands and live cover versions.

Even the infinitely trendier Radio Luxembourg broadcast only at night and suffered from programming too often dictated by record-company sponsors. The Texas consortium knew they could earn a tidy sum from advertising revenue. They had read in the *Wall Street Journal* that already one pirate station, Radio Caroline, was operating and it was doing very nicely, thank you. In its first ten days of operation, Caroline sold £64,000 worth of advertising.

Pirate radio actually had a longer pedigree than most people, even now, believe. Indeed a reunion in the sixties of pre-war pirate presenters saw establishment broadcasting figures like Bob Danvers Walker and Roy Plomley, the founder of *Desert Island Discs*, remembering their rebellious youths.

But pirate radio really burst on to the British consciousness on the Easter weekend of 1964, when disc jockey Simon Dee was the first live voice on Radio Caroline. The entrepreneurs behind that station had named it after an old newspaper picture of the late President Kennedy's daughter smiling from underneath a table as she sent papers flying and interrupted an important meeting. The cheeky, youthful irreverence of the picture summed up the image they wished to convey.

Caroline quickly established its reputation, spawning other off-shore imitators and causing the government to take fright. Though Britain's Conservative government was not ideologically opposed to commercial radio, its Postmaster General, Reginald Bevins, was still able to voice official paranoia, warning that 'our shores [could soon be] ringed by an Armada of pirate radio ships with all the consequential dangers of . . . interference with home programmes and the risk to human life'. A Labour victory in the general election that year increased official hostility to offshore broadcasting as the new government's Postmaster General, Anthony Wedgwood Benn, with support from the Council of Europe, pledged to outlaw the pirate stations altogether.

The American consortium was unperturbed. It would take a long time to pass the legislation outlawing the stations, and in the meantime there was money to be made. Their new station would have a transmitter much more powerful than Caroline's (50,000 watts as against 10,000) and so would reach a larger audience. Also, it would be modelled on their local station Radio KLIF in Dallas – decidedly more hip and dynamic than anything broadcasting in Britain, including Caroline, which had neglected to adopt American ideas such as jingles, news and weather reports and broadcasting through the night.

The consortium put up an investment of £178,000 and dreamed up a way to drastically limit their overheads. They would broadcast tapes of KLIF in Dallas. American radio with American music. Plain and simple. They would call it Radio London to make it sound nice and homely for the British folks, but there would be no need to employ a British disc jockey.

Had that plan gone ahead the life of Radio London would have been brief, and the broadcasting career of Maurice Cole non-existent. But thankfully, the man the consortium had employed to run the station in Britain, Philip Birch from the JWT advertising agency, and his number two, Alan Keen, an assistant advertising manager with the *Daily Mirror*, argued that the explosion of British pop that year made a British-sounding station with British DJs essential.

And so Birch hired Chris Peers, along with other specialists Morris Sellar and Roy Tuvey, to find him some DJs, a far harder task then than it would be today. Then there was virtually no one in Britain with experience of commercial broadcasting. A top Australian 'jock', Tony Withers, whose simple enough catchphrase, 'Hel-lo', was chanted in a rich bass voice, was recruited as chief DJ. A handful of others were found to join him. But more were needed. Peers

recalled: 'I went to Radio Luxembourg, I went all over the place
. . . I used to go round to the BBC and go to producers and say:
"Have you got any tapes of guys who have sent in stuff to you
that you can't do anything with?" Morris Sellar and Roy Tuvey
and I were getting these disc jockeys for Radio London. We ran
through a whole lot of tapes in a little studio up in the East End
of London.'

And then Peers remembered the shy lad from Liverpool. He had
fouled up at the BBC, but maybe he deserved another chance. 'We
put together everybody's tape that we thought was any good, which
we then submitted to Ben Toney. I said: "This is not fair, to put
Maurice Cole's tape amongst these others – although they weren't
all that good – but he's bright enough. He's got enough imagination
to make it."'

He told the Texan, Ben Toney, the station's first head of
programming, and by now based in London, about Cole, stressing
that they shouldn't judge the boy too harshly or compare him with
the other disc jockeys. He had no broadcasting experience, after all.
But he did have potential.

Toney listened to the tape. 'Well, he's a kid,' he remembers
thinking. 'He sounded very young, but kind of clever at the same
time. I thought he had a lot of potential and I had to have an
additional person out there for relief. I thought: I'll take him out
there and pay him £5 or so less than the other disc jockeys and let
him get some experience.'

So, an astonished Maurice was summoned from Liverpool to
Radio London's offices in Curzon Street, Mayfair, and was duly
offered and gratefully accepted £15 a week to be a disc jockey.
Before setting out for the ship he stayed the night at his sister's
flat in London. The Catholic fund-raising agency had provided her
with a penthouse flat in Sloane Street. Cathy, now twenty-one,
had become Kate and was engaged to an Irish businessman, Conor
Horgan, an import-export specialist, who went on to supply Marks
& Spencer.

Events seemed to be going at a frantic speed. It had only been a
few days since Kate's brother had told her he was going to be on
BBC Radio; and now here he was in her flat telling her he had
landed a job in radio, not with the BBC at all but on a ship.

Her last sight of him before he set out for Radio London is still etched on her memory. It was five a.m. and still dark. They stood together on her doorstep, as the little lad with his tiny suitcase prepared to find his way across London and then to Frinton, on the Essex coast, in the blackness.

'You could see from his body language he was petrified,' Kate remembers, 'terrified out of his wits. My heart really went out to him. He looked white as a sheet, and gaunt and thin and nervous. I got up with him, but he couldn't eat. He stood at the door and said cheerio and he had this little suitcase. I remember thinking: poor creature, I hope he makes it with no breakfast. It was dark and he looked so innocent. He was always so young for his age. When he went to the pirate ship he had the experience of a fourteen-year-old or maybe a twelve-year-old. And I thought, watching him go off into the gloom: there goes his lovely innocence.'

Over in America, the consortium was determined to surprise not just the British government, but competitors like Radio Caroline. It also surprised the crew of its own pirate radio ship. Radio London was to broadcast from a former US minesweeper, the *Galaxy*. The ship, registered in the Honduras so that the British government could not impound it, was in dock in Miami. In late October 1964 the consortium told its captain to give it a sea trial. Fifteen minutes before it pushed out of the dock, the captain was told that the 'trial' would be a voyage to England. Its twenty-seven crew, most of whom had never been to England, and none of whom had any desire to do so in winter, were not told until out at sea.

By the time the ship was moored off Essex, half a dozen DJs had been recruited. Birch and Keen were ready to start collecting advertising revenue. And Toney was ready to start directing programmes, though he had one worry gnawing in his mind. The government might try to take official action against the ship and its employees. If the disc jockeys used false names they could not be charged with broadcasting from the ship.

Whether that defence would have stood up in a court of law is open to question. But he asked the DJs he had hired if they would change their names. And, in a spirit of adventure, they all agreed. Peter Ince simply opened a Miami phone book on the ship at the 'Bs' and picked the name Brady. Tony Withers became Tony Windsor, Paul Kazarine became Paul Kaye. The soon-to-be-recruited barrister's son Edward Stewart Mainwaring dropped his last name. And David Wish became Dave Cash.

When it came to Maurice Cole's turn, he decided not to keep even half his original name, as most of the others were doing. He was embarking on a new adventure and he might as well have a completely new name. What though? As he racked his brains he remembered that he'd recently seen a film with one of his favourite comic actors, Edward Everett Horton, a butler-playing star from the pre-war days who later went on to appear on television as a Red Indian chief in a series called *F Troop*. If there was little logic to plucking the name Everett rather than Edward or Horton, there was even less to plucking Kenny out of nowhere. He later told Kate that Ben Toney, seeing his hesitation, had simply said to him: 'You look like a Kenny.'

And so pirate DJ Kenny Everett was born. Still a teenager, at least for one more month, he set out for the North Sea and fame. Liverpool, Catholicism, the priesthood and that skinny, introverted, awkward loner Maurice James Christopher Cole belonged, he hoped, to another life.

4

THE PUKING PIRATE

'I can't understand the government's attitude over the pirates. Why don't they make the BBC illegal as well? It doesn't give the public the service it wants, otherwise the pirates wouldn't be here to fill the gap. The government makes me sick. This is becoming a police state.'

George Harrison MBE, interviewed in
Disc, August 1966

Pirate radio was one of the most exciting manifestations of Britain's cultural revolution in the 1960s. Its mixture of adventure, experiment, humour and dissent, to the background of a three-minute pop record, epitomized the era that spawned it.

It changed the way pop music was broadcast, leading to the eventual birth of Radio 1. It enraged the government. It made hits of songs it championed, songs such as 'Winchester Cathedral', 'Concrete and Clay' and 'Everyone's Gone to the Moon'. It made its own stars, promoting artists such as Tom Jones and arguably even the Beach Boys. It transmitted to listeners the shared dual thrill of flirting with illegality and doing so afloat, in veritable pirate tradition. And it produced a band of disc jockeys who were to dominate radio for nearly thirty years. It was not just a young Kenny Everett who made jokes and played records while feeling acutely bilious. The excessively jolly Jack tars on various ships included Tony Blackburn, Dave Cash, Keith Skues, Emperor Rosko, Ed Stewart, Dave Lee Travis, John Peel, Johnny Walker, Paul Burnett, Simon Dee, and many others who, for better or worse, were to help define standards in pop music and broadcasting over the coming decades.

But as the nineteen-year-old Kenny Everett, revelling in a new job and a new name, boarded the tender at Harwich for the three-mile journey to the Radio London ship out in the North Sea, he felt neither a sense of history nor excitement. He felt like puking. And he did. Thrice.

So overwhelmed was he when he was informed that he would be in the vanguard of a pop revolution, that he had all but forgotten that Radio London was situated not in the city whose name it bore, with its cosy studios and fashionable restaurants and most of all *terra firma*, but on a barely converted minesweeper, where deliveries of food and water were sporadic, where the soon to be rich and famous cult figures shared cabins – and all this on one of the choppiest seas in the world. To add to the stomach churning, the ship was anchored at the bow, and in rough weather the stern, where the studio was situated, could rise twenty to thirty feet and, of course, drop again.

Many years later he recalled that first journey out to the ship in his book *The Custard Stops at Hatfield*, in a passage where there was little need for his customary exaggeration:

'As I was on my way out to Radio London, thinking "This is the life for me, sitting on a boat, bobbing up and down playing jolly tunes and telling jokes," I suddenly became aware of this horrendous feeling deep down within my soul. The feeling soon identified itself as "Here comes the puke" and I was sick three times on the tender on the way out to the ship. When I arrived aboard the ex-American minesweeper they'd kitted out with a transmitter, it was tossing around on the North Sea like an egg-cup in the middle of a gale, and people were hoiking great sides of beef and pork into the chef's department. That smell, coupled with the overwhelming pong of diesel fuel and the non stop swaying movement . . . well, I was a goner. For about two months I lay flat on my back, only getting out of the bunk to throw another cupful or two of yuk down the nearest loo. Or, in dire cases, over the nearest disc jockey.'

Never had the memory of Liverpool been so good. Those first days and nights Everett would often stand on the windswept deck and gaze at the lights of Frinton, vowing to get the next tender back to shore. There was nothing to cheer him up. The cooks, he observed, were all either ex-convicts or Belgians, the distinction meaning little to him, and would cook everything in axle grease;

the all-pervasive smell was awful, and he was constantly sick. The showers were tin, and when the wind was up and you were taking a shower, you were hurled from one tin wall to the other. Unlike the Radio Caroline ship, the *Galaxy* had neither plush fittings nor even portholes.

A *Daily Mirror* reporter who visited the ship in January 1965 wrote a story that sounded as though it came from a war zone: 'Below deck the quarters are cramped with little comfort. Steel walls are painted white and battleship grey. There's a smell of damp seaweed. The men sleep in bunks, two to a cabin. Wash basins are rusty, the showers primitive. There are no baths.'

When purchasing a minesweeper, the Texas consortium had either forgotten, or not wanted to know, that the builders of minesweepers expect them to be blown up, and so don't bother to endow them with creature comforts.

They certainly don't endow them with studios. The makeshift one that was installed in the stern was above some of the tanks, so the sound of water was a constant technical hazard. There was also an echo, and to deaden the sound, several dozen thick blankets were sent down from Radio London's headquarters in Curzon Street. These were strung up by bits of wire to make a tent. Such was Kenny Everett's introduction to the world of watery wireless.

Nevertheless, on 16 December 1964 Radio London made its first test transmission, on 266 metres on the medium wave, and two days later started broadcasting. Its first official broadcasting day was 23 December, and its first record Cliff Richard's 'I Could Easily Fall in Love with You'. But as broadcasting commenced, more problems became evident. Radio London had not yet established relationships with record companies and had no proper supply of records. Pete Brady did have a friend at Decca, and the box of Decca records he acquired featured heavily in those early weeks. One of those was a record called 'It's Not Unusual' by a new singer, Tom Jones, and repeated plays during the early days of Radio London made the song a hit.

The only other source of music in those first days, apart from records the DJs had simply carried on board with them, was the collection of American records that Ben Toney had brought with him. One of these, 'Dang Me' by Roger Miller, also became a hit by virtue of its Radio London plays, and its follow-up, 'King of the Road', a huge hit.

Kenny Everett found that playing the same thirty records over and over again meant that he was hearing them in his sleep. 'When a new batch came, you'd jump on them like a dying man.' But if he was hearing Roger Miller in his sleep, he wasn't alone in being unable to sleep soundly.

'All sorts of rumours were rife,' Keith Skues remembers. 'It was believed that living within such a close proximity to the antenna, the radiation was causing premature baldness. It was also believed that the radiation would cause sterility. As the ship had no proper earthing it was further believed that the vessel acted as one giant cathode, and that through the process of electrolysis the hull was being gradually etched away. Everyone on board the *Galaxy* had visions of the bottom falling away and being drowned in their sleep.'

It was a high-risk occupation being a DJ. But at least the music began to arrive. As record companies woke up to the fact that Radio London was becoming cult listening for their customers, new batches came with increasing speed, and the problem of getting records to the ship was solved. Getting them on board was another matter.

Once, on New Year's Eve, when there were no tenders sailing, Philip Birch hired a helicopter from which to drop a box of records on to the ship. 'It was a frightening experience. The pilot could not see below him because of the 'copter's floats, so I practically had to hang out of the opening and shout directions as the wind buffeted us about.' Few if any listeners could have guessed that to play them a few readily available chart records, the affluent, Mayfair-based managing director of the radio station was dangling a box of 45s on the end of a rope with the pilot bawling: 'Here's a knife. Cut the rope before I get tangled up in the guy lines.'

Meanwhile, below decks on the swingiest, happiest 'Wonderful Radio London', the crew were trying to kill one another.

The crew consisted of a mixture of Europeans and Jamaicans. One day the Jamaicans complained to the DJs that the Dutch, who wanted more of their compatriots on board, had tried to kill them by throwing nuts and bolts into the funnel while they were cleaning it Whatever the truth of it, the Jamaicans eventually left and the Dutch crew, by then numbering over twenty, turned on the six British DJs, demanding their cabins. The DJs managed to fend them off by brandishing their Scottish cook, Jock, a particularly hard nut, who in turn brandished a kitchen knife. But Jock was no respecter of DJs either.

Everett once recalled that on that same New Year's Eve that Philip Birch was dangling above the ship, Jock was trying to carve up DJs below. 'Tony Windsor said something he didn't quite like and he went for Tony. I remember seeing him chase Tony round the mess table with something like a hatchet, something from the kitchen. I threw a glass of beer at him and hit him on the head. He started to come after me, then everybody came running. It took that long to get through to the crew that one of their number had gone berserk. Suddenly there was a great column of engineers and people pinning him down and dragging him into the basement . . . until the tender came out and carted him off. We never saw him again. We couldn't afford to have murder on the boat. That might have irritated the government.'

But, albeit at risk to life and limb, the music was getting to the DJs. If they kept their wits about them they could avoid radioactivity, food poisoning and hatchet-wielding cooks. And one of them, Everett, had found a pastime which made him quickly indispensable and was to affect the rest of his broadcasting career and those of countless others. He was experimenting with jingles: short musical bursts usually repeating the station's name.

He did not instigate the first jingles he sang and sometimes edited; neither, in fact, did Radio London. The station's Texan founders had bought a set of nearly fifty jingles from PAMS (Promotion And Marketing Services), a specialist firm in Dallas. For around $4000 Radio London got a selection of jingles familiar to listeners to American music stations, but a fascinating novelty for Britain. By just changing the name of the station, PAMS converted their Texan jingles into 'Wonderful Radio London'; 'Big L'; 'Wonderful Big L, where you're hearing things'; 'It's smooth sailing with the highly successful sound of Wonderful Radio London' – sung in a Dalek-style electronic voice known as a Sonovox to a musical backing.

The tune was recorded normally but with a lead instrument taking the vocal line. The track containing the instrument was then replayed through small speakers which the vocalist held against either side of his vocal cords. When the lead instrument reached the part that was to be sung, the vocalist mouthed the words and the instrument appeared to sing. It was the same method that was used on the children's record 'Sparky's Magic Piano', where the piano appeared to speak.

The American-made package did throw up the odd anomaly. One jingle was in Spanish, made for stations that transmitted over the border into Mexico. That was never broadcast; but 'Radio London reminds you: go to the church of your choice' was broadcast quite often, even though the message was better suited to the gospel-loving folk of the southern USA than the pop-mad partygoers of the Home Counties.

Everett used much of his free time playing around with the jingles, loving the freedom of invention it gave him. The Sonovox fascinated him as it showed that you could disguise your voice. Even without a Sonovox you could use any number of different voices and different personalities. The very concept of the jingle excited him because it meant that you could delight the listeners with a simple plug for a station or a show almost as much as you could with a record. And whoever was making the jingles could make up tunes, make up catchphrases and sing both the lead and the harmonies. Also, you could be funny. Suddenly, the career of disc jockey had a whole new creative dimension.

While the other jocks were playing cards or chatting on deck or planning conquests for their next shore leave, Everett would more likely than not be listening to the tapes of American radio that came over from Dallas and studying the technique, or even more likely, experimenting in the studio.

One of the engineers, David Hawkins, noted: 'We always found that though Kenny didn't have any technical training, he was interested in both the operation and theory of operation of all electronic equipment on the ship. In fact, sometimes his questioning was so detailed that it made us refer to our textbooks.'

The other DJs rapidly saw Everett's enthusiasm. As Duncan Johnson noticed: 'Kenny would stay up all night and glue tapes together. He would stay up all night doing things and then sleep during the day.' The DJs put him in charge of editing the jingles and adding to them with his own, including trailers that would plug their (and his) shows.

A few months later he was dreaming up jingles which would have seemed too oddball for PAMS in Dallas, but showed the embryonic

Everett absurdist style. One such jingle that he produced contained all the instances of the word 'wonderful' in the station's repertoire of jingles, strung together, with the words 'Radio London' at the end.

Crucially, the station's founders had insisted that for the first time in Britain, and in what was to prove a significant contrast to Radio Caroline, the station use American-style format radio. This meant regular plays for Top Forty records throughout the day (nothing to do with sales – just records the DJs liked, and in the event often anticipating by weeks the official pop charts) interspersed with new releases, an LP track, old hits or 'revived 45s' as they came to be known, and hourly news and weather reports. Every show was to follow this formula with military precision – start the programme with a Top Ten record, then one from slots eleven to twenty, next an album track and then a 'revived 45'.

Radio London was the first British music radio station to have hourly news bulletins. Research in America had shown that listeners suffered guilt pangs if they felt they were listening to non-stop music without being informed about current events. But getting the news was a problem for a pirate ship. That difficulty was overcome with journalistic initiative and expediency. The DJs under news director Paul Kaye nicked it from the BBC. BBC radio had news every hour on the hour; Radio London staff noted it down, rewrote it and broadcast it on the half-hour. It was the one unarguable and brazen form of piracy they employed. But ironically, while they were to be accused, often wrongly, of playing records without paying any form of royalty, or jamming shipping radio waves, the charge of stealing the news, of which they were plainly guilty, was seldom levelled at them. The BBC's only form of revenge was to give out a false news item one April Fool's Day and smile as they heard Radio London solemnly repeat it half an hour later.

On the first day of broadcasting, two days before Christmas, the level of excitement among the tiny band of disc jockeys was high. Only Kenny Everett felt left out. Indeed, he was left out. As he had had no broadcasting experience, the station bosses felt uneasy about giving him his own show; and he did not broadcast on the opening day. But on Christmas Eve it was decided to extend broadcasting hours, and he was given his own programme that night. He was to start as he was to go on, by giving his employers a nasty jolt.

Radio London was dutifully promoting a campaign against drink-driving. Kenny, with chief DJ Tony Windsor watching encouragingly in the studio, began: 'Tonight, I want you before you drive home from the party, I want you to get drunk.' Windsor turned pale. Kenny continued: 'I want you to get quite drunk, no, not quite drunk, very drunk. I want you to get plastered. I want you to get so drunk you can't even find the keys to the car.' He had, ingeniously, saved himself. Windsor gave a sigh of relief and the show continued. Paul Kaye, who had advised Everett to remember the public-service announcements, and noted how he handled it, knew he had witnessed something special. 'That gag made us realize that we had a natural on our hands.'

Christmas Day was Everett's twentieth birthday and to celebrate that and his first show his colleagues hung him by his ankles over the side of the boat, an initiation ceremony which terrified him. But both Radio London and Kenny Everett had arrived. And the youth of England really did believe they were hearing things. Suddenly, out of nowhere, here was the station of their dreams.

Up until then, the dying days of 1964, and nearly halfway through the decade now remembered as the high point of pop and youth culture, young people, indeed people of all ages, might clutch a transistor playing Radio Luxembourg under the blankets at night; but as far as daytime listening went, they would wait, frustrated, all week for the occasional weekend piece of popular music on the BBC. There was the Sunday round-up of the charts by Alan Freeman in *Pick of the Pops*, and the weekend pop mainstays on the Light Programme, *Saturday Club* and *Easy Beat*. But these apart, pop in the mid-sixties and at a time when it was at its most inventive, rarely featured on BBC radio. And when it did, more often than not the tune would be played by a dance orchestra paid up to the Musicians Union. The BBC couldn't quite comprehend that there was any intrinsic difference between 'I Can't Get No Satisfaction' as performed by the Northern Dance Orchestra and 'I Can't Get No Satisfaction' as performed by the Rolling Stones. BBC Radio had had its moments, live sessions with the Beatles notable among them, but the moments were few and far between.

With the pirates, there was suddenly continuous access to pop records, a passport to the culture that had swamped the country, delivered by DJs almost as young as the listeners were – and in some cases younger. They were enthusiastic, they were zany, they were broadcasting increasingly in defiance of the middle-aged establishment which wanted to outlaw them. And Radio London, though not the first pirate station, was the hippest of them all.

Brian Long, a teenager when Radio London started, found a lifelong obsession in pirate radio, and thirty years later researched for pleasure rather than publication an exhaustive statistical document on it. It was Big L rather than the Beatles or Rolling Stones which symbolized the sixties for him and many of his contemporaries.

'Big L became a way of life,' he says, 'and the Big L theme, as it became known, was embedded in the memory as symbolizing all that was new and stimulating. As a teenager in the sixties I was very taken with pop music. My need to hear records was satiated by pirate radio, in particular Radio London. School holidays were spent listening all day long and wherever I went so did the transistor radio . . . I didn't really want to go on the family holidays to Cornwall because reception wasn't available during the day. The highlight of the week was the Fab 40 show on Sunday afternoons and not knowing if your current favourites had dropped out of the chart was crucial.

'If the record wasn't there it could result in you never hearing it again, because a large percentage of records that made the Radio London chart were very obscure. This only added to the variety and excitement of the station, and as there was such a quick rate of turnover and movement in the chart, missing the Fab 40 show, even for one week, would leave you completely out of touch.'

Or as John Peel was to put it later: 'The pirates provided the soundtrack to a lot of young people's lives.'

Radio London's knack for picking obscure records and turning them into hits was remarkable. One novelty record, the twenties-sounding 'Winchester Cathedral' by the New Vaudeville Band, was championed by Big L and became a huge hit in both Britain and America. Stars like Gene Pitney, P.P. Arnold and Marianne Faithfull were hiring boats to come on board to see the phenomenon for themselves.

Jonathan King became a star because of Radio London: his first hit, 'Everyone's Gone to the Moon', was plugged incessantly by the station. Pirate radio, he realized, had created a sense of excitement and adventure which hadn't really existed before. 'By doing all this out on the ocean, going up and down, struggling through enormous odds to get music to their public, the whole music spectrum has taken on a new sort of feeling of necessity. If somebody is really prepared to go through sheer hell just to play you a Tremeloes record, then that Tremeloes record has to be a particularly important thing in your life.'

But for Everett, playing the records was not fulfilling enough. Radio to him had meant the Goons, slapstick and surrealism. There had to be a way to bring humour even into a show that was ostensibly just about pop music. These were the thoughts going through his mind as he sat playing with jingles in the makeshift studio. And he didn't have to wait long to put them into practice.

A week or two after Everett had come on board the *Galaxy*, a new DJ was sent out to bolster the numbers. Dave Wish, a tall, handsome Canadian of British birth, had had a little experience on radio in Vancouver. Admittedly, it wasn't much more than writing and speaking commercials; but to Ben Toney it made the twenty-one-year-old a veteran, and when he hired Wish, who was to adopt the name Dave Cash, he asked him to help Tony Windsor train the other jocks. He also gave Cash a box of KLIF reel-to-reel tapes, and told him to make sure all the DJs listened to them.

As he came on board, Cash was greeted by Everett, eager to hear the tapes. 'He couldn't wait,' remembers Cash. 'He was a big fan of American radio.' The two spent a lot of time together listening to the tapes and discussing radio technique. Everett was studying Cash and learning from him, even though he was only a year older. While Everett excelled in the editing room, making up jingles, he was still a little shy and introverted as a DJ. Cash's technique, perfected on Canadian radio, impressed his pupil. Cash showed him that you could talk on the radio as if you were just talking to a friend and say: 'Hi, how are you doing?', and think always that you were addressing one person. It was a far cry from the BBC, where some presenters still addressed the microphone as if addressing a public meeting.

The programme that had impressed them both on the American tapes was the Charlie and Harrigan breakfast show, a double act relying on quick-fire quips that made its presenters as much if not more vital a part of the show than the records. On one occasion Charlie and Harrigan mentioned a Bic pen, and said to each other: 'We all know what you can do with a Bic pen.' Cash and Everett both recognized the allusion to taking the centre out of a pen and smoking hash with the tube. 'My God,' said Everett to his new friend, 'they're talking about getting stoned on the radio.' Then he looked at Cash. 'We could do a show like this,' he urged.

The two began to prepare for it. Everett and Cash already had their individual three-hour shows, but a *Kenny and Cash Show* was soon also in the schedules. Cash, who wanted to be a novelist anyway (which he now is) started writing scripts, Kenny would provide the Goonish voices, and the two of them began experimenting with sound effects. For a time they lived in the studio. They got hold of a sound effect of an express train running through a station, which they played each time they told listeners to send in an express request. Crude stuff, but it hadn't been done before.

They rapidly moved on helter-skelter to more sound effects and much more ad-libbing. Please don't talk over the records, an anguished listener wrote in to say. Kenny and Cash discussed the dilemma, repeatedly, over the records. Advertisers were also kept on their toes. One afternoon Everett decided to cough through all the cigarette commercials. And then there were sketches, sketches, sketches. Hundreds of them.

The cast of characters that Everett and Cash breathed life into again lent on Cash's knowledge of American radio and TV. The American comic Jonathan Winters had a character called Auntie Maud Frickett. *The Kenny and Cash Show* had an Auntie Doris, who in Everett falsetto, later to become well known on television, lectured the DJs. 'You boys are making a mess. I found a bra in your cabin. Which one of you was wearing a bra?' 'Oh, Marianne Faithfull left it last week.' Actually, Cash did have an Auntie Doris, who was none too pleased when she heard the show.

Cash also introduced Kenny to the work of Gary Owen, a guy who appeared in the *Rowan and Martin Laugh In*, a hit American TV show soon to be shown on British TV. His catchphrase, spoken in a tone of meaningful dramatic doom, was 'Meanwhile in another part of town'. Kenny and Cash had sent to them a demo tape that Owen had made. They were in hysterics listening to it. Particularly one line: 'This programme is brought to you by the Kremmen snuff company. They want you to stick their business up your nose.'

Everett was to store away in his mind the doom-laden melodramatic lines, the inversions of language which made him laugh so, and not least the name of the snuff company. Later on in his career he wanted a space hero for his radio show. Gary Owen's Kremmen snuff company was to live again.

Cash may have been the straight man in the double act, but at that stage he was most definitely the writer on the show. At first he methodically scripted the sketches, and gave them to his partner to read. But after a little while Everett did something which at first infuriated Cash, who remembers: 'He would come and read it, and then throw it away. I would say: "Fuck off man, I need that." But he just said: "No, we'll ad-lib it." It put a lot more pressure on, but after a while I gave up and learned to do it his way.'

Everett was still nervous at the microphone, but Cash helped him beat this, and they and their audience began to enjoy themselves. 'We had this ability to get absurd without going over the top,' says Cash. 'I would sit in for one hour of his show and then we started to build characters and various bits and pieces.' The bits and pieces included highly unconventional items then for a music station. They would run competitions for 'The Most Hated Group' and nominate people to be in 'The Out Crowd', as a counter to the 'in crowd' being so heavily promoted in the fashion-obsessed Britain of 1965. They even had Out Crowd membership forms printed.

The Kenny and Cash Show achieved higher ratings than any other pirate show. They were given a column in a music paper, they made a record, shift rotas were altered so that they could work in clubs on land together, and their joint love of the Beatles, which made them play numerous Beatle records, spurred Everett to make a promo jingle saying that Radio London was 'Your official Beatles station'. Not true, of course, but the fans loved it, and Brian Epstein, the Beatles' manager, made a point of sending records, including *Sergeant Pepper's Lonely Hearts Club Band* and 'Strawberry Fields Forever' to Radio London, and often to Everett, before anyone else.

The show was so successful that the pair even broke away from the sacred American format to devote whole sections to the Beatles or the Beach Boys. The American director of programmes, Ben Toney, was furious: 'You guys break format again and I'm kicking your ass.' Everett's reply showed how quickly he was now gaining confidence. 'What's a format? Is that something you put down and wipe your feet on? You mean a floor mat, you just pronounce it differently because you're a Texan.'

When Cash and Everett went on shore there were screaming girls at London's Liverpool Street station to greet them. When they were holding a club night at the Marquee in Wardour Street, there were queues around the block for tickets. Everett, who never in his career enjoyed live gigs, whispered to Cash: 'You do it, I'll follow along.'

The importance of Cash on Everett's early career cannot be overestimated. But by the spring of 1965, in the studio he had become his own man. *The Kenny and Cash Show* was on from five to six in the afternoon followed by the Kenny Everett show from six till nine. A few months after his first broadcast, the twenty-year-old was in the studio for four consecutive hours.

Outside the studio, though, Everett remained an enigma to his fellow DJs. One week in every three the DJs had shore leave and enjoyed making a few bob extra by spinning records in various clubs around London, where they were already being hailed as celebrities. Everett hated these public appearances, away from the safety of a studio, and did them as little as possible.

But his radio broadcasts with and without Dave Cash were winning a legion of fans. Polls consistently saw him voted one of the most popular DJs in the country. And his colleagues used to listen to his shows in admiration and hysterics.

'He was the funniest man I'd ever heard on radio,' says Ed Stewart. 'He came out with things we all wished we'd said ourselves. He was doing this commercial for a deodorant and he suddenly improvised with "it's wrong to pong". He was always making up jingles, doing the voice and the harmonies, quite unique.'

Off the ship, though, it was a different story. While most of the other DJs couldn't wait for their shore leave, to paint the town red and chat up the girls, Everett rarely joined the gang. He had tax-free money to spend, but he had no idea what to spend it on. One evening he just stood in Piccadilly Circus looking at the bright lights and the throngs of people, wondering why he wasn't having a good time, although he realized years later that that was the last place to go and stand if you wanted to have a good time.

'He kept himself to himself,' says Ed Stewart.' A few of us shared a flat in London and very much saw ourselves as studs. He was never a part of that. One suspected on the ship that he wasn't straight.

I don't think he was quite sure of his sexuality. He never talked about girls. I'm an Everton supporter and as I knew he was from Liverpool I tried to talk to him about football. He wasn't at all interested in that either. He hated stage work. He was shy, a very shy boy.'

Except when he was performing. In the studio he could adopt his funny voices, write and sing his jingles and adopt several different personas. He performed too in the mess. Ed Stewart remembers that he camped it up at the table. 'He had names for all of us. He was Edith Everett. Once he got us all to make up a commercial for Easter. There was Ed Stewart with his hazel clusters, so I became Hazel Clusters. Kenny became Fondant Cream.'

He was also, the DJs could not help but notice, a great practical joker. It was not just the campness and Edith Everett that foreshadowed some of his television characters more than a decade away. One day Ed Stewart was reading the news when Everett walked into the studio with two pieces of chalk up his nostrils. Stewart giggled through the death of Nehru.

But neither could the DJs help but notice that Everett would rather spend time either in the studio editing jingles or in his cabin reading a book. He never joined them to ogle Emma Peel in *The Avengers* on the ship's TV. Homosexuality was not discussed; the DJs were too preoccupied with themselves and having a good time. But Dave Cash certainly knew even back then that Everett, along with two other of the DJs, was probably homosexual; he also knew that he was incredibly innocent and had never had any sort of sexual experience.

He and Everett and Pete Brady shared a flat in Lower Sloane Street in fashionable Chelsea. Everett would sometimes bring friends back, always male, but always friends. It never, as far as Cash saw, went any further. Jonathan King, the pop star Radio London had made, was one such close friend. The American rock singer Harry Nilsson was another. They were, says Cash, boy friends, but literally just friends. 'Kenny was very naive. It never at that stage went any further. He was very affectionate. If he liked you, he loved you. He would often give me hugs. If he disliked you, he hated you. There was no halfway house.'

But Cash recalls vividly that when he brought his then girlfriend, Dawn, back to the flat, Everett reacted very oddly. 'He wouldn't leave the room. I whispered: "Get out, man, get out of here" but he wouldn't go. The next morning he said to me: "I wasn't very happy with you going with a girl." I think it hurt him.'

Meanwhile Radio London's reputation and listener figures continued to soar. Everett had rapidly and unexpectedly established himself as one of the most popular DJs in Britain. And then, in inimitable style, he blew it.

His three-hour daily show was sponsored by an American evangelical outfit, the Worldwide Church of God, based in Pasadena, California. It paid Radio London a nightly fee to play a half-hour tape of its leader, seventy-two-year-old Garner Ted Armstrong, preaching. This lengthy spot, called *The World Tomorrow*, was one of Radio London's biggest accounts. It also came right in the middle of Everett's programme. It was also about religion, one of the things he had come to the pirates to escape.

He loathed it, and was unable to resist taking the mickey out of it with comic references during his show. 'Hello, Vicar' or 'Hello, Padre,' he would say just as Garner Ted's voice was about to come on. Or he would make up his own tapes using part of Garner Ted's fire-and-brimstone sermon. One such tape just had Garner Ted repeating 'Rape, rape, rape, rape'. That little nugget was broadcast by Everett at the end of his show, and one of Garner Ted's lieutenants heard it. He was a marked man. On another occasion he edited a tape so that it had Garner Ted endorsing violent crime, and sent it on to the mainland for use on another sponsored station, where, who knows, it may well have been broadcast and baffled the listeners.

One night in November 1965, Everett made the regular caustic remark about *The World Tomorrow*. Unfortunately, one of the listeners that night was a Mr Garner Ted Armstrong, on a visit to England. He complained and the station's MD Philip Birch went out to the ship to haul Everett over the coals. 'You're a broadcaster,' he reprimanded him. 'You're talking about a guy who is bringing a ton of money in.' Nevertheless, after a week or so, Everett returned to taking the mickey out of Garner Ted Armstrong, who in turn lost his religious feeling for this particular fellow man, and told Birch: 'Either that little creep goes, or I pull the programme.'

And so Everett reached a milestone. In November 1965 he was sacked, for the first but not the last time. In truth he was not sorry to go. A year on the boat had taken its toll on him, and his reputation was such that he was immediately snapped up by Radio Luxembourg, eager to boast an ex-pirate.

But Luxembourg did not suit him. At that time the programmes were sponsored by record companies, and Everett found himself restricted to playing nothing but Decca records. Within a few months he was sacked again, this time with even less justice. He told a newspaper interviewer that he had smoked pot, and Decca, in a fit of pomposity and conveniently forgetting that their chief profit-makers were the Rolling Stones, who were no strangers to pot, demanded his dismissal. By June 1966 he was back on Radio London, and now so much in demand that he was given the breakfast show and on some days was broadcasting for as many as six hours. His salary had also risen from its initial £15 a week to a princely £150.

But the days of pirate radio were numbered. The Labour government's decision to outlaw the pirates politicized and disaffected a whole swathe of the younger generation, and it was a lucky thing for the Prime Minister, Harold Wilson, that by the time he gave eighteen-year-olds the vote for the 1970 election, the debate over pirate radio was all but forgotten. The government never really understood what young people saw in pirate radio. Cabinet papers from 1965 released at the start of 1996 show that Wilson was considering having advertising on BBC radio as a way of competing with the attraction of the pirates – as if it was the adverts rather than the music that turned people on.

During 1967 Wilson received numerous letters from young people urging him to change his mind about outlawing the pirates. These were passed on to the Postmaster General, Edward Short, who had told a conference that year that the pirates could rapidly cause 'chaos in the ether'. His Civil Service private secretary sent out a standard government response:

'Many people have been very disappointed to hear that pirate broadcasting is to be stopped. It seems so harmless and is enjoyed by so many people.

'In fact, despite the repeated claims of the pirates, their broadcasts are far from harmless. The pirates are using wavelengths which we have undertaken to leave clear for the broadcasting services in other countries. By so doing, they prevent people in those countries from hearing their own domestic programmes. They also represent a danger – slight but ever present – to the radio services on which safety at sea depends. Moreover, broadcasting from the high seas is forbidden, all over the world, by international law, and the pirates make almost unlimited use of recorded material, threatening the livelihoods of the musicians and other performers whose work they use without permission or payment . . . The most pressing need is to silence the pirate stations, which are flouting international regulations, earning us such a bad name abroad, endangering shipping and threatening to make broadcasting end in chaos, not only in Britain but over most of Europe.'

Anyone who thinks that this is the paranoia and po-faced fogeyism of a bygone age will be interested to learn that Keith Skues's uncontroversial history of pirate radio, *Pop Went the Pirates*, largely written in 1968, could not be published until 1994, as successive governments were worried that it could be seen to be promoting the cause. Only when they were finally convinced that his tome was not propagandist did they allow him to publish.

Many of the points made in Edward Short's official response were questionable. Not a single complaint was received about interference with foreign stations. And Radio London and other pirate stations did pay royalties to the Performing Rights Society, based on a percentage of advertising revenue; though it is true that the pirates never sought permission beforehand to play the records. The PRS officially opposed this and would sign no formal agreement – but accepted the money.

The pirates actually caused little harm and brought an awful lot of pleasure. An editorial in London's *Evening News* of 17 July 1967 was not wide of the mark when it said: 'It is astonishing how a government that wilfully inflicts the hideous sonic boom on harmless citizens should have taken so much trouble to silence the pop radio pirates. A month from now they will be outlawed and sunk without trace by a ponderous piece of legislation that turns music makers into criminals. They were doing no harm. They gave, in fact, much enjoyment. And although they were said to be a danger to shipping, an interference with SOS calls and thieves of copyright, we have heard less and less of these complaints. The truth is they were a nuisance to a government that likes everything under regimental control, and a threat to Post Office monopoly in particular. And what has happened is a symbol that dreary conformity in misery is now believed preferable to allowing any one to step merrily out of line. Proof that the pirates were performing a service (how wicked that they should profit by it!) is that the BBC launch their "pop" channel on 30 September. But you'll pay for it!'

Paul Bryan, the Conservative Shadow Postmaster General, sounded his own party's warning shot about the birth of commercial radio.

'Despite their protests, millions of listeners will now be firmly told that they must listen to what the government and the BBC think is good for them, and not to what they have shown they prefer. The socialists will not tolerate commercial radio, but the success of the pirate stations means that people want commercial radio in addition to the BBC and there is no reason why they should not have it. It would have been perfectly possible to set up local commercial radio stations at no great cost. A great opportunity has been missed.'

At midnight on Monday 14 August 1967 the Marine Offences Act, making it an offence for a British subject to work for or to supply a pirate radio station, became law. That day, Big L delighted its twelve million listeners in the UK (and four million in the Netherlands, France, Belgium and Germany) for the last time. Pop celebrities recorded messages of support, as did former staff DJs, including Everett.

A nation may not exactly have wept: there was too much else to think about at the height of the Summer of Love. But for a generation which had gained a three-year illicit thrill from pirate radio, for musicians and record companies who owed much of their success to Radio London airplays, and for disc jockeys who had been able to experiment and innovate, cultural life was a little poorer. And the vast number of pop stations from Radio 1 downwards that were to lean so heavily on Radio London's format never quite managed to capture its sense of recklessness, improvisation and discovery.

Listening to a recording of Radio London's final hour — from two to three p.m. on that afternoon — is like unwrapping a time capsule. If the melodramatic melancholy of the DJs giving their final farewells — at least until Radio 1 snapped most of them up a few weeks later — now seems a little over the top, it still adds to a heady, nostalgic mix alongside the fulsome messages from some of the superstars of the day.

There were also, of course, the adverts, solemnly read out by Ed Stewart, hosting the final hour with Paul Kaye, proclaiming the value of a touch-typing course for just twelve guineas, or 'the new idea in smoking': Consulate menthol cigarettes with the then equally trendy new catchphrase 'cool as a mountain stream'. And in the days when sexism was not even a gleam in a sociology lecturer's eye, Ed could take the needle off a sixties rock song and intone with intense sincerity: 'Listen, girls, Look Transparent Cooking Foil lets you *see* when the meat's overcooked.'

Paul Kaye pinched his last news bulletin from the BBC, played the jingle 'News Around the Clock', put on his serious mid-Atlantic voice, announced 'Dateline Monday 14 August', reported a series of attacks by American aircraft in Vietnam and the conviction of TV personality Michael Miles for drunkenness and the ensuing £16 fine. He reminded those who may have just tuned in: 'This is the station that offered the first offshore newscast. I hope I will again be able to say: "Paul Kaye reporting."'

That final hour had started with the most familiar Radio London jingle: 'You're hearing things, you're hearing things on Wonderful Radio London.' Then came Ed Stewart and Myrtle, his falsetto creation with the simple if not terribly inspiring catchphrase 'Hello, dear'. This was followed with a message from Cliff Richard before one of his records, which started fortuitously: 'It's over, didn't even cry. I just stopped living when you said goodbye.'

Whoever chose the records for that last hour – probably music director Alan Keen in conjunction with Ed Stewart – was to make the point forcibly. After Cliff came the Walker Brothers with 'Breaking Up Is So Very Hard to Do', the Beach Boys' 'Heroes and Villains', 'The Last Time' by the Rolling Stones, and Dusty Springfield's 'You Don't Have to Say You Love Me', with its all too appropriately maudlin first verse:

> 'Left alone with just a memory
> Life seems dead and so unreal
> All that's left is loneliness
> There's nothing left to feel.'

Mick Jagger opined: 'We're very sad to see you go and hope to see you one day again. You've given us a lot of good times.' Lulu confessed to feeling 'awful. When I'm in my car I always have Big L blaring.' Beach Boy Bruce Johnston said the group owed a lot of its success to the radio station. Cat Stevens, whose song 'I Love My Dog' was certainly promoted by Radio London, gave his thanks, as did Madeleine Bell. Dusty Springfield brought the older generation into the proceedings. 'I suppose it's sort of sad really,' she said. 'My mum said this morning she didn't know what she was going to do. She said she'll go potty without Radio London.'

Jonathan King even seemed to see Big L as a triumph of good over evil, and its demise a boost for the powers of darkness in his farewell message. He said: 'I'm very attached to the ship and all the people on it. I'm delighted to hear that it's going out with such dignity. All the times it has been on the air it has given, and it has had faith in people, and this is something which is very hard to find in our life and society as it is at the moment. I think Radio London has given so much to the English nation.'

That certainly would have been a more apocalyptic note to end on than the last celebrity farewell, which came, fittingly, from a Beatle. Unfortunately the Beatle was Ringo, who in his laconic, nasal drawl managed – who knows, perhaps intentionally, but then again perhaps not – to reduce the melodrama to a slight irritation.

'This is Ringo,' he said to millions of expectant transistors. 'I'm just saying cheerio to all you Radio London listeners 'cos, as you know, we're going off the air. It's a bit of a pity and the radio will never be the same, but it's one of those things. Cheerio.'

MD Philip Birch attempted valiantly to raise the tone again with a speech that barely mentioned the station's *raison d'être*, music, but instead turned it into a social service. It had in its fleeting three years helped the Royal National Institute for the Blind, Oxfam, Cancer Research and the Lifeboat Fund, and had saved the life of an airman who bailed out over the North Sea. 'As one listener put it,' he concluded, 'the world will get by without Big L, but I'm not sure that it will be a better place.'

The DJs were sure that it wouldn't be. All the big names who had featured in those three years said goodbye: John Peel, Pete Brady and Tony Windsor, the latter managing to say goodbye with a full-throated 'Hel-lo'. A soulful Tony Blackburn dropped his smile for the last time in many years to note that everyone aboard had the same aim: 'to pioneer commercial radio'. Pete Drummond, skating over the small fact that Kenny Everett had been sacked from the station for offending a sponsor, proclaimed: 'Radio London has been a unique station where freedom of speech and music has not been denied to the disc jockeys or to the audience. I doubt you'll ever see the like of it again.'

Dave Cash noted: 'Big L gave the Kenny and Cash programme the biggest boost that ever happened, and if we do get back on another radio station somewhere sometime, the Big L gave us our start and we want to thank them for it.'

Keith Skues, typically the one DJ with statistics at his fingertips and a photographic memory of recent Hansard entries in his head, talked about the Marine Offences Bill and then said it was 'a sad, black day in offshore history. During the past three years the sales of radios have quadrupled. Offshore radio has been directly responsible.' Ed Stewart paid tribute to the station where he had found Myrtle and became Stewpot (adding deliciously that he was especially sad, girls, because no more would he be able to tell you about Look Transparent Cooking Foil, which lets you *see* when the meat's overcooked). A bewildered Tommy Vance had been on the boat for only two weeks, and had probably never set eyes on Look Transparent Cooking Foil, but claimed to be as sad as everyone else.

And then with by far the longest message came twenty-two-year-old Kenny Everett, the length allotted to him a sign that he was now being seen as the station's star product. Aside from the fact that he euphemistically referred to his sacking as a desire 'to move around', his farewell was unusually heartfelt. There were no Spike Milligan inflections, no playing with words, no daft jokes. Indeed, it was to be one of the last times that he spoke publicly from the heart, before a mask of zany absurdity completely took over.

'Hello, Big L listeners,' he said. 'Kenny Everett here. I'm sure you've heard a lot of the messages from the other DJs saying how terribly sorry they are that Big L is coming off the air and what a crime it is. Well, I'm probably Big L's strongest admirer 'cos I was there right from a month before it started broadcasting, and was there up until six months ago, so I've seen Big L go through all its various stages and phases and everything, and I know almost everybody that works there today. And there's not very many weeks go by that a couple of the people who work there now don't come round for tea and we have long chats about the boat because it's a fantastically interesting topic, it really is.

'Big L has occupied my every waking moment since I left it. I don't know whether I'm sorry I left because you know you've got to move around etc. There's not a day goes by that I don't drag out the photographs of Big L and look at them. All the memories come flooding back. It's lovely. All the people that work there, really gassy people, they are too much. I've never met a more dedicated bunch of people in my life than the people who work in the offices and on the boat too. There's a tremendous spirit.

'Big L will always be remembered as the fantastic radio station it is today because it's being chopped up at its prime, and everything that happens like that is usually remembered for years and years and years. I think that if people do their bit and keep on remembering Big L and keep pestering for commercial radio to come back then the same people who are in it now will take over again, and we'll get Big L once again, only this time on land, and it will be clearer. It will be better in every way, so let's keep thinking about Big L and all the tremendous people you've heard on the air like, er, Kenny Everett and Dave Cash, and let's say thanks to Dave Cash too because the *Kenny and Cash* programme was really a gas to do. And Alan Keen has been a lovely programme director and supplied us with some superb records, and that's just about it really. It's just been a gas. And I won't forget it. Hope you won't too.'

And then Radio London bowed out. Paul Kaye, who had been the first voice on the station, was the last, saying: 'Big L time is three o'clock and Radio London is now closing down.' The last record had been an inspired choice: the Beatles' 'A Day in the Life', from the recently released album *Sergeant Pepper's Lonely Hearts Club Band*. Though neither Ed Stewart nor Paul Kaye said so, listeners needed no reminding that this track had been banned by the BBC, its censors believing that Paul McCartney's line 'Made my way upstairs and had a smoke' could only mean one thing, and that thing had nothing to do with cool mountain streams. The unspoken message that this sort of track would be denied their transistors in a pirate-free environment was not lost on the youth of England.

For young Brian Long clutching his transistor radio in the kitchen, it was the end of an era. 'It was unbelievable when it finished. I couldn't really take in that it would happen – until it did. I can't remember what I was doing when Kennedy was assassinated, but I can clearly remember sitting with the radio in the centre of the kitchen table listening to the dying moments of Big L. I still have that radio and sometimes think of all the vibrant programmes that it once emitted.'

To the DJs' amazement, when they had cleared customs at Felixstowe for the last time, they arrived at Liverpool Street station to find 1500 fans chanting 'Big L' and wearing mourning bands on their arms, giving them the welcome usually reserved for pop stars. Keith Skues even had the shirt ripped from his back.

Radio London's final hour turned out to be exactly that. But pirate radio never completely died. Radio Caroline was reincarnated several times in the ensuing decades; and it even gave an expression to the language. Pirate radio fans used to hire small pleasure craft and journey out to see their favourite ships and favourite DJs, often in poor weather. They would tend to carry transistor radios, cameras and duffle bags, and wear anoraks. In 1973 Radio Caroline DJ Andy Archer referred to the fanatics as 'anoraks', a name now given to obsessives of anything and everything.

Inevitably, when Everett looked back some twenty years after the close of Radio London, he hid any natural enthusiasm he might have felt under a mask of zaniness and cynicism. The food was appalling. One morning he had opened a packet of corn flakes only to discover a mass of writhing weevils. And the other DJs had found it hard to strike up a rapport with him. 'On board ship,' he recalls in *The Custard Stops at Hatfield*, the book he wrote with Simon Booker in 1982, 'the studio was in the bilges and our soundproofing consisted of a mass of blankets hung over the dank, rusty, slimy walls. If you listened to the Pirates, it sounded as though we were all swathed in mink and had pop stars coming out of our ears in a haze of champagne bubbles. In actual fact we sat in a dingy, blanket-ridden little cell which would make the poorest scout hut in the land seem like the Café Royal.'

5

KENNY AND THE BEATLES

'Goodbye Kenny, it's nice to see you back. Goodbye Kenny, we
hear you've got the sack.'

Unpublished song by Lennon and McCartney

There were consolations which made the seasickness, the weevils
and the bilges bearable. The obvious one was being paid to play
records, and so become famous and relatively wealthy for doing
something that was already a hobby, if not an obsession.

But there were also compensations even greater than doing the
job, and meeting the people, of your dreams. The school failure from
Liverpool was already spending his shore leaves rubbing shoulders
with the likes of the Kinks and Dusty Springfield. And then, in
the summer of 1966, came a phone call which was to transport
him to Cloud Nine. One night, sitting in his flat in Lower Sloane
Street, Everett answered the phone to find it was Radio London's
programme director, Alan Keen, with a request that would have
been music to the ears of several million young people around
the world. Yet, to Everett's amazement, Keen sounded almost
apologetic.

'How would you like to meet the Beatles?' he asked the
dumbstruck DJ. 'I'm afraid you'll have to go to America with
them, follow them around to about twenty different cities and
spend a few weeks nattering to them about the tour and life and
anything else they want to tell you.'

On that day at least, Everett must have believed there was a God
again. A twenty-one-year-old, music-obsessed lad from Liverpool

was about to make his first trip to America in the company of the four most important and exciting people not just from his home city, not just in his world, but arguably in *the* world. It was, thought Everett at the time, like being told you've won the pools and you're going to heaven to spend it.

The rationale behind sending Everett on tour with the Beatles was a suitably surreal one. In the first days of Beatlemania, George Harrison had innocently confessed in an interview to liking jelly babies. It was a remark that John, Paul and Ringo came to curse him for. From that day on, the group were pelted with jelly babies at every gig they played by fans believing that a direct hit might curry favour with their idols.

For the American tour, Bassetts, purveyor of jelly babies to the Beatles (via several thousand middlewomen), decided they would send a pirate-radio DJ with the Fab Four to report on transatlantic attitudes to hurling the jelly baby, and other matters which seemed of enormous import way back then.

In fact the tour that Everett went on was to have a place in pop history. It was the Beatles' last. The concert in August 1966 at Candlestick Park in San Francisco was the last touring gig they ever played, though neither he nor even they knew this when they set off in a thunderstorm.

The trip had an inauspicious start. The plane carrying Everett, the Beatles and lesser chart stars the Ronettes and Bobby Hebb (who had a British hit with 'Sunny'), began its take-off in awful weather, and one of the engines gave out with a loud bang on the runway. The Ronettes decided it was all too much and disembarked. The rest stayed put, in various shades of green. Everett was still infected with euphoria. He later recalled that his only thought was: I'm going to die with the Beatles.

Indeed, he would have been right alongside them. At the start of the trip Paul McCartney came back from the VIP seats and said: 'Which one's Kenny Everett?' When the DJ identified himself, Paul said: 'Come up the front with us.' Paul was protective of him during the whole tour, and it was a kindness Everett never forgot. Even though he and John Lennon were to become close, Everett never really appreciated John's acerbic wit. But he would never brook any criticism of McCartney, because of that early gesture of friendship.

The plane finally made it to America. But a rather worse problem awaited. What Bassetts didn't know was that Everett, though a zany and spontaneous DJ, was no great shakes as an investigative journalist. Uninspired opening gambits like 'How's it going then, John?' received the inevitable riposte: 'You're not a very good interviewer, are you, Ken?'

But fortunately for him, the Beatles continued to take pity. This was not wholly in character at a time when the group could be devastating to journalists, finishing off with a barbed put-down of anyone who didn't match up to their ready wit and off-the-wall humour. But something about Everett appealed to them. He loved music, he loved them, he loved joking about, he was a working-class kid from Liverpool. He was as near as dammit 'one of us'.

In the first few days of the tour Everett just retreated into his all too familiar shell in fits of despair and embarrassment that he wasn't up to this interviewing lark. Paul spied him in one of these black moods and made another remarkably generous gesture. Taking the DJ into the bathroom of the hotel, he said: 'Why don't you just ask me one question and I'll rabbit on for ages? Then you'll have enough material for ages.' He rabbited on for an hour, and with careful rationing this filled most of the broadcasts back to England for the duration of the tour.

Judged by today's technology, the way Everett recorded his material on that American tour was basic, to say the least. He would hold a microphone up in the air at one of the stadium concerts, tape the sound of the Beatles on stage singing one of their hits, almost drowned out by the screams of teenage girls all around him. Though ludicrously primitive, it probably gave one of the more accurate impressions of being at a Beatles concert.

If the recording methods were rudimentary, the transmission process was pure Heath Robinson. Everett would say a few words of commentary to complete the tape, then rush to his hotel and ring fellow DJ Paul Kaye in Harwich and play the tape down the phone. Kaye recorded this by holding his telephone earpiece to a microphone. Then he would take his tape on the tender to the pirate ship. The consequent snatches of concert, Everett commentary, McCartney interviews and jelly-baby commercials were spliced into a seamless whole. If it still exists somewhere it would be a priceless possession for Beatles collectors, though the sound quality might defeat even George Martin, the group's legendary producer.

In America, on that hectic last tour of thirty-one towns in thirty-two nights, Everett was accepted into the Beatles' inner circle. This allowed him to experience at first hand the sort of measures that had to be taken just to get the group to a concert venue at the height of Beatlemania in America. Even the jelly babies, Everett's *raison d'être* in America, were more troublesome there. George Harrison remembers: 'It was terrible. They hurt. They don't have soft jelly babies but hard jelly beans like bullets. Everywhere we went I got them thrown at me.'

And everywhere they went with Everett in tow, he marvelled at what was becoming increasingly like a military operation. Going to Shea Stadium, the security men got wind of a rumour that the Beatles' fleet of limousines was going to be ambushed by fans. They stopped on a dark highway outside New York and transferred to a large army truck, which transported them past the fans.

Worse was to come at Philadelphia, where the fans charged the stage. The Beatles and Everett took refuge in a caravan, which became engulfed in a sea of teenagers and rocked violently. Once again he took a morbid solace in the fact that he believed he was about to die with the Beatles.

Back in Britain, as 1966 turned into 1967, his relationship with the group took a predictably psychedelic turn. And his relationship with one of the most important members of the Beatles' entourage took an unpredictably romantic turn.

Peter Brown, who was to be immortalized by the Beatles in song in 1969 with a name-check in 'The Ballad of John and Yoko', was Brian Epstein's best friend and personal assistant. He went on to run the Beatles' company, Apple Corps, for a while, and when the group broke up in 1970 he moved to New York, where he became a successful business consultant. His clients now include Sir Andrew Lloyd Webber's Really Useful Group and the BBC. Like Epstein, he came from Liverpool, where they both ran record shops; they were both homosexual; and they both adored the Beatles. Like Everett, he came from a Catholic family. 'I had rejected religion when I left home,' says Brown, 'but nevertheless our shared background was a sort of bond between us.'

In 1967 Brown was sharing a flat with Epstein in Chapel Street, off Belgrave Square, close to Everett's Chelsea flat. The two of them met, probably at a Beatles gathering, shortly after Everett left Radio London in February 1967.

Brown was four years older than Everett and infinitely more worldly-wise. He took Everett under his wing, and took him to stay with him in the country, where the Beatles would sometimes join them. Everett loved being with them, even if sartorially he was an odd man out. Brown recalls: 'I don't think he had much experience of socializing and he was thrust in among rather high-profile people. He wore very, very square-looking clothes. He used to wear a rather naff sports jacket with a shirt and tie. Everyone else would wear rather hippyish clothes. I used to tease him about it.' It didn't matter.

Rapidly it became a physical relationship, Everett's first – and also the last with a man for a very long time. They were together for six months, Everett often staying with Brown at the Epstein home. They saw each other all the time. Yet, despite the fact that Peter Brown was not closeted about his gayness, Everett never spoke about the relationship afterwards. It has never been referred to in any of the hundreds of newspaper articles on him. Even his future wife, who knew he had once had a crush on Brown, never knew it was a physical, serious relationship. Certainly, it seemed to leave Everett as confused and uncertain about his sexuality as he was before he met Brown.

Peter Brown remembers a full, intense and completely physical relationship on both sides: 'I was the first relationship Kenny had with a man,' he says now. 'It was 1967 and very promiscuous times. We quickly got together and had a sexual relationship. It was full-blown right from the early stages. The physical relationship was one I was sort of in control of. He was totally adorable and vulnerable. The first time for anybody is very physical, very affectionate. And if you've reached twenty-two, as Kenny had, you are very needy.' Brown never noticed any of the insecurity or guilt feelings that Everett was to experience over his sexuality in years to come.

'We were a couple,' he explains now. 'I suppose he thought it was all right because the Beatles approved of it. There wasn't a stigma attached to being gay in our circle. I lived very comfortably and securely in that kind of world. We were together less than a year, but it was a unique period. We did a lot of going down to the country and doing acid at Brian's Sussex home. Brian was very fond of Kenny. Brian didn't have relationships that lasted more than five minutes. He was subjected to having to deal with a string of boyfriends. So he liked the fact that Kenny and I were a couple. Kenny had a bad trip once and George Harrison took care of him. George was stoned himself, but he looked after Kenny. Kenny loved the Beatles but I don't think he ever realized how much they admired him. It was definitely a mutual admiration. He never realized how special he was.'

The relationship ended on 27 August 1967, the day Brian Epstein took a drug overdose and died. Brown was completely shattered by his best friend's death. Reporters had been outside his flat all day. In the evening another friend, the late Tommy Nutter, the designer, who had a tailor's shop in Savile Row, phoned him to ask him if he was coping OK. 'No, I'm awful,' Brown said. Nutter went round to comfort him and they were together for four years. He replaced Everett.

Brown remembers: 'I don't think I confronted the situation terribly well. Kenny was a shy and most adorable person. I do feel some guilt over my handling of the relationship. I was the more mature person and the more experienced. But I can't underestimate the effect of Brian's death. I had lost my best friend and there was the question of what was going to happen to the Beatles. It was a very traumatic and very difficult time for me. Kenny always used to say I dumped him for Tommy. Although one relationship followed the other I didn't consciously do it. But Kenny gave me a bit of a guilt trip about our split. He gave me something else too. It was a large wooden spoon. He gave it to me because he thought I was a mixer. On the bowl of the spoon he had written "Love Kenny". I still have it hanging in my kitchen.'

Whatever effect that first relationship had on Everett, he kept it to himself. It is one of the most curious aspects of Everett's story that after he and Brown drifted apart, it was as if that six-month relationship had never happened. Homosexuality was once again a problem, a part of himself that he refused to come to terms with. It is possible that he tried to put it out of his mind as he still had embedded in his thinking the idea that homosexuality was a sin whatever the Beatles' circle might think. Other 'sins' though, he, in common with much of the youth of the Western world, went helter-skelter to embrace.

On the American tour the young Everett had turned down all offers of drugs, even though pot was passed around as a matter of routine, and Paul had on one occasion talked rhapsodically about LSD. Everett had nodded sagely, even though he hadn't understood a word. Back in Britain, things were to change. On Weybridge golf course, with John Lennon.

John, and his friend from schooldays, Terry Doran, had been spending the evening at the Speakeasy, the London club where every sixties pop star and hanger-on worth a Scotch and Coke went to be seen. The pair bumped into Kenny Everett outside the club and started to chat, but were spotted by some fans, who ran towards John. The three of them rushed into John's car. Everett recalled the incident years later in *The Custard Stops at Hatfield*: 'The two of them were obviously on something because John was talking completely incomprehensible drivel, and Terry was not only understanding what was being said, but replying in the same off the planet drivel.'

Everett lay in the back of the car, not even sure if the other two were aware he was there, but curious to see John's mock-Tudor Surrey mansion. He followed them in and gazed wide-eyed at the vast pastel carpet, the suits of armour and medieval altarpieces. With grotesque disregard of his surroundings, Doran rustled up some Heinz tomato soup. Everett recalled thinking: Wow, John Lennon eats Heinz tomato soup. How ordinary. I thought he'd have turtles' eggs flown in from Bangkok, and caviar freshly rolled on the hips of Filipino virgins.

He spent the night there, and for breakfast the next morning Lennon suggested they take LSD. Then he suggested going for a walk. 'I remember it was raining,' wrote Everett afterwards, 'very gently, the sort of upper class, fine rain you could only find in posh places like Weybridge. It was very quiet, and the air smelled of pine trees as we wafted along, dressed in psychedelic cloaks. We walked on to the golf course, and suddenly a helicopter landed. I've no idea why, and it's just the sort of surreal thing you'd imagine when you are tripping, but it definitely happened. Or was it a bird?'

Perhaps it was a walrus.

For Everett's trip with John Lennon may have influenced one of the best-known lyrics in pop. A few months later, in September 1967, Everett was allowed in to the Abbey Road studio to witness the

Beatles recording 'I Am the Walrus'. It was a seminal moment in the group's recording career. Their manager Brian Epstein had died of a drug overdose just nine days before, and this was the first song they recorded after his death. It was one of Lennon's best, composed at the piano in his Weybridge home, a protest laced with psychedelic imagery directed against his schoolteachers ('experts/textperts') and against the establishment in general, at a time when it was beginning to round on the young and the drug culture, arresting Mick Jagger and Keith Richard of the Rolling Stones for possession, and, with huge consequences for Everett, banning the pirate radio stations.

It was quite a session to be present at. John had been singing until he was nearly hoarse. At one point George Martin said to him: 'Look, you've been singing now for about seven hours, you're beginning to sound hoarse. Why don't we do it tomorrow?' But John insisted on continuing, which explains the even rawer than usual sound of his voice on that track.

As Everett watched, John got to the line: 'If the sun don't come you get your tan from standing in the English rain.' He stopped singing, turned to Everett and said: 'Reminds me of that day on the Weybridge golf course, eh, Ken?' Everett looked blank. 'You remember, the Weybridge golf course, the rain, get a tan from standing . . . oh forget it.'

Ken's easygoing relationship with John and Paul was not always quite so easygoing with George. One spat occurred at a party thrown by Brian Epstein. It was at the house in Sussex where Winston Churchill planned some of the campaigns of the Second World War. It was a party which those who were there recall rapidly turning into one enormous acid trip. Terry Doran contrived to fall out of a window and remain unhurt; people were wandering around solemnly declaring they had found the meaning of life.

Brian Epstein had bought a grand piano especially for Paul. But Paul didn't turn up, so Derek Taylor, the band's press officer, sat at the piano playing Ivor Novello songs, while those around him tripped the light fantastic. Those who were there remember it as a typical sixties party. Probably it was only typical of parties where the host was Brian Epstein and the chief guests the Beatles.

But the evening started relatively innocently, with Everett smoking joints with the Beatles in the inglenook. At the time George was deeply into his Indian mystic phase, which was responsible for persuading the rest of the group to spend time with the Maharishi and for sitar-led music, conspicuously out of character for Beatle albums, on tracks like 'Within You Without You' on *Sergeant Pepper*.

Everett was in depressive mode and was talking in the inglenook to John, George, Ringo, Klaus Voormann (of Manfred Mann) and a girl he had not met before about how suicidal he felt. The girl passed a joint around, but when it reached George he just held it while he attempted unsuccessfully to soothe Everett with talk of religion, love and the meaning of life. 'It's all around you, Ken,' he drawled meaningfully to a less than interested Everett, who could only think that George, whose garb consisted largely of bells and beads, sounded like Tinkerbell whenever he moved. The girl became irritated with George. This was hardly good counselling, she thought, for 'this little boy who just wanted to die'.

She also became irritated with George for talking about sharing love instead of just sharing the marijuana. She reprimanded him with unintentional wit: 'George, you're hogging the joint.' Love and peace went out the window as Harrison rounded on her. 'I don't need to hog joints,' he hissed. 'That's very unChristly of you,' she responded coolly. Everett laughed to see the Beatle taken down a peg, and to his surprise he was not the only one laughing. John Lennon laughed till he nearly fell off his chair, and Ringo patted the girl on the back. Both of them obviously relished seeing George's mid-sixties saintliness punctured.

Everett was rapidly becoming the Beatles' favourite disc jockey. Indeed, so favoured was he that Lennon and McCartney took a break from recording the album *The Beatles* at Abbey Road to record a jingle for his Radio 1 show. If there were a competition for DJ one-upmanship, which of course there is most days, then having the Beatles do your jingles is a pretty good start. Prophetically, the jingle was a joke song about Everett getting the sack.

The scene in the Abbey Road studio that day on 5 June 1968 was a remarkable one. Everett had gone there to interview John Lennon. He arrived with a friend from EMI Records, nineteen-year-old Tony Olivestone, who had a tape recorder and held it while Everett did the interview. One of the first surprises that Olivestone got that day was that Everett played Schubert in the eight-track tape machine in his car on the way there. 'All I listen to when I'm driving is classical music,' Everett told him.

When they arrived at Abbey Road, the Beatles were recording 'Don't Pass Me By', the first song on a Beatles album to be composed by Ringo Starr. But the attention of both Everett and Olivestone was caught by the sight of the still largely unknown Yoko Ono, lying on the floor next to John and saying never a word the whole time they were there. 'I couldn't believe what I was seeing,' says Olivestone. 'John Lennon was sitting on the floor strumming a guitar. And there was this apparition all in white next to John. Most people didn't know of her existence at that stage. She never spoke the whole time we were there. In fact she never moved.'

The interview showed an increasingly strange John Lennon leaving Everett straining to catch up with his changes of subject and tone. Most of the interview that Everett got that day was never broadcast. Only one tape of it still exists, a reel-to-reel, and Olivestone has it. If the world had heard it, they would have got a different view of the Beatles. The interview cum rap session dashed frenetically between contrasting facets of the group: lovable moptops, psychedelic trend-setters, surreal humorists, and most notably, though this side was never broadcast, cruel and tasteless.

Robert Kennedy, candidate for president of the USA, had just been murdered in cold blood in America. Lennon, mainly, with the others not slow to take their cue from him, laughed and joked about the assassination. Even in 1995, twenty-seven years later, when the music magazine *Mojo* printed a section of the interview in a Beatles tribute edition, it dared not print the Kennedy references.

The interview is fascinating, showing as it does, Everett's rapport with the group:

John Lennon: So, Kenny, how are you going?

Kenny Everett: Oh, it's wonderful. First a few questions, then I'd like you to sing me a goodbye jingle.

JL: Goodbye jingle.

KE: What can we expect from you in the next few months?

JL: A lot of brown paper bags, Kenny, actually. We're working very hard on that at the moment, the boys and me.

KE: Anything tuney?

JL: Oh yeah. There's a lot of tunes to be found in the bags actually . . .

(The Beatles giggle and mumble about Robert Kennedy being shot.)

JL: They're not laughing about the Kennedy assassination on the air, are they, Kenny? On the air! Ha ha ha.

KE: We're getting all this, you know . . . Is there any particular record out at the moment?

JL: Oh yeah, let me think . . . (sings) When I was a little baby my momma used to smash me in the cradle, picking those old cotton fields back home.

KE: Did you come back [from India] with anything incredibly fantastic?

JL: Yes. A beard.

KE: I saw a photograph of you in the *Daily Mirror* wearing a sheet.

JL: That's called a venoos, Kenny – what are you talking about? I got it in Morocco.

KE: It looks like a sheet.

JL: Well, venooses do look like sheets so that the lower classes in Morocco won't get too put out, having only sheets to wear.

KE: Have you got anything to say that our listeners would understand?

JL: How about: 'Good morning'?

KE: About anything you've recorded so far? Something that they'll comprehend?

JL: No, dear, we've just done two tracks, both unfinished. The second one's Ringo's first song, which we're working on at this very moment

KE: He composed it himself?

JL: He composed it himself, in a fit of lethargy.

KE: And what do you think about it?

JL: I think it's the most wonderful thing I've ever heard since Nilsson's 'River Deep Mountain Dew'. (He strums and sings about Kenny Everett.)

KE: This is straight out of your head?

JL: This is *ad nauseam*, Ken. Straight out of the mouth that bit me.

KE: How's business with Apple?

JL: I couldn't ask for any more tapes or bits of paper.

KE: Ask me a few questions.

JL: So, Kenny, what are you doing?

KE: I'm having a daily show come on soon.

JL: Really, so they haven't sacked you?

KE: If you were stranded away on a desert island, what one gramophone record would you take with you, excluding the Bible and *Sergeant Pepper* as obvious choices?

JL: One gramophone record? It hasn't been made yet.

KE: When you produce something of such a high standard as your last album [*Sergeant Pepper*] undoubtedly was, don't you think that you've really got to strive to produce something a little bit better?

JL: It only got high because everybody said how high it was. It was no higher than it was when we made it.

KE: There's hidden meanings in that one, ladies and gentlemen.

JL: No, what I mean, Kenny, is that, you see, it doesn't pose a problem to us. It was so long ago, we've forgotten what it was about anyway. I don't think I ever did listen to it, since we made it, properly. I played it just after we made it, and that's it really. But I like to hear it on the radio.

KE: All right. Shall I play it?

JL: Yes, that would be nice.

KE: Do you think Paul and you could do a duo harmony jingle?

JL: Well, you'll have to get him.

(John and Paul play and sing repeatedly: 'Goodbye to Kenny Everett, he is our very pal.')

JL: Play Tiny Tim, Ken. Play Tiny Tim. He's the greatest ever man. You see if I ain't right, Kenny Everett. (sings) Oh, Tiny Tim for president, oh Tiny Tim for Queen.

George then comes and joins them, saying: 'It's nice to be on the air again. Beatle George speaking. Got the sack, did you?'

All the Beatles then sing a jingle: 'Goodbye, Kenny, see you in the morning. Goodbye Kenny, see you at the dawning. Goodbye Kenny, it's nice to see you back. Goodbye Kenny, we hear you've got the sack.'

JL: There you are, Ken, you've got an LP there.

KE: It's been a pleasure.

JL: You're wrong, Ken, it has *not* been a pleasure.

KE: Can we have a rousing chorus of 'Strawberry Fields Forever' in jazz tempo?

John and Paul then speak the words of the song in a Noel Coward camp tone.

Later that year Everett produced the official Beatles Christmas record for their fan club, or, as it said on the cover: 'Kenny Everett had a nice time mucking about with the tapes, and deserves to be called producer.'

And, a year after that bizarre interview at Abbey Road, John and Yoko chose Everett to relay one of their world-peace-in-a-bag messages to the public. Curiously, Everett, the wackiest DJ of the age, found it hard to relate to John and Yoko's avant-gardism and became quite irritated with it. Yoko asked him to make sure the message from her and John reached all national newspaper editors. Reluctantly, he did so. Only one paper printed it in the end. Though a natural anarchic comedian himself, Everett was baffled by John and Yoko's antics. But even more curious and even more revealing was his reaction to Lennon's death.

Though John was the Beatle with whom he definitely had the closest relationship, he wrote about his murder quite soon after the event in a notably detached and unemotional manner. What he wrote said little about John and even less about their friendship, but it revealed plenty about the writer's unwillingness to deal with emotion.

'It was obviously a shock when the news came through that John had been murdered,' he wrote, 'but I didn't get as worked up about it as most people. Having met the guy a few times, I figured that his philosophy would have prepared him for whatever was going to happen next . . . It's not as if he was only halfway through and hadn't produced his best work yet. There were a couple of good tracks on his last album, *Double Fantasy*, but I don't think anyone could reasonably expect him to keep churning out classics. He'd done his bit, and that was that.'

It was a strange farewell from the DJ who, more than any other, paid homage to the Beatles on radio during the sixties, and indeed long after. I well recall listening to Everett's Radio 1 show when *The Beatles*, better known as the 'White Album', was released at the end of 1968. His infectious enthusiasm knew no bounds as the little snatches of songs, almost indeed jingles, that connected tracks for the first time on a Beatles album were plucked by Everett to punctuate his show and whet the appetite for what was to come.

That year Everett was a regular visitor to Apple Corps, the company set up by the Beatles with the aim of being a philanthropic business and somewhere that struggling artists and musicians could bring their wares. The results were predictably disastrous. And for Derek Taylor, the Beatles' press officer, surrounded by unwanted tapes, unwanted freeloaders and occasionally unwanted hell's angels, the sight of Everett would always cheer him up.

'He used to come around to Apple and hang out on the sofa by my desk,' says Taylor. 'We smoked. He could rarely remember why he came. We would just prattle on. In that stressful atmosphere it was a great relief. Anyone was welcome for a drink and a smoke, provided they didn't insist on a recording contract. Kenny was particularly easy to get along with because he was unthreatening, and he was a Beatlemaniac. A genuine, unreconstructed Beatlemaniac.'

The Beatles played a greater part in Everett's story than he realized. Not only had they taken him to America and given his fledgeling career an almighty boost; they had granted him access to the Abbey Road studios, and given him interviews and first plays of new releases to make his colleagues green with envy. A freshly minted copy of 'Strawberry Fields Forever' and 'Penny Lane' was sent by Brian Epstein to the Radio London ship and Everett was the first DJ in the world to play it. After *Sergeant Pepper* was made, George Harrison invited Everett round to his house and played it to him. Everett was knocked sideways. 'Do you think we should release it, Ken?' asked a solemn Harrison. 'Well, yes, I think perhaps you should,' gulped Everett.

It was even a Beatles record that got him his first warning of dismissal, after it had prompted a delicious Everett on-air *faux pas*. On Radio London in the summer of 1965, Everett and Ed Stewart were strolling on deck one evening, sniffing the sea breezes and twiddling a knob on a transistor radio. Suddenly out came the sound of Paul McCartney singing 'Yesterday', the first time either jock had heard it. 'I said: "Kenny, listen to that. That sounds like a musical orgasm,"' remembers Ed Stewart. 'Kenny was as innocent as hell. So the next day he plays Yesterday and says on air: "This song gives Ed Stewart a musical orgasm." There's an immediate ship-to-shore phone call from 17 Curzon Street, the station's headquarters in London, and Philip Birch, the managing director of Radio London, said get that man off immediately. He wanted him sacked.'

Stewart was in charge of the ship that day, and he managed to soothe Birch with an explanation that amazingly happened to be the truth. Twenty-year-old Everett, the likely lad from Liverpool, had just repeated the word 'orgasm' because he thought it had a nice sound. He did not have the faintest idea what it meant. (He was not the only naive waif on board that ship, incidentally. Tony Blackburn nearly got the sack when he read out a listener's joke: 'Why don't fairies have children? Because they're always going to gobblin' parties.' Blackburn, who didn't understand the double entendre or why his fellow DJs were killing themselves laughing, was completely flummoxed when he received a severe reprimand.)

If the Beatles were an important force in Kenny Everett's life, they also figured after his death. He adored their music, and he was for a time a member of the inner circle. Appropriately enough the Beatles were present, on record, at his funeral in April 1995. Weeks before he died he had asked his agent, Jo Gurnett, to ensure that John's 'Strawberry Fields Forever' was played at his cremation. It was the record for which he had the most affection. He recognized its Liverpudlian allusions, its evocation of the psychedelic era and its mould-breaking production and technical innovations. And, of course, it featured John and the rest of the band at the absolute height of their powers.

Knowing the Beatles changed Everett's life. And in a way that was to be infinitely more far-reaching than even seeing America, having his first gay liaison or taking acid for the first time. It was through his friendship with them that he was invited to that party at Brian Epstein's home where George Harrison flew into a temper, just as his relationship with Peter Brown was fizzling out. The girl who had caught his eye in standing up to Harrison was a former singer in a female duo, and a well-known face among the sixties London in crowd. She was at the time the lover of the pre-Beatles, smouldering, lip-curling, British rock and roll sensation Billy Fury. She barely noticed Everett, though he did register just long enough for her to think: That boy looks really ill. He looks like a stick insect.

But he noticed her. And the next day he found to his great astonishment that he was experiencing a feeling quite alien to him. He couldn't get her out of his mind. Could this be what he had been told would happen? Could this woman be the 'cure' that would banish those impulses he had, and make him at last 'normal'?

Over the next decade, in a haze of genuinely romantic courtship, drug-induced euphoria and perverse viciousness, he would find out.

6

LEE

'To Lee, the only woman in my life. A jewel, a flower, an essence of all that is good and lovely. An island in a sea of horror and agony, of despair and crippling fatigue and boredom. She and she alone can bring happiness and solace into my worthless and empty life. I would kill for her – kill, d'you hear, KILL!'

Entry in Everett's diary

While Kenny Everett continued to lie on the floor at Brian Epstein's party soliloquizing about ending it all, Lee Middleton was busy. As one of the few people at the party not tripping, she joined her pop-star chum Lulu in the kitchen at five a.m. to fry some eggs. In this she was disturbed by John Lennon, dressed in kaftan and poncho and with, she all too vividly remembers, a weird and threatening look in his eye. He was in an odd and dangerous mood, and she was afraid of him. She hid under the table, cuddling up, appropriately enough, to Cynthia Lennon, John's wife, who was one of her best friends. 'With some men when they look at you, it's flattering,' says Lee. 'But with John, around that time, the way he would look at you, you knew you had to avoid him. And the best way to keep him away was to be near his wife.'

Lee's life in those days was lived out against a celebrity backcloth. She, much more than her husband-to-be, was cherished by the stars who lent on her, came to her for advice and always wanted her at their parties. She met Everett at a Beatles party in the mid-sixties. She saw him for the last time at Elton John's fortieth birthday party in March 1987. When Everett turned against her and vilified her after their divorce, he was shocked to find that Elton John and other celebrity friends dropped him to remain loyal to Lee. She counselled a devastated Cynthia Lennon after Cynthia came home from a holiday to find Yoko Ono installed in her home, and an equally devastated Maureen Starr when her marriage to Ringo broke up. But her own marriage to Everett was as stormy as that of any of her famous friends; and the traumas of her own marriage she had to keep secret for a long time. Yet, for all this, there were a few years when the two of them were passionately and intensely in love.

Audrey Valentine Middleton was born on 14 February 1937, one of three daughters of William Middleton, a Sheffield fireman, and his wife, Elsie. If Everett found the Liverpool of the fifties constricting, he could be glad he wasn't born into his wife's generation. Lee, who was nearly eight years older than him, experienced the real wartime and postwar austerity. Clothes and food were rationed throughout her youth. Banana-flavoured semolina was served in the Middletons' two-up two-down house as a special treat, there being no actual bananas. Her female teachers, deprived of nylon stockings, used leg paint, which invariably went patchy shortly after being applied.

From the age of eight Audrey experienced *déjà vu* and had dreams which came true, including one of a schoolfriend being fatally injured. But it was not something that at that time she gave much thought to. The priority for a working-class teenage girl in postwar Sheffield was to get a husband. Audrey idolized her father, a strict but loving parent, who in turn adored his wife. Young Audrey would pray at night that her future husband would be just like him.

She was still a teenager when she married, her choice being a junior professional footballer, Alan Bradshaw, also in his teens. The wedding, like her later one to Everett, contained elements of farce. At the last minute she told her mum she did not want to go though with it; but her mum had ordered 100 trifles from the Co-op, so she had to. Port was spilled down her wedding dress, which was trod on and torn by an uncle with two left feet at the post-wedding dance. The wedding night saw no consummation, partly because husband and wife were flummoxed to find Audrey's dad had sewn up the sleeves and legs of her pyjamas as a practical joke. Consummation on the honeymoon was swiftly followed by cystitis, which was in turn swiftly followed by a much-confused young hubby heading off for national service in Germany while Audrey, who now worked in the office at Sheffield's Empire Theatre, went back to live with mum and dad.

Before long she had run away to London, changed her name to Lee and was living with her new boyfriend, Alex Most. The crush on Alex was intense, only to be shattered when he turned out to be bisexual and left her temporarily for a well-known composer of musicals. Lee amused herself with a series of sugar daddies and took some less than salubrious jobs in nightclubs, though paradoxically one kept her clean. This striptease job was 'the shower-bath act', which involved her having to shower on stage five times a day. At the time her future husband was studying to be a missionary.

Lee was soon spotted by a producer at Hammer Films who, seeing her resemblance to the actress Billie Whitelaw, cast her as her double in a film. She was also singing professionally and her career was beginning to blossom. Then she got pregnant by Alex. She was not ready for children and so decided to have an abortion back in Sheffield. It cost £10 and was in the proverbial backstreet. Lee describes it as 'a filthy house with a dingy woman at a table holding a huge douche; a plastic washing-up bowl lay on the floor. She had me put one foot on a chair and did the deed over this grubby bowl.' A week later she was bleeding, in terrible pain and in labour. Afraid to send for help in case she was sent to jail for her illegal termination, she was eventually ambulanced to hospital, where she was told the foetus had been dead for a fortnight and septicaemia had set in.

She still did not pause for breath. As soon as she had recovered, she returned to London and became one half of a singing duo, Lee and Michelle, 'curvaceous blonde bombshells' as the advertising posters put it, complete with Brigitte Bardot hairpieces. Lee, like many of her generation, made up for a youth spent in postwar austerity by flinging herself headlong into the economic and cultural youth explosion of the early sixties. She became a typical good-time girl of the period, flirting with suitors who included aspiring actors Michael Caine and Terence Stamp, and becoming an integral part of the Soho coffee-bar set that spawned numerous pop stars, film stars and authors. It was a circuit that tended to live in a haze of late, late nights and purple hearts. One morning Lee had breakfast with Keith Moon of the

Who. His breakfast consisted of a sandwich of bread, butter and pep pills washed down with Buck's Fizz. But Lee survived, though her £10 abortion had a much higher price: she could never have children.

By 1960 Lee had a persistent suitor, and one who would have made her the envy of thousands of pubescent girls, had they known. Billy Fury was one of a clutch of British singers who modelled themselves on Elvis Presley but was rapidly becoming a star in his own right and was Britain's number-one sex symbol. The couple moved in together (very secretly, as pop stars were not meant to have girlfriends in those days) and planned to marry, even though Fury warned her he had heart trouble and was not expected to live to old age (he died of a heart attack in 1983). Theirs was a volatile eight-year relationship punctuated by Fury's various affairs, including one with the actress Amanda Barrie that would enrage Lee, and another with one of Lee's closest friends that ended their common-law marriage. Meanwhile Lee had become a creditable solo performer, appearing as 'Lady Lee' on the cabaret circuit, but her recording career was accident-prone. She covered Dionne Warwick's 'Anyone Who Had a Heart' but failed to release it before the Cilla Black version. She raved to Alex Most, by this time a platonic friend, about a new song she was releasing, 'Something Tells Me I'm into Something Good'. Alex in turn raved to his brother, the record producer Mickie Most, who got one of his groups, Herman's Hermits, to release it first. It went to number one. Though she never had a hit record, Lee knew, and was courted by, the leading figures in the music industry. The Beatles' manager, Brian Epstein, was a close friend and invited her to his party one weekend. Fury was away, so Lee went without him and entered to find George Harrison 'talking intensely to this strange, thin person, the thinnest person I'd ever seen'.

Everett began to visit Lee at her home. The psychedelic era was dawning, and weekend parties tended to be LSD parties and last literally all weekend. One time Fury came home to find Lee and Ev, as she always referred to him, high on LSD, on the couch together. She had her leg across him and he was playing the 'piano' with her leg as a keyboard. The singer lived up to his name, and exploded: 'What's going on between you two!' Lee thought that particularly amusing. She enjoyed Everett's company, just as she enjoyed the company of her other gay friends; for she assumed right from their first meeting that gay he was. 'He would sit and watch me make up and dress like an adoring son. He used to follow me around like a little creature. He was always there. I think he fell in love with the glamour of it all. I was fairly attractive in those days and used to dress very glamorously. Billy Fury was a big star and Ev wasn't anybody really. Then we became sort of like sisters, going everywhere together and always laughing.'

That wasn't quite true. Between the laughing, Everett would revert to his depressive state. Many a soirée at Lee's home was dominated by his monologues on how he wanted to die; how he was thin, unattractive and fancied men. God had given him every handicap, he told her. Indeed, the first time she saw him after Epstein's party was when he came to her house, again tripping, to inform her that he was going to kill himself. Lee snapped him out of it, saying: 'If you are going to do so, could you please vacate my premises, indeed vacate the area, because it would be extremely inconvenient for us all.' She went on to tell him: 'You're not unattractive. But you have to give good value in life. If you keep boring on about how you're pathetic and how you want to commit suicide, no one will want to be with you.' It was a very direct form of counselling, but it seemed to work. 'He stopped talking about suicide and started to live,' says Lee, adding without any conscious irony: 'He didn't start talking about suicide again until after we were married.'

When she and Billy Fury drifted apart, Ev was there constantly, a best friend. 'He surrounded me,' says Lee. 'But then he always loved a good tragedy.' He was also prone to strange mood swings and became aggressive towards her and, most particularly, to boyfriends who happened to be there. He went out of his way to humiliate them with a waspish wit. Ray Williams, a record producer at CBS, was one of several who courted Lee (he arrived with a marriage licence one day, to propose) only to find this strange, out-of-work pirate-DJ friend of hers knocking at the door in the middle of the night, a licensed court jester all too ready to use a lovelorn suitor as the butt of his jokes.

'One by one, Ev destroyed them,' says Lee of her suitors at that period. 'It was a planned strategy. He would arrive at odd times of night, knocking on my door. He'd bait them, make them look small and spend all his time running them down. Whatever they did, he would belittle them. He was very good with words, brilliant with words. He had Ray Williams in tears a couple of times. I began to realize that I only wanted to be with him.'

Occasionally Everett would turn his waspishness on Lee. Once, after he had broken a fan and some precious beads at her home in a fit of gratuitous spite, she banned him from visiting. But he bombarded her with 'forgive me' letters until she relented. He must have been fascinated too by Lee's lifestyle at that time. The house she had shared with Fury in Ockley, Surrey had fourteen acres of grounds and was known as a tripper's paradise: the lawns would often be dotted with people on LSD.

Their friendship grew; they had the same sense of humour and Everett began to confide in her about his confusion over his sexuality. He had had a couple of homosexual 'encounters', he told her, one of them with the Beatles' PA, Peter Brown, though he did not go into detail and Lee was left not knowing how far the relationship had gone. Everett appears never to have confided that to anybody.

He did tell Lee he found homosexuality distasteful. 'Men aren't built for men,' he muttered. And as they got to know each other better, he confided more. He hated the fact that he was homosexual, he told her. 'Homosexuality is a mortal sin, and I know God will punish me for it,' he said. This time Lee's counselling was not of the pull-yourself-together variety. She assured him gently that it wasn't a mortal sin; it wasn't a sin at all. She had many homosexual friends, and many of them were happy and fulfilled. But Everett wasn't convinced. He talked about wanting to be 'cured'.

Their relationship became one that seems so 'sixties' that it could almost belong in a spoof send-up of the era. He bought her a six-foot Casa Pupo paper sunflower and insisted they take it regularly to the countryside for air. They sat out on village greens and knitted together. And all that was when they *weren't* taking drugs! (Everett was a skilled embroiderer and would give his closest friends embroidered shirts he had made for them.) And they talked. He told her of his anger; anger at what he called his skinny, weedy physique (in fact he had a charming, boyish face and was attractive to men and women alike, but curiously never accepted this fact); anger at religion, particularly his; anger at his physical desire for men. 'He blamed God for how he was born,' Lee remembers him telling her again and again. 'Well,' she replied, 'he made you very cute. You get away with murder, mate, being so cute.'

They went in his Fiat on a motoring holiday in Italy. She believed they were going as chums but began to note that he treated her as if they were courting, becoming angry and sulky whenever she got chatting to another man. Everett's driving was such that he had three crashes, one with a car, one with a lorry and one a collision with a deer. When they returned, the customs man asked them if they had a receipt for the car. Lee took the official to examine the scratched and dented heap. 'Would we really want to smuggle that?' she asked.

The holiday went well as they drove through France in gales of laughter, listening to Beatles cassettes and booking into rooms with two single beds. Then, in Italy, the mood changed. They were given a room with a double bed. 'Ev became very nasty to me,' says Lee. 'He began attacking me verbally. We had our first fight and I didn't know why. I never connected it with the double bed. We finally got stoned out of our bonces and were up all night. But if Ev felt threatened or foolish, he would attack. If he felt he was going to be rebuffed, or someone was going to turn him down, he would attack. That grew to be the habit. He would attack before you could. He was rather like a frightened little animal. And that was his way right to his death.'

Back in England, Everett was involved in his first television series, Granada TV's *Nice Time*, in which he completed an unlikely threesome with Jonathan Routh of *Candid Camera* and feminist writer and academic Germaine Greer. The director was John Birt, later to become director general of the BBC. On this series Everett developed a crush on a cameraman. It was to be the first of numerous unrequited crushes on straight men. Lee, whom he had employed as his secretary so that she could travel everywhere with him, was hurt and bewildered, but by now felt too involved with her odd friend to think of leaving him, despite this early warning of his behaviour.

'Ev and I shared rooms, but always had single beds. Since our first fight in Italy it had happened often – he'd attack me for no reason, so I thought. I think he was courting me, but often he hated me for it. We'd definitely formed a powerful love for each other, but every now and then we'd find ourselves confused and irritated. I couldn't understand my feelings for him. I was obsessed and thought of no one else and I reckon he was like that with me. We could have been the perfect couple because we got on so well, so I guess we were both praying for a miracle, one that would make us lovers.'

First they became lovers in a hippyish virtual reality. 'It's a strange thing to say,' she says now. 'But I think tripping was his way of trying to come closer.' Tripping one night, they stood on opposite sides of the room, and felt as if they were making love. 'It is an extreme feeling, like he reached across the room in light to me,' Lee remembers vividly. It was indeed a strange feeling, and one that could make her fortune if she could bottle it. The real thing also occurred under the influence. On another trip in her flat and just before dawn.

'He suddenly looked at me and lit up. He declared I was the most beautiful thing he'd ever seen. I lit up in turn and that's where our agony began. When I say we lit up it's an understatement. I'd had some experience of falling in love, but this was different. It was like being elevated. He was looking at me and seeing me for the first time and the power of feeling in the room was astonishing.'

The next day Everett flung open the door of his radio producer Angela Bond's office and announced: 'I've done it.' He added that the woman was Lee and, yes, he was going to get married to her, which would have come as news to his intended. Phone calls to most of his other friends followed to announce his feat. It was a not uncommon syndrome with gay men. Many of Elton John's friends were similarly roused from their beds to hear news of his wedding-night consummation.

Lee and Ev moved in together into a flat in London's highly fashionable Holland Park. They shared a passion for animals and the flat was soon inhabited by a chihuahua, three kittens, a macaw and a Great Dane. The parrot, who was deeply attached to Lee, took against Everett and acted out a daily routine which could itself have sprung from a comedy show. When it heard Everett approaching, it flew over to the plate rack beside the kitchen doorway, hung upside down until Everett reached the kitchen, then swung out and bit him.

It was a laugh for them, as most things were at that time. 'He was terribly romantic,' says Lee. 'He would do lovely things. He was exquisite. People never understood how romantic he could be. I would come in and the house would have little notes stuck all over it, notes with hearts drawn on them and "I love you". Often it was because he had done something foul, but he always got away with it.'

They were in love, and on the phone most of the time they had to spend apart. Lee was as obsessed with him as he was with her, though she says now: 'It was extreme, but it was not the right way to love a man. I loved him like a mother would. I would protect him and fight for him.' It was not an easy situation for Everett either. The insecure and sexually unsure lad was stepping into the shoes of Billy Fury, a renowned sex symbol. And he knew that he had not lost his desires for men, confused and only half acknowledged though they were.

But for a while, quite a long while, these desires were to be forgotten, or at least submerged. One evening in the spring of 1969, they were with two close friends, Don Paul, formerly of the Viscounts pop group, and his flatmate Alan. Everett turned to them and said: 'Do you think I should marry Lee?' It was an idiosyncratic way of proposing, but proposal it was. Don and Alan considered the matter and agreed it was a good idea, at which point he took her outside, stood underneath his favourite magnolia tree and proposed again without seeking the opinion of a third party. Three months later, on 2 June 1969, they were married.

One of the wedding guests, Angela Bond, remembers it as 'a typical sixties wedding'. But in truth that decade can have produced few weddings as outlandish as Kenny Everett's. Lee remembers it more caustically: 'The whole wedding set the style for the marriage – a farce – but it was one of the best parties ever thrown.'

The couple had forgotten to tell Everett's parents that he had changed his name by deed poll. So in the middle of the ceremony a startled Mrs Cole shouted: 'It's not legal.' By that stage she was one of the few wedding guests still sober. As the couple wanted to make a quick getaway for a three-day honeymoon between filming sessions for *Nice Time*, they had the reception before the ceremony at Kensington Register Office. A carriage with two white horses and footmen ferried them there, while a red double-decker London bus was chartered for the guests, all of whom were to hold a single red rose. Lee carried her little chihuahua instead of a wedding bouquet.

Someone whispered to Angela Bond: 'Is she marrying the dog or what?'

The catering at the reception was masterminded by a sex-change chef formerly called George but for the wedding reception to be addressed as Lorraine. She/he was only halfway through the necessary operations and still had stubble on her chin and a deep voice despite being decked out from head to toe in net and chiffon. Somebody – and suspicion fell on George/Lorraine – spiked the wedding punch with speed, which gave the guests, including the future director general of the BBC, a lunch they would not forget in a hurry. 'They were all out of it, raving like mad,' remembers Lee, 'John Birt, Germaine Greer, they were all there.'

Lee's dress was made from a lace tablecloth to which she had taken a fancy in a department store. When the saleswoman fetched it she said: 'It seats eight, madam.' More than one newspaper had a headline the next morning: 'The Bride's Dress Seats Eight'. But Everett certainly saw the whole mad jamboree as his lucky day – so much so that he decided not to shave again after the wedding, and wore the familiar beard for most of the rest of his life.

Then off they went on their honeymoon to Jersey – all four of them. Lee's good friends Don Paul and Alan accompanied the happy couple, none of the four thinking it at all unusual. As it turned out, it gave Lee someone to chat to on the wedding night. Everett, who had not touched the punch, fell fast asleep. The other three, high on speed, talked in the suite's sitting room all night.

After the honeymoon the couple rented the country home in Newdigate, Surrey of Peter Asher, brother of Jane and half of the singing duo Peter and Gordon. Asher was moving to Los Angeles, and the Everetts and their menagerie marvelled at the mansion, with its eight-acre lake, rowing boat and swimming pool. It was modelled on a Japanese house complete with pools and bonsai trees. John Lennon had once borrowed the house and written 'Bungalow Bill' there. Despite its opulence, the house was only burgled once. The Everetts returned one weekend to find that a burglar had visited, but had taken an odd booty: an electric kettle without its lead and other useless items. Two years later Billy Fury confessed to Lee that he had done it, bitter that she had married Everett. (A few years later, when Fury was recovering from open-heart surgery, he moved in with Everett and Lee for nearly a year.) After he had his first heart attack, Lee went round to the house where he still lived with her former best friend, Judith, though Judith and Fury now argued and fought fiercely. They lived in the small gatehouse to Oliver Reed's estate in Ockley, where Reed bred his shire horses. To Lee's horror, she found a house that was filthy. Dogs' muck was ground in on the kitchen floor. And every single wall was covered with the name 'Lee', painted in two-foot-high letters. The home lives of sex symbols are not always as we imagine them. When Fury finally split from Judith he used a fail-safe method to ensure the split was final. He sent Keith Moon round with a shotgun to get his clothes.

The Newdigate house witnessed an even stranger event. Ken and Lee held a seance with the BBC producer Bernie Andrews, a cameraman and the cameraman's friend, whom they had never met before. The glass spun wildly round the alphabet, spelling out the name of the cameraman's friend and saying that his ex-fiancée had just died, that she had gassed herself because she was still in love with him. The young man, pale and shaking, rang up the girl's father, who told him it was all true. Everett, who had always mocked Lee's claim to psychic powers, said quietly: 'I can say no other way, but that I've been wrong. There is life after death.' The next day, Lee went to the College of Psychic Studies in London, and began a celebrated career as a medium.

Everett, in what Lee remembers as his happiest phase, spent evenings with her reading books about psychic phenomena. Much leisure time still revolved around soft drugs – indeed on a daily basis – and antics that shocked the Everetts' more stolid friends. When Lee's seventy-eight-year-old mother came down from Sheffield to stay she was much taken with the cakes that were specially made for her, not knowing that they were hash cakes. She came back an hour later with a big grin for a second helping, 'the happiest I'd ever seen her', says Lee.

Some of Everett's working hours were spent on TV series such as *The Kenny Everett Explosion* and *Ev*, good grounding for him but not really revealing his full talent or the success that was to come his way on television half a dozen years later. The filming sometimes took place at the couple's London flat. Lee would walk in to find a sketch being filmed which, for example, involved the antique music stand on their grand piano being ignited; or, on one occasion, to find her husband in bed with six fat ladies, who rose in unison to chase him round the room. That convinced Lee that they should get their own house in the country. They chose a fourteenth-century farmhouse in Cowfold, West Sussex, which they bought for £19,250, with much renovation to be done. In a short film, now unfortunately lost, cameras recorded them moving in, on top of a bus with Marc Bolan singing his latest hit, 'Ride a White Swan'.

Heady, over-the-top, extravagant and euphoric days. As indeed befitted a man who, since meeting Lee, had secured a job with the new national pop-music radio station, where jollity was on tap all through the day and no one was allowed to be anything but wonderful or feel anything less than fab.

7

A SACKING AND A COVER-UP

'She probably crammed a fiver into the examiner's hand.'
Kenny Everett's speculation to Radio 1 listeners in 1970
on how the Minister of Transport's wife passed her driving test

It is part of Kenny Everett's story that he was sacked from Radio 1 for a joke he told about a Cabinet minister's wife. Every single obituary that followed his death in 1995 recycled the episode. Mary Peyton, the wife of Conservative Minister of Transport John Peyton, had probably passed her advanced driving test, he told his listeners, because she bribed the examiner.

He did indeed say this on air. And it suited everyone involved that this was perceived to be the reason for his dismissal. The BBC had to protect the good name of a government minister from a clear libel. Everett looked a martyr to establishment cronyism. His listeners could side with his cheeky, irreverent humour. Some had car stickers demanding their favourite DJ's reinstatement. Even the Labour Party got in on the act, complaining that the BBC was protecting the Tories.

It was a good story. And it held sway for twenty-five years. But it wasn't true. The BBC got rid of Kenny Everett for a much more important reason, and one which threatened the Corporation far more seriously than a silly jape about a driving test. It was because he threatened to go public on the restrictive practices and deals with the Musicians Union that were frustrating not only Everett and his listeners but making the much-vaunted BBC pop station Wonderful Radio 1 a pale shadow of its pirate forebears.

Everett had been in on the birth of Radio 1: he composed and recorded the promotional jingles for the new station and had even played a part in its conception. As he left his studio for the last time, in 1970, he probably thought back to a lunch at Verrys restaurant, the then fashionable stars' eating place at the top of Regent Street, in the spring of 1967 with Robin Scott, the founder-controller of Radio 1, and Johnny Beerling, then a senior producer and later to be a highly successful Radio 1 controller himself.

Scott, known as the 'White Tornado' because of his shock of white hair and bursts of enthusiasm as he ran down the corridors of Broadcasting House, knew back in 1966 that BBC radio would have to change to catch up with the pirates. The Home Service and Third Programme would stay as Radio 4 and Radio 3; and the Light Programme would have to be split in two, with 'sweet music', as he described it, on Radio 2 and Radio 1 becoming the brand-new pop station. By early 1967 most of the plans were laid. The BBC knew the government's anti-pirate legislation was on the way; it would poach most of the pirate DJs to give it street cred (besides, the studios of Broadcasting House were not exactly heaving with trained disc jockeys) and it would start transmitting a month after the pirates were outlawed.

Everything was ready. Hadn't Frank Gillard, one of the BBC's most senior figures, already made a giant leap into the sixties by declaring he would henceforth be known as Director of Radio rather than Director of Sound Broadcasting? Auntie was ready to swing.

But Beerling was worried. He had made a secret trip out to Radio London ('Go if you really want to, old boy, go, but I don't want to know anything about it,' Mark White, head of the BBC Gramophone Department, had warned him when he told him he was going). And on the ship Beerling gazed in amazement. 'I saw this man Everett doing everything. In the old way of doing things, the DJ sat in one room with a script. Someone else played the records and somebody else controlled the sound. Yet I see this man who has control of everything.'

It was a shock to the system, both Beerling's and broadcasting's. Why, when he had produced *Housewife's Choice* the links between records were all scripted like miniature talks; he would select the requests, the lists of records, dig them out of the library and give them to the presenter, Bruce Forsyth or Dickie Henderson, who would prepare a script, liaising with Beerling. The script would then be typed by the production secretary, and it would contain every word and ad lib in the programme, along with the complete timings of all the records in the show. There would then be a 'real-time' rehearsal with all the records played and all the scripted links read out. Then Beerling and the presenter – perhaps Pete Murray, David Jacobs or Don Moss – would do it all again for real.

Beerling went to see Scott and urged him that before he went any further with his plans for the new pop station, he must meet Everett. 'He has come from nowhere to become a cult figure,' he added. Scott was hooked, and the lunch at Verrys was fixed.

Over lunch Everett listened to the two older men describe the station they were planning. Immediately he saw that one key ingredient was missing. 'If you want your Radio 1 to sound like pirate radio, you must have jingles,' he told them, 'and you must have them done by PAMS of Dallas.'

And so the BBC for the first time had jingles, and went to Dallas to buy them. To Radio London listeners they were pretty familiar. 'Wonderful Radio London' was inverted to become 'Radio 1 is Wonderful'. Even Tony Windsor's 'Hel-lo' lived on, though this time spoken by Tony Blackburn on his radio show, which also featured Arnold the dog and the corny jokes that had been his trademark on Radio London. Most of the other Big L DJs, the occasional one from Caroline and a few such as Pete Murray, Jimmy Saville, Alan Freeman, Jimmy Young and David Jacobs from the Light Programme, staffed the new programmes.

During the summer BBC listeners and viewers were warmed up to the idea of the new station by 'promos' advertising Radio 1. Beerling and Scott knew whom to entrust with these.

Everett had already, with uncharacteristic boldness, taken to hanging around at Broadcasting House and was becoming known. More than a decade later he confided to his friend the Thames TV cameraman Ray Gearing, the formula for infiltrating the BBC bureaucracy: 'You could always get into the Beeb,' he said, 'as long as you were carrying something under the arm. I used to carry a ten-inch tape spool. You won't be stopped as long as you have something. You then wander around the corridors until you find an empty office – make sure you get one with a telephone. Then start paging yourself regularly, and after a while people will feel they know you. Then, when you apply for a job, everyone thinks they know you and you're in.'

The Radio 1 promos were composed and performed by Everett. From September, Everett said, 'there will be light [excerpt of big band music]; there will be pop [a blast of *Sergeant Pepper*]; and then there's always [a snatch of chamber music] oh, hmmm, excuse me ' Ten years later, when Radio 1 broadcast a history of the network's first ten years, the presenter, Alan Freeman, referred to these promos and said: 'Kenny was one of the network's most valuable assets.' His departure from Radio 1 was not mentioned.

Teenagers with placards protested outside Broadcasting House against the end of the pirate stations. On one famous occasion they were confronted live on air by the *Today* programme's Jack de Manio, who advised them benignly to go and chat to the Postmaster General. The 'borrowing' from the pirates was undeniable. As Screaming Lord Sutch, chairman of the Monster Raving Loony Party and briefly a pirate radio station owner, perceptively put it: 'The BBC have copied the best ideas from the illegal stations. They've turned out to be the biggest pirates of them all.' The BBC was quick to point out that the pirates had leant very heavily indeed on American music radio.

Anyway, things were happening too fast to worry about. This was a brand-new national pop station set against the background of the most permissive moment in Britain's history. As Johnny Beerling remembers: 'There was great camaraderie in those days, the time of the morally lax swinging sixties, when anything went and the pill was the governor of morals. Aids and herpes hadn't been discovered, and the worst thing that could happen was a dose of the clap, and a penicillin injection up the bum would soon cure that. There was, of course, the great Radio 1 Crab-lice scare of 1967, when a number of secretaries were unfortunately afflicted with those intrepid little creatures, and justifiably blamed the influx of the heterosexual (and there were one or two) pirate disc jockeys.'

The estimable Beerling's memory conjures up some wonderful backstage cameos of those early Radio 1 days. How Terry Wogan had millions of poor housewives on the floor every afternoon performing strenuous exercises to 'fight the flab'; exhorting them to 'stretch those muscles, ladies', while Wogan himself, somewhat overweight (before he slimmed down for the telly) ate a cream bun, contenting himself with sitting back in his chair, making the appropriate straining noises.

Just after seven a.m. on Saturday 30 September Johnny Beerling watched from the producer's booth as Tony Blackburn played the Move's 'Flowers in the Rain'. The Bee Gees, the first live group on Radio 1, waited in the next room with Keith Skues, who would introduce them on *Saturday Club*; and the establishment embraced pop.

Fleet Street was bemused but largely positive. The *Guardian* wrote: 'As the sycophantic celebrations of young men whose talent lies in peddling adolescent dreams are part of a rather frenetic attempt to appear young, Fleet Street mainly welcomes the BBC's attempt to turn hip.' A particularly penetrating comment came from George Melly in the *Observer*. He wrote: 'It was all go at Auntie's first freak-out. The solemnity with which the conventions evolved by the pirate stations have been plagiarised is almost Germanic in its thoroughness; the little bursts of identifying plug music, the comperes gabbling over the opening bars of the records, the fake excitement, ("Beautiful song, beautiful words, must make it.") even the deliberate amateurism and fake fear of the sack, are all there. And yet somehow the effect is of a waxwork, absolutely lifelike but clearly lifeless.' And there was an astute observation made by David Lewin in the *Daily Mail*. He predicted that the Top Ten would no longer consist of the most popular records but rather the most popular DJs. 'It wouldn't be what they play, but who plays it.'

The bizarre mix of BBC establishment and pirate irreverence was unique. While DJs gabbled frenetically over the intros to records, Robin Scott was giving a lunchtime lecture about the new networks. It was still a time when pop radio was taken seriously enough for BBC executives to give lectures about it.

'There was,' he said, 'some idea that the new service would be for the "sweet music" audience.' But there was already a good deal of this on the Light Programme and it was abundantly clear that if the new service was to be dynamic and attractive, it must go for pop. 'There is no doubt at all in my mind that to have reduced the percentage of pop would have cut the BBC away from the majority of the audience, both existing and potential. We should not forget that the young housewife of twenty-seven, perhaps with two children or more, was a seventeen-year-old when rock 'n' roll music first hit this country . . .'

Scott was bullish in the face of accusations of ripping off the pirates. In a section of his lecture quaintly entitled 'Are Jingles Fun?' he declared: 'We have been accused of imitation, but in fact the pirates copied American formats. We already had some jingles, even on the old Light Programme, but it's difficult to SING the charms of the Light Programme.'

For the pirates, learning BBC ways could be, literally, a painful experience. When Ed Stewart signed off from his first show, his producer, Angela Bond, threw her pencil at his face and it caught his nose rather sharply. 'What did I do wrong?' he squealed in surprise. 'At the BBC we give producers name-checks,' she said. Neither he nor any of his colleagues forgot again.

In fact, as Radio 1's bosses later realized, the station really started a year or two too late. The frontiers of contemporary music were being extended away from the hummable three-minute pop record that had dominated youth culture from 1964 to the end of 1966, and into a more confused phase of the hippyish, lengthy, drug-induced explorations of Pink Floyd and their contemporaries, pop, jazz and even classical fusions, to be followed a year later by the progressive rock of Led Zeppelin, none of which was suitable for the Radio 1 format − or so the controllers decided, probably wrongly. Nevertheless there were still enough three-minute pop tunes to go round. Radio 1 was an instant success, and its presenters, Stewart, Blackburn, Skues, Peel, Emperor Rosko, Jimmy Young *et al*, household names.

But where was Everett? He was hosting *Midday Spin*, an hour-long record review programme, once a week. The programme suited the BBC for more than one reason. First, it was pure pop, rather than the ridiculous hybrid of the Rolling Stones followed by a Strauss waltz that had epitomized the Light Programme. Secondly, if the DJ gave the briefest review of each record (such as 'here's an interesting new release from EMI') the corporation did not have to make a royalty payment.

As one of the most popular and most talented DJs in the country, and in his small way an architect of the new network, Everett felt ill used. He later said: 'I did an hour of this every Tuesday lunchtime for a while, seething every morning as I'd hear Tony Blackburn doing his three-hour, daily breakfast show. Aaargh!' Dave Cash, for one, believes that Everett's hatred of the BBC sprang from these few weeks at the all-important start of Radio 1, when he seemed to be given a low-profile role.

But *Midday Spin* had an advantage for Everett that cannot be overemphasized. It brought him into contact with a remarkable woman, who was to succeed Cash as the central influence on his broadcasting career. The programme's producer, Angela Bond, was to be Everett's producer for most of the next three years. And she was to be a lot more than that. She was to be, at times, his inspiration, his sounding board, confidante, and a cross between a mother and an older sister. She built his confidence, gave him techniques and phrases that were to become synonymous with him, even brought him down from his LSD trips. And she doted on him, her affection undimmed even by a desperately unhappy Everett rushing into the Managing Director of Radio's office in 1970 and demanding successfully never to work with Angela Bond again.

The daughter of a sea captain, Angela Bond was born in Hull and brought up in Hull, Shanghai and Hong Kong. Her personality is an intriguing mixture of Yorkshire bluntness and an all-embracing earth-motherly kindness and compassion, with an infectious passion about both music and radio. Although now retired, she still helps train Radio 1 broadcasters in computer techniques, and she still has the latest rock CDs piled high all over her living room. To rise as she did as a female producer on a pop station in the sixties was quite a feat. Had she been male she might have risen even higher. Had she been male it is unlikely that the BBC could have neglected to include her in the Kenny Everett tribute programme it recorded after his death – a shameful omission.

When Angela Bond was a DJ in Hong Kong in 1963, her eleven-year-old daughter, Suzie, wrote from boarding school, where she listened to Radio Luxembourg under the bedclothes, that there was a 'fantabulous' new group called the Beatles with a record out called 'Please Please Me'. Bond got hold of it and Hong Kong heard the Beatles for the first time. In Hong Kong she also sang in a band in which the young Ed Stewart was the bass player. By 1964 she was working in the Light Programme's Gramophone Department. At first she wore her colourful hats in the building – hats she was to wear in the producer's booth to make Everett giggle – until a colleague whispered to her that at the BBC only the lesbians wore hats.

In 1966 Bond and her colleagues Johnny Beerling and Derek Chinnery, the latter two both later to become Radio 1 controllers, scripted a manifesto for the start of a BBC pop radio station. Bond was delegated to type it.

One aspect that she, in particular, was pushing was that the new station should not use star names as DJs, but use accomplished broadcasters and make them stars. 'Let's get people with broadcasting talent and turn them into faces,' she said. The best pool to pick from was clearly the pirates. Her other proposal was for a pilot programme of *Midday Spin* which would introduce listeners to the concept of DJs playing records, rather than the customary mix of records, cover versions and dance bands. The ideal time was lunchtime because kids had their transistors clutched to their heads during their meal break.

One afternoon in 1966 when the planning was well advanced, Bond was in Mark White's office in the Gramophone Department and said to him: 'We are going to give that guy Kenny Everett a go on *Midday Spin*, aren't we?' White replied: 'Well, no, because he's rather difficult to handle and we can't think of anybody who will be able to handle him.' He then grinned and said: 'Why, are you volunteering?' Bond replied: 'If it means the difference between having him and not having him, then yes, I'm volunteering.'

When Bond and Everett met they knew at once that they were on the same wavelength. 'I knew I had this sensitive little white light,' she now says. 'He had this wonderful, mischievous sense of humour. He would look at me from the corner of his eye like a little imp.'

After *Midday Spin* Bond and Everett took over the Sunday-morning show to huge acclaim. A long-running in-joke that Everett played was to take the mickey out of Michael Aspel, or Aspirin as he called him when he handed over to Aspel. 'Oh, here she comes,' he would say of Aspel, 'and she's carrying a beautiful new handbag made of lettuce leaf, with a diamanté and radish-encrusted tiara tilting fetchingly over his left eyebrow.' Overseas listeners who did not receive the Everett show could never understand why Aspel was laughing as he introduced *Family Favourites*.

The success of the Sunday show lured the BBC into a mistake.

They wanted to capitalize on the ratings and took Everett away from Bond for a nightly show, *Foreverett*. Bond begged them not to. Her charge could not sustain a daily show, she told them. It was of a standard, replete with sketches and multiple mixes, that would be too draining on a daily basis. Also, he should not be competing against prime-time television at that stage in his career. They did not listen. She told friends that the BBC had showed a lack of understanding of a creative talent in its formative years. Everett continually came into her office and unloaded his worries. Other producers, he said, were trying 'to get inside my whole body and work it themselves'. He was unable to perfect his pre-recorded content for a daily output. And yes, it still rankled that Tony Blackburn had radio prime time while he, to his mind, had been relegated. Other concerns poured out: his suspicion of the BBC establishment; his hatred of hypocrisy; his feelings of inadequacy; his dislike of his own appearance, particularly his 'short, skinny legs'. His programmes, Bond rapidly realized, were his escape from these problems.

After six weeks the BBC realized the importance of Bond to Everett and asked her to take him back as other producers couldn't handle him. She said yes, but on one condition. They must be given the prestige Saturday-morning spot, ousting what was once the cutting edge of pop on BBC radio, *Saturday Club*. That made the front-page splash story in *Disc* magazine. The issue of 23 November 1968 had the headline 'Saturday Club Is Axed For Everett'. Next to a page-deep picture of Everett in a blue, Chinese-style dressing gown he had borrowed from Angela, the story read: 'Kenny Everett, Radio 1's golden boy, has landed the plum Saturday morning spot . . . Since May Kenny has run his own *Foreverett* show five nights a week and the Beatles have led the in crowd of pop people praising him.' The story quoted Everett saying: 'Paul McCartney's been on at me for ages to do it.'

That McCartney cared either way, and that a weekly music paper could consider a new radio show for Everett the biggest news of the week, were testimony to the massive cult following that Everett had built up in a year. What those listeners did not know was that these facts bore testimony too to the partnership he had with Angela Bond, a name they would almost certainly not have recognized.

From the start it was Bond, not Everett, who would pick the records to be played. She would make three piles, a 'goodie'.pile, a 'baddie' pile and in the middle a mixture of off-the-wall sounds that Everett might like. They would get together a day before the show to make a selection. Trusting her own instinct, Bond would persevere with records that even the artist's record company urged her to ignore. On one occasion Pye told her they had many better records for her to play than 'Do You Know the Way to San Jose' by Dionne Warwick, to which she had perversely taken a liking. She would not be deterred from her goodies, a word she liked so much that when the show gave away prizes, they were described as BBC 'goodie bags'. So was born a phrase which every parent who throws a party for a small child has reason to curse.

While Bond chose the music, Everett would be in the BBC archives picking out ancient sounds, dialogue by thirties actors like Jack Hulbert, big band sounds from Benny Goodman, snippets of classical music. Bond quickly realized his love of gadgetry and what he could do in a studio, so she had a special room built for him where he could experiment with tapes, with sounds, with sketches, making unprecedented and unnatural mixes. There was a ring modulator with which could make his Dalek voices. They called the room the 'wireless workshop' – Everett put up the lettering – and it was there that he was most likely to be found. 'He loved the technical side,' says Bond. 'He lived, breathed and ate it.'

Together they delighted in mixing the genres. Everett came in one morning saying he had just been to his first classical concert. 'Oh, Angela, it was great. A sixty-piece orchestra.'

She found him more classical music. And more. He took it up to the wireless workshop and made it into tapes to insert into the programme. She played him some of the top pop songs of the moment, then the classical themes which had clearly influenced them. He was fascinated. When he heard something he had never heard before and loved it, he endowed it with a sense of wonder. And he particularly loved music from the twenties and thirties, an era Bond concluded he should have been born into. She suggested he use some of the classical themes on the programme. 'I'll tell you what,' she said, 'how's about getting all the tuney bits out of the classical pieces?' He did; and he kept the expression 'tuney bits' in use right until the end of his career. The ideas were often hers, but she was the first to admit that no other disc jockey could have presented them like Everett did. His talent amazed her.

She knew of the success of the *Kenny and Cash* sketches and characters and began to suggest some. One was an old man in the BBC basement grunting: 'Oy, I'm just looking for some records.' Kenny in turn developed one of his best creations, Gran, a fun granny born out of Everett's goonish toothless falsetto whereby he kept himself company on his programmes.

Then one day in the canteen Bond was chatting with a colleague who had brought in her husband, a resting actor with a refined, but rich and fruity voice. Bond turned to Everett, seated beside her, and said: 'What a marvellous voice. You must have him on the show. He could be your butler.' Everett's eyes lit up: 'Yes, and I'll call him Crisp.' The Jeevesian butler, trying to calm the young master disc jockey, while at the same time being pursued by Kenny's frisky Gran, became a staple of the show.

Every show seemed to see a new experiment. 'I'm going to get twenty records in,' said Everett at the start of one, whizzing through a tape of intros mixed together that he had prepared. 'It's up to you, sir,' said Crisp respectfully, while fending off Gran with 'Back in the broom cupboard, madam' at the same time as Everett played one of his favourite revived 45s, Johnny Cymbal's 'Mr Bass Man', having mixed it the night before so that he could sing the deep bass 'bah-bah bah-bahs' with Cymbal.

Everett and Bond were putting records in the charts, just as Kenny and Cash had done on Radio London. They championed Jeff Lynne's group the Idle Race and their record 'The Skeleton and the Roundabout'. In return, when the Idle Race went to America they sent back a package addressed to Bond. It was a tiny box with a reel inside it. Printed around the edge were the words: 'This is an amazing new machine which can sound like any instrument. It is called a Moog synthesizer. Love, The Idle Race.' Angela made a tape of it. 'Wow, can we play it?' Everett asked. The BBC was not supposed to play any music not released in England; but to be the first people to play a Moog synthesizer on British radio, they broke a rule. They had agreed: the shows had to be parties where everybody was invited in.

The age's leading commentators on pop scrambled for a new vocabulary, quickly realizing their traditional one was inadequate to describe Everett's shows. Words like 'disc jockey' and 'funny' told only a fraction of the story. In the *Financial Times*, Tony Palmer wrote: 'Kenny Everett, disc jockey of the year, is 5ft 5 inches tall and he fidgets. His ambition is to die, come back and tell everyone what a gas it was ... Most pop people consider Everett the first real genius of radio. "Everett is Here" is run by him, an archaic butler called Crisp, whom he just happened to meet in the BBC canteen, and Everett's sexually maladjusted Granny who is 300 years old – a victim of the disease called loving.'

'Sibelius is what it's all about,' Palmer concludes mystically. 'Endlessly inventive, musically subtle (he often rescores hit songs for an eight-part choir and then sings all the parts himself), infuriatingly entertaining, his Saturday jamboree has a spontaneous lunacy which confuses the teenies, annoys the mums and dads and delights many ... It also disrupts BBC officialdom which has made several attempts to put him out of business.'

Gillian Reynolds, writing in the *Guardian*, said: 'He is by BBC definition a disc jockey, but his programmes are consistently funny and inventive, owing something to the Goons, something to Wodehouse, but most to Mr Everett's infectious sense of humour. On Thursday evening, Crisp and Granny took the show over for a good 15 minutes, jamming the door against Kenny with empty bottles and slugging away at a bottle of scotch ... The records were almost an intrusion in the extemporaneous and irreverent flow.'

Bond would come in in the mornings to find notes left by Everett in the stylish calligraphy he had practised copying out from the Bible at school long ago. 'Happy Noo Year Dahlin, [signed] Ev, Queen of the waves' was one. Once he had to alter a cheque to her. He was too unworldly to know how to do it. She told him he must sign his name again. He did several times all over the cheque. Once she left his BBC publicity picture on her desk. In the morning she found that he had drawn a beard on it, a year before he was to grow the real thing on his face.

She recognized he was a tremendously creative person and needed to be kept on a loose rein and given his head. This led to the pair of them being continually summoned to the office of Robin Scott, Radio 1's controller, for breaches of the peace.

Bond tried to keep him on the right side of the boundary. She took him aside and said: 'Look, Kenny. You know what the BBC's like. Don't say shit, bugger, arsehole, piss, cock, fart. It's got to be in good taste.' Everett liked her style, but didn't take much heed of the warning, though he did remember her final line about everything having to be in good taste, and stored that away for later.

Everett's favourite trick, which was to prove his undoing, was to comment on the news. The Radio 1 news usually ended with a light item where the newscaster said: 'And finally . . .' Mrs Peyton's driving test was just such an item. After another that said an Olympic high jumper had jumped a new record height, Everett said: 'Into what?' Once he introduced newsreader Peter Jefferson, saying: 'Here comes Peter Jefferson with his airplane', referring to the American rock group Jefferson Airplane. He then listened in horror as the newscaster gave details of a plane crash. Rarely could he resist sitting opposite the newscaster of the day and trying to make him laugh. Nearly always his remarks were inconsequential. But to the BBC they were heresy. They had never, never, come across anyone like him before. To make funny comments on the news. It beggared belief.

But as Bond began to know her charge better, and he opened up his heart to her, she perceived that he wasn't laughing outside the studio. On one occasion he appeared on a television show, his first TV appearance. He came in the next morning, angry and close to tears. 'I'm no good on television, Angela,' he moaned. 'Look at me. I hate my body, I hate my body. These short, skinny legs.' And as his fame grew, he confided that there was another aspect he couldn't cope with and remained unable to cope with. 'I can't stand it when people come up to me, the public. I hate it.'

There was something he hated far more, something which began to explain all his mood swings and uncertainties. He did not, he told Bond, want to be gay. He wished he had been straight. He was affectionate and loved deep friendships, but permissive society or no permissive society, he was a virgin. And he did not want a gay relationship. He had been pursued by homosexual disc jockeys on the Radio London ship, he told her, and he didn't like it. (Peter Brown seems to have been excised from his memory.) She had noticed herself that 'blokes wouldn't leave him alone'. At the same time he was taking LSD and often looked much the worse for wear. It was remarkable that the most popular Radio 1 show, with all its subtle ingredients, was being broadcast at all.

On one, and only one, occasion it wasn't, at least not with Everett. Around midnight on a Friday night, Bond received a phone call at her home. It was Everett in the wireless workshop: 'Ange, I can't do the show. I can hardly walk.' He was being pursued at that time by a man from a music publishing house and he didn't know how to cope. He was in tears as he told Bond: 'He won't leave me alone.' He went on: 'I haven't done it yet. It's like everyone else can fly, and I can't.' He continued to pour his heart out. His family didn't understand him. His parents were puritanical. They were strict Roman Catholics. He couldn't talk to them. What was he to do?

Realizing that he was involved in a traumatic turmoil over his sexuality and was possibly on drugs as well, Bond phoned Dave Cash and the two of them met at dawn at the BBC and constructed a new show. Though Everett had been going through internal hell for some time, and would continue so to do for some time, it was the only show he missed.

Listeners were unaware of Everett's inner turmoil. The show grew ever more popular, with regular audience figures of five million. But his unhappiness was beginning to come out in other ways. He started giving a number of press interviews complaining about BBC stuffiness, about the equipment (the turntables seemed less solid than Radio London's in the middle of a gale at sea) and particularly about the needle-time agreements with the Musicians Union, who demanded a fixed percentage of live music – between twenty-five and thirty per cent – which meant that Radio 1 could play only so many records and had to fill in with bands coming into the studio to record cover versions of current hits. Vince Hill sang the Hollies. The Northern Dance Orchestra played the Beatles. 'How can you have the Northern Dance Orchestra doing cover versions of the Beatles,' declared an exasperated Everett. 'They sound terrible. Worse than that – they sound like the Northern Dance Orchestra.' And he declared it on air.

The BBC made him sign a pledge not to give any more interviews. But Bond could see he wasn't at peace with himself, and watched, frightened, not knowing where the next outburst would be aimed. In the spring of 1970 Everett made a clearly libellous remark about a well-known recording artist's wife being pregnant by another man. After the show Bond took him aside. 'Lovey, you've got to be careful,' she counselled. He stormed out. That was the last straw.

Even Angela Bond was now the BBC and not his friend. To her astonishment she learned that he had gone straight to the managing director's office and said: 'I don't want to work with Angela Bond any more.'

The management gave in to him. Bond was rueful: 'I'd made him into the biggest thing since sliced bread. And there he was on self-destruct. He absolutely hated the BBC by this time.' Two executive producers, Derek Chinnery and Teddy Warwick, took it in turns to produce him. And to see how different he was from their other charges.

Chinnery found Everett working on tapes in the wireless workshop right until the last moment. It was a five-minute walk from there to the studio and Everett cut it so fine that he often spent the first record rewinding the tape he had just lovingly made. Once there was ten minutes to go before the Rosko midday show, and Everett had run out of tapes, gags and sketches. He said to Chinnery: 'Let's stop. Rosko's here. I'll hand over now.' Chinnery was horrified: 'Why Kenny? Play a couple of records, for God's sake!' Everett did so with great reluctance. 'He felt his role was more than just playing records,' Chinnery found. 'He had to have something productive or amusing to put in.'

By now the BBC was locked in negotiations with the record companies and the Musicians Union to try to increase the amount of needle-time, the number of records the MU would allow the BBC to play instead of having live performance. But, as Teddy Warwick remembers, time after time a negotiating session would start with the MU delegation protesting that one particular BBC employee had been insulting the Musicians Union on air.

The BBC's upper echelons took fright. Warwick couldn't understand why. Surely an international corporation like the BBC could absorb and even exploit one maverick.

'It was getting to the situation where he was seriously upsetting negotiations,' says Warwick. 'That was just as much the reason for Kenny being fired, after numerous warnings, as the story about the Minister of Transport's wife. My view was that Kenny should be seen as a sort of court jester as far as the BBC was concerned. And the BBC is a big enough organization to allow itself a court jester, and even if Kenny occasionally said things that the BBC didn't like, this role suited him and it suited us, and I think the BBC would have gained a lot of respect by having somebody who was as talented as he was, who occasionally seemed to step out of line.'

Out of line he did indeed step on his Saturday show on 18 July 1970. The newsreader reported as the final item the news that Mrs Mary Peyton, wife of the Minister of Transport, John Peyton, had passed her driving test. Everett gave his soon to be famous reaction. Listening at home, Derek Chinnery thought: Oh God, we'll be in trouble now.

Two days later, on Monday 20 July, Douglas Muggeridge, controller of Radio 1, formally terminated Everett's contract. But it was the late Ian Trethowan, Managing Director, Radio, whose decision it was to sack him. Chinnery asked if Everett could 'take a short holiday' as one or two other DJs had after misdemeanours in the past, but Trethowan was adamant: 'He goes.' The debate continued in the next day's papers. Everett told the press: 'The remarks were said humorously. Obviously I didn't mean them. I didn't think anyone would take them seriously.' A BBC 'official' retorted: 'We would have regarded these remarks as indefensible regardless of whom he was talking about.' The press also reported that Everett had said in a recent interview that he thought some BBC Radio 1 output was 'awful, really revolting'. Questioned about this, Everett replied: 'Several DJs were asked what they thought of BBC pop programmes. I said I thought they were rubbish. But I think the real reason I was fired is the remarks I made about the minister's wife. It's an ad-lib show and I saw no harm in my remarks.' Over to the BBC official, who hit back by saying that Everett had broken undertakings he had given over a period of more than a year. 'We believe in giving our DJs as much freedom as possible, but in the case of Kenny Everett, we have too often had to weigh this freedom against our public reputation.'

At Radio 1 they knew exactly what they and radio had lost. Angela Bond and the other producers fired off a round robin to the BBC top brass lamenting the decision to sack Everett and begging for his reinstatement. On 23 July Johnny Beerling wrote to Ian Trethowan, and received an uncompromising reply. That private exchange of letters, reproduced here for the first time, shows the difference in outlook between those running the pop station and those in the real corridors of power at the BBC. Beerling wrote:

A SACKING AND A COVER-UP

Dear Mr Trethowan,

Some months ago you were kind enough to invite me, along with some of my colleagues, to an informal dinner where we freely gave our opinions on various aspects of radio. I would now like to presume further on your time for a moment or two, to express some personal opinions about the unfortunate Kenny Everett affair.

Firstly I believe it is impossible to sit back and say nothing when a decision is made which I believe is damaging everything we have been working to build up in Radio 1. My reasons for thinking this are as follows:

As the producer who has been responsible for a large number of the various Everett programmes, I can hardly deny that, during his BBC career, he has been a source of controversy and occasional embarrassment by some of his comments both on the air, and to the press. But against this one must weigh his talent. I quite genuinely believe that he is the most talented and creative disc jockey/entertainer of our time, and certainly he has produced some of the best radio ever to be broadcast on Radio 1. He is a performer who loves the medium of radio more than any other, and in dismissing him from our employment in which we have the monopoly, we do more to support the case for setting up an alternative system of broadcasting in opposition to the BBC than any Free Radio campaign.

By this dismissal we have received universal press coverage, and in the eyes of our young audience we have been relegated ten years back into the 'Auntie BBC' era. In fact, we all lose. Everett his job, listeners are deprived of one of their favourite DJs and BBC radio some of its hard-won prestige in the eyes of its listeners.

To use a football analogy, if Georgie Best misbehaves on the field, the Football Association does not sack him and permanently damage the Manchester United team. They suspend him for a month or two. Respectfully, could that not have been done, or be done, in this case?

Yours sincerely

Johnny Beerling

Senior Producer, Radio 1 Club.

On 5 August Ian Trethowan replied:

Dear Johnnie,

I had your letter just before I went off for a week, but I hope that in the meantime you have been somewhat reassured about the Everett affair. I hope that for a start you realise that no broadcasting organisation in its senses would fire a very popular disc jockey without the most careful thought. The position was, as I believe you now know, that he had given a specific undertaking in writing, and that he had been warned categorically that if he broke that undertaking he would be out. He then did break the undertaking, so we felt we had no alternative but to end his contract. One consideration in our minds was that if we had not done this, if a 'final warning' appeared to mean nothing, then producers would have found it very hard to deal not only with Everett but with other D.J.s.

That having been said, I must confess that I would have wished it did not appear that we were sacking him because of his remarks about a Minister's wife, even though that remark was clearly actionable and could have cost us thousands. We tried to make it clear to the press that this was not a decisive factor − and that anyway the driving examiner had been equally libelled − but it was probably too much to expect that we would be believed! As for the future, I certainly do not rule out the possibility of Everett coming back to BBC Radio in due course, but I am afraid that under the circumstances we had no option but to act as we did.

Yours,

Ian

(Ian Trethowan)

Managing Director, Radio

On being sacked, Everett phoned Jonathan King, who organized the press coverage. Everett's doorstep was besieged by reporters, and he cunningly bought a crate of champagne to give them, in the hope that it might ensure sympathetic coverage. He probably could have spared himself the expense. In the event, everyone outside the portals of Broadcasting House wanted to champion the people's DJ against the great BBC monolith.

Gerald Kaufman, the Labour MP, wrote to Lord Hill, chairman of the BBC governors, asking if the dismissal of Everett involved a change of policy by the Corporation. Kaufman drily pointed out that personal attacks of extraordinary virulence, though often couched in humorous terms, had been made on members of the Labour government without such immediate and stringent action. Lord Hill replied that Mr Everett's remark about Mrs John Peyton passing the advanced driving test would have been equally offensive if made about any member of the public. Apologies similar to that sent to Mrs Peyton had gone to the driving examiner concerned and to the Institute of Advanced Motorists. He added: 'We have made it clear that this remark was not the main reason for the action taken. Mr Everett has, on a number of occasions, made remarks about broadcasting matters of a kind likely to be damaging to the BBC and its relations with outside bodies.'

The following Saturday the *Daily Mail* invited Everett to write a personal article about his broadcasting philosophy. It started in typically make-believe vein: 'I'd arrive at the studio at 9.30 bearing armfuls of tapes, records and requests, there to be greeted by my butler, Crisp, at the door . . .' But then he did give a genuine insight into his methods and personality, and his frustration with those who did not understand them: 'For the next two hours I'd be living off my wits and hoping the adrenalin would keep flowing. For apart from the records and jingles, everything I said was either instantly thought of or made up while the previous record was playing.

'I'd take anything that came into my mind, for instance a joke about the Transport Minister's wife which got me the sack, and just pour it out into the microphone. I would try to edit my cracks about two seconds before they came out. But mostly my mouth works faster than my mind, so at times things came out sounding like an insult quite unintentionally. That's why I relied on the British sense of humour to work it out for me.

'I hate DJs who just say, "That was Ricky Twinge and the Midwives. The time is now 10.15 on your groovy platter station, Radio 1. And now a great big biggy from a really outsize band – 'You're too much' by the Stoatcatchers." It's meaningless. What I said was nonsense, but at least it was occasionally funny nonsense. Not just boring old clichés.'

Everett retired to his tent, or rather to a Sussex farmhouse, with Lee, and never hosted a live show on Radio 1 again. But it's an ill wind that blows nobody any good. The one beneficiary of the affair was a promising twenty-one-year-old lad called Noel Edmonds, who Beerling still remembers as going to ridiculous lengths to disguise his lack of inches. Edmonds was given Everett's show, and rapidly sounded uncommonly like him, his patter and cast of characters striking listeners as a touch derivative. Poor Edmonds, who was an innocent party, began receiving hate mail; and his producer, Tim Blackmore, becoming alarmed, told him to make the show more distinct from Everett's. It was a baptism of fire for Edmonds, who would open the newspapers to read supplications like the one in the *Evening Standard* on the day of his first show which said: 'Heaven help poor Noel Edmonds, who, from today onwards, has been given the unenviable job of governing in the ten till twelve spot in the wake of the deposed enfant terrible of Broadcasting House.'

Edmonds, then still unsure of himself and a decade or more away from becoming a multimillionaire, himself gave an interview, in which he said: 'I doubt whether many people will take to me because I'm the one who's taken over from the one everybody liked.' Reading the interview, Everett could only think: 'What a complicated sentence for someone planning to make his living from being a disc jockey.'

Angela Bond, meanwhile, wondered what would become of her boy. She would see him from time to time in the coming years; but never for long. More often than not it would be at a London nightclub, Stringfellows or the Hippodrome, where he would rush up to her, purse his lips and say in camp tones: 'Ange, come and meet my new husbunnnd.' She was to meet fleetingly a number of young men so described.

But she and Everett never again had a proper conversation. She was never again to work with him or have any influence over him. Poor, lost boy, she thought to herself, when he was sacked. And at that moment she realized what he had reminded her of during those three frenetic years. The impish DJ, so talented, so funny, so naive, so vulnerable, and so unsure of his sexuality, should have been broadcasting from Never Never Land. He was one of the Lost Boys from *Peter Pan*.

8

CAPTAIN KREMMEN

'I would head for the studio, and the mixer from the kitchen was in there, and it was full of water. And he was underwater, talking, with a microphone dangling in it . . .'

Lee Everett on the creation of
Captain Elvis Brandenburg Kremmen

In later years Everett consistently played down the effect on him of being thrown out of the BBC. He laughed about how an offer to do a show for London Weekend Television arrived the same day that he was sacked from Radio 1. How he had had enough. How he hated the restrictions of the Beeb. It was one of many myths that he propagated successfully about his life and it was completely untrue. In fact, Lee remembers that he was 'inconsolable' when he was fired. Certainly he enjoyed pushing the BBC's endurance to the limit, covertly relishing the repeated summonses to Robin Scott's office to be reprimanded. His adrenalin flowed when he was testing the boundaries of establishment patience and provocatively crossing them. 'I liked saying naughty things,' he later admitted, 'because I wanted to be noticed.'

But the LWT series *The Kenny Everett Explosion*, where the producers did little more than stick Everett in front of a camera, hoping he could improvise just as he apparently did on radio, unsurprisingly failed to make him a household name. Radio 1, about to introduce the travelling road show and other innovations, was at its peak. Everett was a radio broadcaster at the height of his powers. BBC engineers would send tapes of their shows to their American counterparts to show them the cutting edge of radio.

By now Everett's humour was instantly recognizable. It was a mischievous mixture of *Goon Show* voices, his own campy, effeminate, prima-donnaish falsettos rising to a climax on the last syllable (accompanied on television by a wide-eyed conspiratorial leer) and particularly his parodies of old-fashioned clipped BBC English pronouncing contemporary pop language – his fruity vowels when he said 'Feeaabbulous' were a trademark. He was the only DJ to bring a sense of parody to the world he loved. ('Hello, Cat,' he said when interviewing Cat Stevens, enunciating it so deliberately that for the first time the name sounded ridiculous.) Then there was the cast of characters invented by Everett and Angela Bond, linked to surreal situations that outdid even the Milligan-inspired Goons. All this was laced with an anti-establishment irreverence and underpinned by lateral thinking about current pop hits: mixing them with well-known classical pieces, turning them into jingles, slowing them down, speeding them up.

And, as if casting a protective shadow over all these strands of humour, was Everett's innocence. Although mischievous, it was never offensive, so that it had a special appeal to women. Very often he went to the borderline, but at that border there was nothing more explicit than, to use one of his favourite phrases, 'naughty bits'. His was the language and the innuendo of the music hall or the pantomime matinée. He shared with Benny Hill the dual ability to say an everyday phrase and make it sound mischievously suggestive, yet tell a dirty joke and not make it sound remotely dirty. 'Put your hands up, ya bum,' says the sheriff to a bank robber in one of Everett's Wild West sketches on radio. 'Put my hands up my what?' replies the aghast robber.

On radio, he had perfected a show that was simply unique – the culmination of a week's work of writing sketches, mixing tapes, composing jingles, singing four-part harmonies (the former church choirboy had perfect pitch) and 'phasing' – a technical innovation that he, like the Beatles on their records, loved to experiment with. It involved starting two machines simultaneously, then slowing one down to create a dreamy, psychedelic effect. Another of his innovations was to separate the channels on stereo records. He saw that there were some instruments to the right, some to the left, and the voice in the middle. He worked out that if you added the signals together and inverted them you got 'cancellation'. So he would take the latest Beatles record, invert the channels, and the voice would disappear. He could then sing along to the record and sound as if he was the original vocalist.

It was not always easy to discern where the genuine record finished and Everett's improvisations began. Once, when there was a Musicians Union dispute, he played a current hit and in the middle shouted: 'Musicians' strike, everybody out!' Gradually, as the result of an arduous but loving session in the wireless workshop, individual instruments began to desert the record until just the singer was left. At the end the singer, exhausted by his lack of accompaniment, burst into an uncontrollable coughing fit. Somewhere along the way he must have been replaced by Everett, whose cough it obviously was. But it was impossible to hear the joins.

Everett cherished the tools of his trade, which were a means to an end for other DJs. As Radio 1 stalwart and pop historian Paul Gambaccini noted: 'With disc jockeys almost all of us endure the equipment. It is a necessary evil, which we cope with to deliver our message. But Kenny was not only a master of the equipment, he used equipment as tools to enhance his art. You listen to all those little playlets with characters like Captain Kremmen, and he is master of the studio. He therefore is really in control of another dimension of the art which the rest of us never really come to terms with.' Johnny Beerling puts it most lyrically: 'He could milk a performance out of a machine. He had a wonderful lightness of touch with the controls. He would have made a great airline pilot.' Beerling correctly ascribed the superiority of Everett and some of his colleagues to the pirate ships. Trapped on board for a fortnight at a time, the DJs were either broadcasting themselves or talking to each other about broadcasting. It concentrated the mind.

Wherever he worked, Everett was regularly consulted by technicians, rapidly achieving the status of the guru of wireless wizardry. At every station where he worked, those seeking advice would know to find him in a studio or *ad hoc* wireless workshop, rarely in a pub with other people.

Rejected by the BBC, Everett decided to make his home his studio. And every home he lived in had a room where he made programmes, a wireless workshop replete with cartridge machines, equalizers, signal compressors, quadrant faders, multi-track tape machines, amps and other gadgetry over which Everett would wax both lyrical and serious to specialist journals, displaying a passion far removed from the wacky image he reserved for mainstream interviews. And he didn't altogether mind working in a studio at home. His early hero Jack Jackson had, on a whim, moved to the Canary Islands and had the latest releases mailed out to him. There was something to be said for 'sending the show in by phone'. Nevertheless, the years from the summer of 1970, when he was sacked by the BBC, and October 1973, when Capital Radio started, were to be a dismal waste of his professional talent.

Everett might have slipped totally into the slough of despond, and lost his house into the bargain, had not Lee taken him in hand. She saw the very real likelihood of their being unable to keep up the mortgage repayments because Everett's main income had been lost with the BBC sacking. 'You bloody well get into that studio, mate,' she ordered him, as she sat him down in it and literally ordered him to make programmes. Meanwhile she arranged for BBC local radio stations to take the programmes on a syndicated basis. And so the best disc jockey of the age was to be heard on Radios Bristol, Brighton and Medway, interspersed with interviews with local bowls-players and anglers – something he certainly wouldn't have done if he had been happy to leave the BBC anyway and move into television, as he was still maintaining to Sue Lawley on *Desert Island Discs* in October 1993.

Having 'proved himself' on the local radio circuit, he was for a time given a weekly show on Radio 1; but it was recorded at his farmhouse, and the tape driven up to London. Even then the BBC were taking no chances. On one occasion Everett played a record by the Four Tops called 'Ain't No Woman Like the One I Love', and announced: 'That's the Four Tops with "Ain't No Woman Like My One-Eyed Love".' This, perhaps in anticipation of protest from one-eyed women, was excised.

Derek Chinnery had been instrumental in arranging Everett's return to Radio 1. Ian Trethowan had told him to do whatever was needed to keep the station in the forefront, then gulped when Chinnery told him the name of the man who was needed. 'I had to fight to bring him back,' he remembers. 'Ian Trethowan was against it, and finally agreed only if the show was pre-recorded. I wanted to give him a live show. He was never as productive on a recorded show. There's something about the adrenalin that flows when it's live.'

In 1973 Everett was still in love with radio, so much so that he told his producers at LWT's *Up Sunday* programme that he never wanted to do any television again – ever. 'I'm used to radio,' he told them. 'Radio is nice and straightforward; it gets it over simply; it's got a nice atmosphere and radio can make you feel really jolly. Television, though, consumes your whole body. It requires no brain power at all. It's like playing tennis alone.'

In September of that year the now-defunct magazine *Deejay and Radio Monthly* visited him at his farmhouse and asked him about his techniques for compiling a radio programme.

'First I select a pile of decent records,' he answered, 'get a couple of NAB spools of new tape, put them on the machine and start. I stop after every record, do a bit of editing, a bit of multi-tracking, a jingle or two and then put another record on. It's like knitting a pullover really.'

A month later he had a real challenge of a pullover to knit. The Conservative government had, to the BBC's discomfiture, legislated for the start of commercial, independent radio. One of the first stations was Capital, a music and talk station for the London area.

That is putting it at its baldest. Capital did what no station had done since the old BBC Light Programme; and what no station in the present age of themed radio is ever likely to do again. It credited its listeners with a broad enough range of interests to be able to stomach – indeed desire – music, drama and documentaries on the same station. Capital's first chairman was the socialist actor and film director Richard Attenborough, and the first programmes director was Michael Bukht, later head of Classic FM. Together they forged a station that not only played the sort of upmarket classy pop that Radio 1 sometimes neglected. (Simon and Garfunkel's 'Bridge Over Troubled Water' was the first record played on Capital, Joni Mitchell's LP track 'Chelsea Morning' the second). It also had classical music programmes, jazz, award-winning documentaries on aspects of London life such as homelessness and the police, and dramas. Aidan Day, a Radio 1 producer recruited to be director of music, was not alone in maintaining: 'The assumption that someone who likes the Rolling Stones doesn't like a well-written play is absurd.'

A pop show on Capital could be, and was, followed by a George Bernard Shaw play directed by Richard Eyre, later to become the head of the National Theatre. The station broadcast only to the London area, but its polymath approach won it an audience of five million.

Day had known Everett at the BBC. And after the DJ's sacking he used to send him, to the undoubted bewilderment of listeners, coded messages via *The Emperor Rosko Show*, which he produced. Capital's programmes director, Michael Bukht, asked Day what he thought the chances were of hiring Everett. Day phoned Everett at three p.m. and the DJ got straight in his car and was at the Capital office by seven o'clock. For a man who was artistically deeply frustrated, it was a godsend. It was a godsend for Capital too. Everett was just the sort of big name they needed, certainly the biggest name they had.

His brother-in-law, Conor, a successful businessman, realized this immediately and urged him to demand shares in the new station, a demand that would almost certainly have been granted. But he was startled to find that Everett turned on him sharply, saying: 'No. Money is a dirty word. Business is a dirty word.' There still could be no greater professional dream for him than radio and music combined. Further ambition, particularly financial ambition and financial planning, were not on his agenda.

Everett rapidly began to do the promotional jingles for the station. Dave Cash, who was also recruited, remembers that this resulted in the station being cast very much in Everett's image. It was dubbed in the jingles 'Cuddly Capital', a reflection of Cuddly Ken, as Everett liked to refer to himself on air.

Michael Bukht saw the publicity value in saying that, unlike the BBC, Capital would make no attempt to gag Everett. Ironically, the DJ would probably have liked to be gagged now and again to inspire his creative juices. Knowing he wouldn't be sacked for irreverence, he baffled his bosses with goonery.

Once, he announced that his programme guest was the American singer Harry Nilsson. Everett fired questions for nearly two hours, but no one replied. Bukht, who was listening at home, was just about to phone the studio to protest at this milking of a joke when Nilsson said: 'Thanks, it's been great to be on the show.' He just hadn't fancied joining in with the interview. Nilsson was certainly talking, though, while the records were playing, delighting Everett and Day with a story of how he had been on the LBC radio station the night before, and had been fascinated by the 'delay button', which prevents bad language being broadcast. Nilsson tested it by swearing every other sentence, which resulted in listeners hearing the announcer say: 'LBC, where news comes first' every few seconds, over the unbroadcastable bits of Nilsson.

On another occasion Everett almost gave the station bosses apoplexy by announcing that the prize in a competition was a Ferrari. It was against IBA regulations to give away such a large prize and there could have been hell to pay, were it not that Everett had the prize at his side all the time: a Dinky toy version of the high-performance car. Another time Everett invited Dave Cash and fellow DJ Roger Scott to his studio in his London flat in St John's Wood. He was doing a sketch about 'The Thing That Ate Birmingham', Birmingham being a perennial target for Everett and his London audience. The Thing turned out to be an echoing burp which reduced Scott to fits of laughter. On the next day's show a bewildered audience heard no Thing, just Scott's hysterics.

At first Everett was still taping his weekly programmes at home, and driving them up to London, sometimes arriving only minutes before the show was due to start. But Capital soon changed this, deciding to give Everett the breakfast show he had once so coveted at Radio 1, to boost the London station's ratings. But he was not to be alone. Michael Bukht astutely decided to revive the Kenny and Cash combination from pirate days, and the old formula was to delight a new generation. Posters advertising 'Kenny And Cash For Breakfast' appeared all over London. Everett's reputation was once again supremely high in the music business. In 1975 a nervous Freddie Mercury, the lead singer with Queen, sent him a demo tape of the group's new single 'Bohemian Rhapsody'. Mercury explained he was worried that it was too long. What did Everett think? Just as when George Harrison had played him *Sergeant Pepper*, Everett gasped and told him: 'Release it, release it.' Dave Cash remembers that Everett was the first guy to bring in Queen to the station. 'He played their first record, "The Seven Seas of Rhye", endlessly. He was involved with them from the very beginning.'

In 1975 the *Sunday Times* included Everett in their feature 'Makers of the Twentieth Century', writing perceptively: 'Everett is probably

the most accomplished and inventive British disc jockey. This makes
him chief of a brotherhood which at its best is awesomely stupid
and at its worst practically certifiable. All their characteristic faults
– making interminable humourless jokes, talking over the top of
music, pretending to be scarcely out of their teens – have been
turned by Everett into a freeform style that is often palatable, despite
his rather unnatural fondness for the sound of his own singing voice
... Capital, being little endowed with talent, has virtually built its
image around Everett ...'

Certainly Everett seemed very happy at Capital. His show was
winning awards. He was given his head, and to his delight, the
station was committed to playing classier rock music and LP tracks
rather than still being committed to pop singles like Radio 1. Only in
one respect was his thinking opposed to that of his colleagues. When
the station began, Bukht, his chairman Sir Richard Attenborough
and, particularly, Dave Cash, wanted Capital to break the mould in
a distinctive way. It was to be a station with a social conscience. With
great success, Capital operated helplines, a jobfinder and a flatshare
line, aided the homeless and raised large sums of money in its Help
a London Child campaigns. 'We should do something to help the
community, rather than just take their money,' said Cash. For Cash,
as for so many others, the sixties meant, with an awful pun, a joint
legacy. 'I got a social conscience along with a taste for marijuana.
The two things went hand in hand.' Everett couldn't understand
this. He had a taste for marijuana. But a music station was there to
play music. There was no place for politics, particularly a political
philosophy with which he disagreed. He had often jokingly, and
not always jokingly, called Cash a commie.

When preparing their breakfast show now, which artistically was
at an absolute peak, the two of them were frequently at odds over
politics. 'Do we have to do the helpline?' Everett would plead. 'I'd
much rather read out this funny piece that I've found in the *Sun*.'
Cash smiled to himself. Here was the guy with the image of being
Cuddly Ken, who would happily have ditched all Capital's efforts
to help people.

But Cash also noticed a dichotomy in Everett's attitude, and says:
'On the one hand he hated all the social conscience stuff. But when
listeners phoned in to say how wonderful Capital was and how it had
helped them get a job or get their child an operation, Kenny would

be over the moon, and genuinely touched that he could have been responsible for this. Half the time on the air he was more socialist than I was.' Yet as the seventies progressed, Everett started singing the praises of Margaret Thatcher to Cash, who secretly wondered if she wasn't a mother substitute for him.

Later, after the strain of the breakfast show was to prove too much, Everett, at Sir Richard Attenborough's suggestion, reverted to a weekend show, which he prepared at the home in the Cotswolds that he and Lee had, by this time, moved to.

It was here that Everett dreamt up one of his most enduring inventions: a space serial to insert into his (and later other people's) shows, starring Captain Kremmen, a name that had lodged in his subconscious some years earlier. He would record it on Friday nights, or sometimes at dawn on Saturday mornings, the day of his shows, and drive it up to London on Saturday mornings, often arriving at the studios with only minutes to spare before he presented his show. Captain Elvis Brandenburg Kremmen of the Star Corps and his buxom and beautiful assistant Carla reinvigorated Everett – a fan of the early BBC serial *Journey into Space*, the *Dan Dare* and *Flash Gordon* comic strips, the *Eagle Annual* and other intergalactic adventures since childhood – and captured the public imagination. It also led to comics, a book and other merchandising, including T-shirts.

Apart from towards the end of the Kremmen period, when Everett was snorting cocaine and drinking heavily as his personal life collapsed, the adventures of Kremmen and his wars against the man-eating Krells were inspired lunacy. Everett accurately parodied the transatlantic apocalyptic pomp of the space serial narrator, while the adventure he told was inevitably one of cosmic idiocy and often had only the most tenuous links with space travel. In one episode Kremmen was trapped inside his spaceship by a man-eating blancmange. In another 'nerve-noggling episode', with guest star Doug a l'Orange, listeners heard the following: 'I wrenched off my space tunic.' 'Captain, [gasp] what's that scar on your shoulder?' 'Oh, that. I got that months ago in a car accident. I wrapped my car around a tree and was trapped in it for ages. Luckily two cars happened along and saw my plight.' 'Golly, who was in the cars?' 'Mr and Mrs Smith and Mr and Mrs Ball. Fortunately I was pulled out by the Smiths.'

Having both Everett and his studio at home made life for Lee as bizarre as a Kremmen episode. Every household object became a potential sound effect.

'When he was doing Kremmen,' she recalls, 'he drove me insane. I'd have someone round for tea, and he'd come up and say: "Oh, Lee, how can I make the sounds of eyeballs being ripped out?" It was my tea towels being ripped up. And I'd go into the kitchen and find there was nothing in the kitchen. I went in to do a cake one day, and the mixer and everything had gone. I would head for the studio, and the mixer from the kitchen was in there, and it was full of water. And he was underwater, talking, with a microphone dangling in it, and all these tea towels. His sound effects drove me mad.'

Everett created more than eighty episodes of *Captain Kremmen*; and in addition to the books, T-shirts, newspaper strips and merchandise, the Captain and his left-hand lady Carla also surfaced in their creator's TV shows in comic-strip form; the bearded Everett look-alike Kremmen ensuring 'monsters slain, worlds conquered and baddies captured while you wait'. All the voices were Everett's and the eye-catching graphics came from Cosgrove Hall Studios, an early success for a British animation studio that was to gain international acclaim.

On TV, as on radio and in the comic strip, the humour remained idiosyncratically Everett, mixing the adventure of space wars with a down-to-earth, domestic, cuddly response, the absurdity of the juxtaposition making the gag. 'We need your help,' says the space commander in desperation to Kremmen. 'Well, you can't have her,' he replies. 'She only comes twice a week.' Showing Carla the new spaceship that travels faster than the speed of light, he explains: 'Say we went to Mars, this ship goes so fast that we'd arrive before we took off which means we'd have time to come back and wave goodbye to ourselves' – the graphics madly keeping pace with the whole scene.

Kremmen was gorgeous, funny, fantastical stuff. It was only after Everett's death that his close friend Eric Gear discovered it may have contained one curious link with reality. For nostalgic and sentimental reasons, Gear was listening to some old Kremmen tapes. He had heard them many times before over nearly two decades. But suddenly it struck him for the first time that the descriptions of the space hero – rugged, handsome, muscular, tall and devastatingly attractive to women – were not just plucked out of thin air. They were everything that Kremmen's creator fantasized about being.

At Capital, Aidan Day rapidly came to love working with Everett. 'He could create pictures in sound in a way that I had never heard before. For example, in Kremmen there was an evil, revolting monster. In order to get the noise it made he stuck a load of Pepsi down DJ Tommy Vance's throat and he belched, and he slowed down the tape of that to make the noise of the monster.'

Everett loved Capital's eclectic mix of music. With Robin Ray, who hosted a classical programme, he would do a battle of the bands, pitting a group such as Cockney Rebel or Queen against Beethoven. Everett's eagerness to mix the genres has Day speculating now that he must be organizing a jam session in the sky with Mozart, Freddie Mercury and Harry Nilsson.

Often his off-the-cuff remarks had Day guffawing in the producer's box. After a Rod Stewart song, Everett commented: 'Great record, but have you ever thought how Rod Stewart looks like a lavatory brush?' At the time Stewart's spiky hair sticking out over his thin neck made this an apposite simile.

He also started a 'bottom ten' of the worst records ever, inspired by a classic of the genre, 'I've Got to Get Back to My Baby' about a man whose girlfriend dies. He digs up the body, and the record ends echoing out of the grave. That topped the bottom ten, but Everett had the humility to put not far below it a record he had made with Dave Cash on Radio London. The bottom ten later became an LP of the world's worst records, with Everett's face on the cover.

Everett took to Day. He was particularly interested that Day was a Catholic and his brother was a priest. From time to time Everett would disconcertingly throw into a conversation the notion that 'there must be more than this, there must be an afterlife, someone with a harp up there'; but if Day attempted to prolong the conversation, Everett would quickly turn it into a joke.

Day took Everett to his first opera, *La Bohème*, at Covent Garden. Everett was entranced, and not just with the music. He was very taken with the tenor, 'besotted' as Day remembers, and throughout the interval talked of how he was 'divine'. Like most people who worked closely with Everett, Day knew he was gay.

And yet what many of those same people could not see during

Everett's golden years at Capital was the turmoil that filled his mind. He was the most celebrated DJ in the country. He was rich. He had famous friends. And he was married to a glamorous, exciting woman. What could he possibly have to be depressed about?

9

MARITAL MELTDOWN

'If you were on a desert island, would you attempt suicide?'
'Nah. I've done that one.'

Everett interviewed by Sue Lawley on
Desert Island Discs, October 1993

In the summer of 1975 Everett and Lee were invited to spend the day with Dave Cash and his wife at their home in Hillingdon on the edge of London. Cash's wife, Monica, was an actress and played in one of the funniest scenes in the history of cinema. As Cecily Pigeon, she was one of the 'coo-coo pigeon' sisters, Cecily and Gwendoline, who were the dates of Jack Lemmon and Walter Matthau in *The Odd Couple*, and were reduced to tears by a depressed Lemmon while Matthau was in the kitchen mixing the drinks. Early in the sixties she had also starred in Britain's first TV soap opera, *Compact*.

Cash remembers telling Everett: 'This is the lady I love. I want to spend my life with her.' By 1975 Dave and Monica had a baby daughter, Emma, and during the afternoon of the visit Monica took Lee into the kitchen for a chat, leaving Dave holding the baby. Emma showed her appreciation in the way babies do. Dave changed the nappy, chatting to Everett all the while. 'I like being an active father,' he told him. 'Look, I even enjoy changing diapers.' But Everett didn't chat back. He sat quietly and ill at ease, saying little then or for the rest of the day and putting a dampener on proceedings.

When they lunched the next day at their favourite Italian restaurant near the Capital Radio studios, Everett was still awkward and quiet.

Cash asked him what on earth was the matter, and what had been the matter the day before. 'Was it something I said?'

'Just the sight of you changing nappies,' replied Everett. 'I don't feel easy with it at all.' He added that things weren't right between him and Lee, and he was thinking of coming out of the closet.

As it happens, he didn't for some years. Nevertheless, it was then that Cash decided to have the conversation that had been brewing between them for ten years. 'Ken said: "I'm going to be gay," and I replied: "Well, I'm a family man. That's where I'm at and I'm very happy with it. I feel as ill at ease with the gay community as you do with my world."'

For some reason Everett was deeply uncomfortable seeing Cash in the bosom of his family. Perhaps it reminded him that it was a life that would soon, albeit by choice, be denied him. Whatever the reason, Kenny and Cash that day reached an agreement suggested by Cash. They would meet socially twice a year for lunch, and it would just be the two of them. 'You don't bring your boyfriends, and I won't bring my wife,' said Cash. They kept rigidly to the agreement, meeting twice a year right up until November 1994. When Cash phoned early in 1995 to arrange the next lunch, Everett was too ill to talk.

By 1975 Everett's discomfort at witnessing a friend enjoying domestic bliss with his wife and baby came as no surprise to Lee. For three fairly idyllic years after getting married she was hopeful. They both desperately wanted the marriage to work. But then, she explains: 'The gremlins came back. He felt that sex with me and a proper marriage would cure all that. But it didn't, because his fantasies were still there.'

It was in 1972 that he started to give expression to those fantasies. Lee had got in a carpenter called Charlie to do some work on the Sussex farmhouse. Charlie's wife, Sonya, gave riding lessons, and Lee began to take up riding. Soon she was bitten with the riding bug, and she and Sonya decided to go into business, breeding and training horses. Everett and Charlie, whom Lee remembers as a very weak man, began to take LSD trips together (Lee had by this time ended her long flirtation with drugs) and to listen to music in Everett's studio. Sonya was both pregnant and busy with the horses and didn't notice anything untoward. But Lee remembered the cameraman on *Nice Time* and recognized the warning signs.

Her husband had developed another crush. She confronted him with her suspicions, but he angrily denied the charge and accused her of being stupid. Shortly afterwards they had some gay friends to stay for the weekend. After an evening drinking home-made wine, Lee went to bed and left Everett and the gay visitors downstairs. But she could hear their conversation through the old floorboards. She lay in bed numbed as, to her amazement, he lamented how he didn't find his wife attractive, but still fancied men.

It was not just the content of his speech, but the tone that horrified Lee. 'He was talking as if I was forcing my attentions on him against his natural desires. I just couldn't believe my ears as he went on and on about his desperation for a man. Why couldn't he have told me all this? These people weren't even close friends of ours. Why was he making a fool of me? I realized that this is how he must have gone on to other gay friends. He probably did it all the time. In fact, when I investigated, I found I was correct. He was making a fool of me to everyone.'

Lee was mortally hurt. Over the next year or two she began to change. Her interest in spiritualism was already making her into a more serious and deeper woman than the sixties swinger Everett had first met. As she now began to devote herself to trying to make the marriage work, she became more reclusive and spent inordinate amounts of time nursing her increasingly lovesick husband – lovesick for other men, nearly always unattainable heterosexual men. But the stress began to tell, and the glamour-puss of just months before began to look older and strained. For she was spending an increasing amount of her private life helping her husband through his emotional traumas, and of her public life denying any hint that these traumas might be taking place. But taking place they were. Everett continued to be ashamed of his homosexuality. He started to take sleeping pills, and after taking them developed a dangerous habit of going for a drive along the country lanes. One morning at six a.m. Lee found Everett and all three cars, a Mini, a BMW and a Land Rover, missing. He later arrived back on foot. He'd driven one car into a ditch and then, still only half awake, come back to fetch another to try to pull his first car out, and then the third car to rescue the other two. All three ended up in the ditch. For a short while Lee took up again with her lover of long ago, Alex Most, but rapidly returned to Everett.

She noted what was to remain an astonishing feature of her

husband. Whatever traumas he was going through, however suicidal the depression, however black the cloud, when he walked the few yards from his bedroom or sitting room to the studio in his home he became an anarchic comedian. Whether he was able to completely switch off his personal torments or whether, as is more likely, they drove his talent, the fact is that much of his best work was produced when he was close to despair. Not just the Capital Radio shows and *Captain Kremmen*, but also his rise to international fame with his Thames Television sketch shows, all occurred during a period when he would make the shows (often at home in the case of radio, and in London when it was television) then switch back to an imploding marriage and a seemingly never-ending torment over his sexuality.

When he eventually began to win the latter battle, there was still a strange and secret contrast. He could be Cuddly Ken in the daytime, a cult television figure for the under-twelves, and then at night indulge in a frenetic lifestyle of potentially dangerous sexual practices. But then other comics, entertainers and film stars have over the years had lifestyles that contrasted outrageously with their screen images. It was Everett's achievement in the seventies of being at a creative peak as a comic while living on the edge of oblivion that is so remarkable. However much pain he was in, says Lee, he still used to go into his studio and turn out amazingly funny things. His pain used to turn into humour.

The Charlie episode had not yet run its course, though. Lee decided to sell up in Sussex and buy a sixty-acre hill farm in Carmarthenshire. Charlie and Sonya came along too. While Lee and Sonya did the hard physical work, Ken and Charlie spent most of the time getting stoned, though Everett did rather take to milking the cows. It was the one job he always volunteered for: he found it therapeutic and the cows seemed to like his lightness of touch.

Generally, though, he had time to kill. This was the in-between time after Radio 1 and before Capital, and television work was also thin on the ground. Nor was the Welsh countryside exactly a natural habitat for Everett. A man whose life was in the London pop and media milieu which sparked off his talent was hardly likely to be happy on a bleak and remote hillside, in a house with no running water, surrounded by horses, sheep and cattle. When his family visited they came away depressed. This was not the place for him.

At home in Liverpool with Cathy, Mum and Dad.

The first Radio 1 line-up. Ev is behind Terry Wogan.

Posing with his producer Angela Bond.

deejay

and Radio Monthly

No. 11 September 1973
(inc. August)

EXCLUSIVE: RONAN O'RAHILLY SPEAKS O

Noel Edmonds · Disco Picks · Soul Sounds

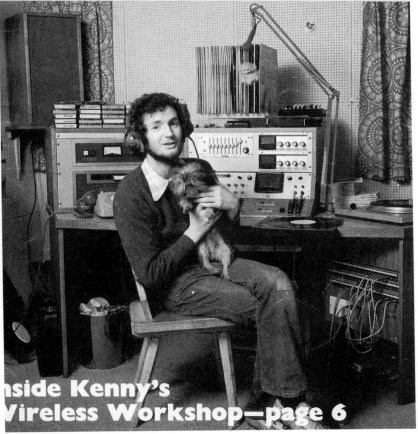

nside Kenny's
Wireless Workshop—page 6

Dominating *Deejay* magazine.

Marital bliss . . . Over
the threshold and into
the wheelbarrow.

Topping the rating with *alter egos* (clockwise from top left) General Marvin D. Bomb-the-Bastards. Gizzard Puke, Cupid Stunt and Marcel Wave.

Party political broadcast Ev-style.

With Cleo Rocos.

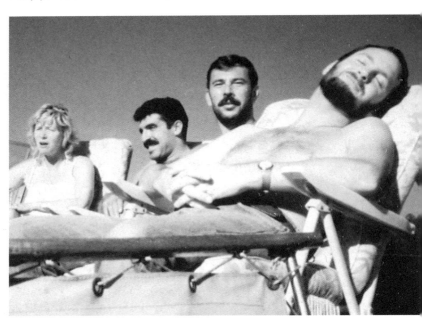

The famous *ménage à trois*: Ev with Nikolai and Pepe.

Off-screen happiness: with his adored sister Kate before the Gay Mardi Gras in Australia, 1994.

On a walking holiday with the Gears.

A kiss from a fan after he reveals he has the Aids virus.

His funeral contained the Requiem Mass he so wanted but believed he could never have.

He wanted more order in his life, a much more regular domesticity, or so they believed. Sure enough, there was an explosion waiting to happen, though when it did it could hardly be blamed on the rigours of farming.

One morning Sonya, pregnant with another child, rushed crying into the kitchen, threw buckets of water across the room and begged Lee to leave with her and set up a farm on their own. She told her she had just seen her husband and Everett sauntering across a field holding hands. Sonya went off to stay with her parents. Lee stayed to run the farm and confront the situation. Then, to get away from it all, she accepted an invitation to the launch party for Elton John's record label, Rocket, in Los Angeles, where she ended up singing backing vocals for Elton with her friend Dusty Springfield.

Elton met the flight at Los Angeles with six ra-ra girls with pom-poms and a ten-foot moving poster of the Queen. The party was at Universal Studios, with cowboy shootouts going on all around. Lee and black singer Noni Hendryx decided to swap identities with the help of wigs, make-up and body paint, and fooled everyone. In the middle of the party Everett arrived, wanting a reconciliation with Lee.

When they returned to England, things seemed to improve. Everett, who was by now doing his weekly show for Radio 1 and presenting (a scripted) *Top of the Pops*, was kept busy. Nevertheless, he was still taking excessive amounts of sleeping pills, mixing them with alcohol, throwing up in the night and going for early-morning drives. It could easily have proved fatal; indeed this was a period that Everett was lucky to survive. And Lee knew he was still going off from time to time to meet Charlie. Worse, he was giving him money and some of their joint possessions. The stereo was one of the first items to disappear. 'A pot of money went Charlie's way and a lot of our belongings,' says Lee, 'so I have very great resentment. Apart from the fact his wife was lovely and in such a terrible state and pregnant.'

The launch of Capital Radio more than occupied Everett. Getting up at five a.m. for the breakfast show and having to be in bed most nights by nine, having taken sleeping pills, left little time for extracurricular activities. He and Lee were getting on much better, though they had separate rooms in their rented house in London and for the rest of their marriage rarely shared a bed again for long. With the rampant success of his Capital show, the madcap side of Everett was returning. Once he phoned Lee in Los Angeles, where she was visiting Dusty Springfield. Lee told him how she and Dusty had just struggled to carry a drunken Mama Cass home to bed, and how, bearing in mind Mama Cass's weight, that had been no easy task. Only after a few minutes did Lee realize she had been talking live on air to the breakfast show.

For their next move the couple bought the actor Hugh Griffiths's old house, a converted pub in the Cotswolds village of Cherington near Stratford-upon-Avon, complete with fourteen acres of land, a barn and even an old jailhouse in the garden, at the bottom of which flowed a stream. It was a beautiful setting, and it did wonders for Everett. He always looked back on it as the house he was most happy in, and in later years he would drive friends out to show it to them and tell them so. When they moved there, Lee once again hoped it would be a fresh start for their marriage. They may have pulled back the bed covers to find a mouse nest with three baby mice nestling in the mattress, but she could cope with problems like that. Everett told Lee that the Charlie episode had 'got it out of his system'. He desperately wanted the marriage to work. He wanted, he told her, to be 'cured'. The next few months were blissful, then Everett started mentioning Stuart, a jolly, down-to-earth, moustachioed South African engineer who was working at Capital.

Stuart was heterosexual, and Lee was by now recognizing a pattern. 'He would drool and moon for a long time over a man. Invariably they would be straight and there was no hope of the love being returned. Then one night he would get stoned and confess all to the object of his love, and suffer a painful rebuff. He'd go into a suicidal depression, and I would have to nurse him out of it. What always won was my pity. I felt sorry for him. He had such black depressions that I would see this black cloud come into the room and the whole room would go dark.'

The crush at Capital was on a completely straight man. There was no hope of the infatuation being answered. Everett got more and more depressed. Stuart was invited to the house on a number of occasions and took a fancy to one of Lee's friends. Lee instinctively disliked Stuart. It was obvious to her that he knew her husband had a crush on him. Yet he was happy to take their hospitality. She learnt from her friend that Everett had again been saying needlessly cruel things about her. He had told Stuart that Lee had only married him for his money.

At this she blew up, and confronted her husband. How could he say such things about her? He hadn't got a penny when they met. He was an out-of-work pirate-radio DJ. 'Our whole bloody marriage I was always juggling to keep the finances straight,' she now says.

She left the London flat and moved to Cherington on her own, living more and more like a recluse. 'All he did was get crushes on straight men, because he knew he was safe. I was nursing him through traumas all the time. For years and years he was in pain.

'I needed to try to move away from the permanent pain marriage was giving me. Physically, I'd gone from being a very attractive woman to a drab, lifeless old lady. The unhappiness was showing on my face drastically. I felt washed up.'

Everett came to Cherington at weekends, and they had furious fights, sometimes physical, though even those were not without an element of slapstick. Once, after they had both gone to bed in their separate rooms on opposite sides of the large house, Lee exploded, ran down the corridor, threw herself at his door, splintering it and landed at the foot of his bed with parts of the antique door showering down on her. 'And another thing!' she panted. At that they both dissolved into fits of laughter.

Then, one night in May 1975, Lee took a call from Aidan Day. He explained that he was at her husband's London flat, from where Everett had rung him to say that he had taken an overdose. Day told her that an ambulance was taking him to the Royal Free Hospital in Hampstead. At the time, Lee had Everett's mother and father staying with her. They were still unaware of their son's homosexuality. Lee had covered up well. But they knew him to be a depressive, so the overdose came as no great surprise.

Lee's response amazed Day. She said she wasn't prepared to come immediately, but would do so the next day. To Day, it seemed a peculiarly unemotional response, but he let it pass. Nor did he tell Lee on the phone what he had found in the flat. On the floor, by a mess of empty pill jars, was a drumskin with a heartfelt farewell letter written on it from Everett to Stuart, the Capital engineer. The next day it was still there and Lee burst into tears when she saw it as she arrived with Everett's agent, Jo Gurnett. The two of them looked at each other without speaking, and destroyed the drumskin, allowing Everett to claim in interviews for years to come that he had overdosed on Mandrax purely by accident because of the jet-lagged state one gets into doing an early-morning breakfast show.

When Lee got to the hospital she found her husband 'sitting up dressed on his bed, totally confused and upset at still being alive. He looked like a little boy, so small and helpless.' By this time the press had gathered outside the hospital, so Lee and Jo smuggled their charge out via the laundry chute.

The press followed them back to the St John's Wood flat and leant on the doorbell until it was answered. Lee went out and made a statement telling the agreed story, saying it had all been a mistake and the breakfast show had made him overtired. She also managed to make a joke, saying she and her husband had a new foal and were going to name it 'Sleepy' after her husband's big sleep.

Everett's mother had even written herself a small part in the drama as press interest had grown since the news broke. She would answer the phone pretending to be the cleaner. The woman who never gave an interview spoke to a clutch of tabloid journalists many times over the space of a few days without any of them realizing who they were speaking to.

Michael Bukht baffled the press with the science of breakfast-show stress, saying: 'He has been doing the six-thirty to nine-thirty a.m. show – which means his day starts at four-thirty every morning – for the past eighteen months. He has been very tired and was due to go on leave next week. When he telephoned, he said he had taken some sleeping pills and they hadn't worked too well. So he took some more. Then he realized he had taken too many.' To make doubly sure that no reporter went off with a suspicious thought in their head, Jo Gurnett dutifully told the newspapers: 'It's ridiculous to say there are any problems between Kenny and Lee. They're a deliriously happy couple.'

The ploy succeeded. The confused suicide attempt of a desperately unhappy man was portrayed in the press as a mistaken binge by a guy living life in the fast lane and having to cheer the nation at the crack of dawn every morning with zany improvisations after a night on the tiles. Besides, putting it any other way would have bewildered the readers of those papers.

Sir Richard Attenborough, chairman of Capital, told Everett to take time off to recuperate, and ensured that when he was better he was given a weekly show to take some of the strain off him. But then, to Lee's astonishment, Everett invited Stuart to stay for the weekend. The two of them went for a drive, and Everett confessed his feeling for him. He suffered a shattering rebuff. He told his wife that Stuart yelled at him that he was a 'pervert'. Lee remembers Everett returning to the house 'like a broken doll' and taking to his bed. He became ill.

'Ev was devastated,' she recalls. 'It sent him into this spiralling black cloud that got worse and worse. And I nursed him. If I found that John [Alkin, her present husband] had another woman, I'd be really ferocious. I'd be totally female. But with Ev it was different. All I could see was this poor little thing suffering. I just felt so sorry for him. He was so sad.'

Though at the time Lee was suffering from chronic asthma and arthritis, she devoted herself again to looking after her husband. She began to gauge his state of mind by covertly reading his diary. It was full of outpourings for Stuart; but she could at least chart how depressed he was; and gradually he began to recover. One day the entry read: 'Lee's a brick.' It wasn't quite the paean of praise she had hoped for from the man she still loved. But it was better than nothing.

But she was still worried about his pill-taking. As well as the sleeping pills and the Mandrax (now illegal) he was taking Tuinol, an extremely powerful barbiturate, and he still suffered depressions. Lee went to a spiritualist church in Stratford-upon-Avon to pray for him. The medium at the altar, Peggy Foster, said she would very shortly receive help through a book. The next day, collecting Everett's sleeping pill prescription at the chemist, she saw a British Medical Association booklet, *Sleeping But Not Sleeping*, about sleeping pills and their side-effects. She and Everett read it and found it described him exactly, saying a side-effect of continuous use of sleeping pills was severe depression. They both determined to wean him off the pills. One withdrawal symptom was weeks of severe nightmares.

He would wake up night after night, screaming that a hag with jagged teeth was trying to eat his feet. Lee, who had been living in a separate part of the house since his suicide attempt, returned to sleeping with him because he was afraid to sleep alone. Some nights they played cards through the night, because he was afraid to sleep at all. But the cure worked. For the first time in over a decade he stopped taking sleeping pills.

And he totally changed. 'The terrible black cloud lifted,' says Lee. 'We went away on a second honeymoon to Jamaica, and he became very sexual with me. It was like he was totally cured. We started again. We started marriage again. It was marvellous.' Back in Cherington, he began to take an active part in village life. With Lee he organized parties and badminton tournaments, and even helped to run a village magazine, as well as swimming galas with underwater wheelbarrow races. For the Queen's Silver Jubilee celebrations in 1977 there were concerts, barrel races and bonfires. He became a keen walker, going on long hikes with Lee's brother-in-law and, later, with his friend and bank manager Eric Gear. It was a particularly sunny period for Everett. He was becoming physically healthy, was enjoying his home life, minding the garden, helping in the kitchen and working on Captain Kremmen and its merchandising spin-offs. 'He became the lovely daft creature I had originally married,' says Lee.

How contented a time it was for Everett can be surmised from the fact that, at his wish, following his death, some of his ashes were buried in the garden of that home in the Cotswolds.

To cement the marriage further, the couple had decided just before the cure from sleeping pills, when he was in the depths of depression, that they should adopt a child to give them a shared purpose. It was an odd decision. Neither of them particularly liked children. Everett told a newspaper that 'they slobber, are messy and scream all the time'. When he and Lee went to visit his sister, they would ask if they could come when the kids were in bed. Everett would pick up his tiny precocious niece, Joanna, by the scruff of the neck and place her at arm's length on the floor, saying in the campest Noel Coward tone: 'You'll make somebody a *wonderful* wife some day.'

Children had never seemed to figure on their agenda. But by this time Lee was clutching at straws. 'He was so unhappy,' she says now, 'and I thought it would give him something to live for. I couldn't give him babies, and I never wanted children, ever. And I went through one period when I thought perhaps he'd have had more chance if he had married somebody who could give him babies. I went into hospital to have my tubes fixed and everything but it didn't work. Underneath, I never wanted them, but I just felt that if he just had a marriage where he had a baby, it might have given him something to live for, some reality in life. And he felt that too. And so we put in for adoption.'

They applied to an adoption agency, were interviewed and offered a selection of mixed-race two-year-olds. For a while they were interested. But at the last minute they changed their minds. Both realized together it was not really what either of them wanted.

It would not be true to say that it was always solely a case of Lee going out of her way to show tolerance of her wayward partner. Everett had to learn to live with his wife's increasing involvement in the paranormal. She sold her entire record collection and all her marijuana and gave the money to the local spiritualist church. (Little did the church realize how its new-found wealth was raised.) She gave up drugs for good, and became teetotal. She had discovered that she had powers as a healer and was to build up quite a reputation for it, now working for the Institute of Complementary Medicine. She went to sessions where she regressed into her past lives, in one of which she saw herself as a Japanese girl having her head cut off by a marauding warrior. (She has assisted regression for the likes of Elton John and Tony Blackburn.) Three times Lee was told by other mediums that she had been her husband's mother in two past lives. She readily believed this as her role with him became more and more like a mother's, protecting him, guiding him and clucking over him.

She became increasingly conscious of people's inner thoughts, once embarrassing even Everett by bounding out of a jolly dinner party because she sensed that the friends laughing and joking really bore ill will towards each other. Before leaving she blurted out to each person what they were really thinking. Everett screamed up the stairs after her: 'That's that. You've really gone insane now.'

She began to believe it herself and arranged again to visit Peggy Foster, the medium who had told her that she would find a cure for her husband's addiction to sleeping pills. She went with a neighbour, and later recorded what happened that morning in her book *Kinds of*

Loving. She wrote: 'That appointment proved to be the turning point of my whole life . . . In that hour and a half the feeling in the room was astounding – a power, a sort of light descended on us. We felt wonderfully well, though I was in reality anything but. I was told what was going to happen to me, but I didn't understand until later when it actually happened. I was told I was ready to work for the Light, that I would be guided to bring forward the gifts – brought into this life with me, which had of necessity lain unremembered. I would have to be patient as there was much work to do. First, my body was to be healed. I was to stop drinking and every morning for the next three mornings I had to stand by the window and breathe deeply for three minutes: I would be healed in these three days.

'I went home and stopped smoking. I've never smoked from that day, and I used to smoke 20–30 a day; I didn't have a drop of alcohol for a year and three days later I had no trace of asthma . . . As far as I'm concerned my life really began on that day, not back there in 1937 . . . At first Ev scoffed and sent me up unmercifully, but one day I told him that if he made me make a choice of him or this path, I'd have to choose the path. He looked into my eyes and knew I was telling the truth. From then on he left off the send ups.'

But, just as Lee had to cope with a husband who changed dramatically from the man she married, so it cannot always have been easy for Everett, keeping up with the dramatic and disorientating changes in his wife's life.

Lee's reputation as both healer and regresser grew with her book, radio appearances and her own London clinic; and many people came to the house in Cherington to be healed or taken back into past lives. One woman from the village turned out to have been a Spanish nun raped by soldiers in a previous life.

It is an unorthodox picture of English country life: a cottage where Everett was in his studio, his head in water, his hands ripping up tea towels as he prepared the sound effects for the next Kremmen adventure, while Lee was down the corridor regressing a matron from the Women's Institute who sobbed and screamed as she relived being raped and murdered in a nunnery at the hands of marauding Spanish soldiers.

Nevertheless their marriage was going through a happy and settled period, and they were becoming devoted to each other once again, this time Everett nursing Lee and cooking for her after she had a hysterectomy. Even so, with his ever-present forgetfulness the meals sometimes didn't arrive until several hours after they were promised – an episode of Kremmen having been recorded in the interim. But Lee could cope with late meals.

And then she noticed that he was mentioning a man's name rather too often. It was another crush on a heterosexual acquaintance. This one even came round for dinner with his girlfriend. When Lee met him she saw with a sinking feeling that he was moustachioed, muscular and dark, like most of Everett's other crushes.

While Lee had despised both Charlie and Stuart, this one was worse, and she still shudders when she thinks of him. At the end of the evening he came over to her and told her he now expected to go to bed with her; that surely was part of the deal. She fled into her bedroom and locked the door with tweezers. But similar incidents were to happen again in the future. The sort of people her husband was developing crushes on were not always going to be the sort to whom one would want to give house room.

Everett again began to sink into a depression. He invited the crush and his girlfriend for the Christmas holidays, but Lee was rude to them and they departed. Everett accused her of ruining his Christmas and went to bed. She accompanied their mutual friend Tommy Vance, the DJ, and his wife, Cookie, to a party. There Lee got chatting to John Alkin, a tall, blond actor, whose face is instantly recognizable from the TV series *The Sweeney*, in which he played an often-seen Flying Squad assistant to John Thaw and Dennis Waterman.

Lee had known Alkin slightly for some years and had given him healing when his marriage was breaking up. Still unhappy and confused, she flew off to America to stay with friends, but once again Everett rushed out to her and flew her home.

This time, however, the downward spiral was irreversible. Everett had become heavily dependent on cocaine. The habit was making huge inroads into his and Lee's bank account, at times to the tune of £1000 a week. It also brought out an unpleasant side of him, a vicious temper which on occasion culminated in fist fights between husband and wife. 'He got heavily on to coke and then we had a really bad time,' Lee says. 'His eyes would go black like he was the devil, and he'd become vicious. I've got masses of apology letters from Everett, saying he regretted how vicious he had been.'

Yet, for all the personal crises, Everett's career was progressing apace. It was now 1978, and he had been booked to do a series for Thames, one that was to make him a household name. Lee decided to give the marriage one more go. To Everett's chagrin, she sold the house in the Cotswolds, and they bought a London flat with a Victorian walled garden, in Pembridge Villas, Notting Hill Gate. They shared a bedroom, though with single beds. They went on a health kick, swimming and playing badminton together every day. But it was not to last.

Jo Gurnett, Everett's agent, threw an anniversary party, and Lee returned from the toilet in the middle of the evening to find Everett dancing with a gay man. The two were caressing each other and not caring who saw. This time she decided there would be no more attempts at repairing the marriage. She wrote in her own book later: 'They were mauling each other. I felt I was going to vomit. I'd known for ages of his drives, but to see them was another matter. I can't describe how I felt: first sick, physically sick, then cold inside as if someone had died. How could he have done this to me in front of everyone, in front of me?'

A few weeks later it happened again. At a London nightclub, Legends, Everett took another man out on to the floor and danced slowly with him. The late Russell Harty, the television chat-show host and friend of Everett and Lee, was there. He came up to Lee and hugged her. That was the moment when she realized that she was an object of pity and that the marriage was finished.

She went away for a holiday with some girl friends. When she returned she and Everett talked things through and decided to live apart. He bought a flat across the road, though he kept a key to the marital home. She agreed, for the sake of his career, to keep up a pretence for the press and public that they were still living as man and wife. That pretence was to last a further four years.

One night Everett and Lee went out for a meal with Freddie Mercury. At the restaurant, Everett was eyeing the waiter. 'I really think the waiter is fabulous,' he remarked. Lee thought it was time to act. She saw he was gay and went over to him: 'My husband really likes you,' she said. 'We're going on to Legends. Would you like to join us?' His name was John Pitt, and he was an exceedingly quiet, gentle boy from Australia. He said yes and ended up moving in with Everett and staying for more than a year.

Meanwhile Lee flew off to New York to see friends, and there she too embarked on a radically different lifestyle. Her old unconventionality suddenly returned with a vengeance. She met and entered into a lengthy lesbian relationship with an internationally famous American tennis player. The tennis player never 'came out' and still does not wish her name to be known in this context. Everett took it in his stride. 'He was fine about that,' says Lee. 'He'd come to the airport with me and give parties for my girlfriend.'

Lee was now in the bizarre position of acting out in London a charade of being happily married while her husband was living across the street with another man, and in New York a charade of being just friends with a tennis star when she was living with her in a fully sexual relationship. Everett now became her friend and confidant, making transatlantic phone calls to her every day. He was, Lee saw, relieved she had fallen for a woman. Had she fallen for a man at that time, he would have been deeply hurt.

Lee and the tennis star even indulged in a camp wedding, declaring themselves married. The *News of the World* heard about it and reported it under the headline: 'Kenny Everett's Wife Marries In Lesbian Ceremony.' Everett and Lee said the story was rubbish. But on this occasion *The News of the World* had got it right. That strange affair lasted a year. Just before Lee and her girlfriend finally split up, Lee again met John Alkin at a party. This time he moved in with her and stayed. At first Everett was furious. Lee taking up with a woman was one thing. Another man was a blow to his pride. There were some nasty rows, but when he got to know John he got to like him very quickly. The tennis player remained friends with Lee, and once, when she was in London, she offered John Alkin a ticket for the Borg–McEnroe final at Wimbledon in exchange for an afternoon out with her. Alkin, instantly likeable and by far the most level-headed of the people who then surrounded Everett, took the ticket. He and Lee were to about to enter an unshakeable and lifelong relationship, though he recognized that her marriage to Everett had been unusually powerful. Both Lee and John acknowledge even today that it still exerts a curiously powerful grip on her.

Though she was living with John Alkin, Lee was still emotionally and indeed financially linked to Everett. On one occasion there was a particularly furious row in front of John Pitt. 'Look, Ev, I've bought a fur coat from Harrods today: £1600.' 'What!' he screamed. She squared up to him and replied: 'Do you know what, this £1600 will still be keeping me warm in thirty years. This £1600 would go up your nose in a week.'

After the row Lee went on holiday to Israel with John Alkin. A girl friend rang Lee and told her Everett had filed for divorce. He had gone to Freddie Mercury, who had taken him to his lawyer. Lee returned home to find divorce papers accusing her of adultery. Lee wrote to the lawyer informing him of the actual domestic arrangements and the lawyer washed his hands of the case. Freddie Mercury was temporarily furious that he had been taken in. Everett's temper subsided, and divorce was forgotten about for the time being. But the couple hardly spoke for three months, until Christmas Day, which Everett was spending with Freddie. Everett said he was unhappy because, for the first time, Lee hadn't sent him a birthday card. 'Phone her,' Mercury replied. So he did. And he stopped taking cocaine.

But in 1983 Everett and Lee did decide to divorce, basically because Lee and John wanted eventually to marry. At first nothing changed. Everett still came round for many of his meals, as he had done since he moved out; and even after he stopped doing so Lee would prepare and freeze meals for him in bulk, which he would pay her for – an unconscious exercise in feminism as she became one of the very few wives in Britain to be paid for cooking for her husband.

Everett's sister, Kate, had been friendly with Lee during the marriage and rang her up to say: 'You're not divorcing the whole family, are you?' 'No,' Lee replied, 'only your little brat of a brother.'

When news of the divorce reached the press in September 1983, the *News of the World* arrived at Lee and John's house beside the Thames in Berkshire for an exclusive interview. The couple ingeniously escaped by going to the end of the garden, getting on their boat and sailing away for three days, though it did not stop the newspaper running a story headlined 'Lee Escapes With Live-In Lover'.

Everett, who clearly knew the story was about to break but forgot to warn his wife, proved that he was no slouch in maintaining an image and guarding his career. He ensured that he was pictured leaving his apartment with glamorous actress friend Cleo Rocos on his arm. If there had to be innuendo in the papers, then it might as well be Everett the Casanova for the time being.

Of course, in reality, during the period leading up to the divorce Everett and John Pitt had been living across the road from Lee and John Alkin. Everett approved of Alkin. At first, he tried his usual trick of making jokes at his expense and trying to humiliate him as he had done with all of Lee's suitors in the past. 'He would make witticisms that verged on sarcasm,' remembers Alkin. 'Then he would wait for your response, wait to see the whites of your eyes. I passed the test.' Alkin managed to give as good as he got. The two became close friends and spent a lot of time together.

Indeed the occupants of the two flats became a virtual family of four. Immediately after Everett and Lee's divorce, the two of them sat down with John Alkin, who interviewed Everett on his feelings about his divorce, his marriage, his career and his future. The tape, never broadcast, is kept by Lee at her home and is a poignant mixture of affection, humour and confession. At one moment Everett and Lee laugh that one day they will reveal all in a book. At another Everett says he is still 'in love with her mentally'.

Talking about the divorce, Everett at first treats it playfully, saying: 'I feel great because it really means I can pursue my homosexual pursuits. The only thing that was wrong with Lee and I, apart from the fact that she goes up in the air about everything, is that we are not physically compatible. She's a chick and so am I. [Laughter]'

But he rapidly became more serious, saying how his coming to terms with his sexuality had brought him a new confidence and his former 'desperation' had gone. Because he was now relaxed he was able to form relationships with some ease, rather than desperately striving for them and failing.

'Freedom now means the ability for me to choose any man I desire the look of. My relationship with Lee is better since the divorce. It was my fault because Lee told me before our marriage: "We can't get married because you're a faggot" and I said: "Oh no, after a couple of years or months it will suddenly all fall into place and I'll go, of course: 'Women, big tits, fab, cuddly.'" But it never happened, so we were never physically compatible for the whole ten years.

'We are mentally compatible because we go up and down like yo-yos. But when I was married to Lee I felt trapped in a situation that was wrong because I'm a homosexual and Lee isn't. If we were only physically compatible, if I fancied her as much as I fancied some of the leather-clad moustachioed creatures in Heaven, then our marriage would have lasted till the end of time. It would be the great romance of our times. It would be Bogart and Bacall. But God said: "Forget it, you're a faggot."'

Looking back at his former self, he concluded: 'I have no shame in saying now I was a total fuck-up in every way. I couldn't converse with anybody. I was too busy thinking: What's it all about? Who am I? And it's only just now I'm beginning to sort myself out. I feel confident.'

Even after the divorce, as well as dropping in for meals, for long periods Everett brought his washing. And on every visit, often daily, he would monopolize her. When he had to leave to go to a meeting or to the studio he would more often than not call up on his mobile phone to continue the conversation he had been having with her. Everett and Lee even went out for romantic candlelit dinners on their wedding anniversary. 'He wanted me for his laughter, his talk, even his affection,' says Lee. 'But for the sex side he went to the fellers.'

Once though, Everett and Lee attended together the funeral of one of her relatives. He comforted her afterwards. They were alone, and to their surprise they ended up in bed together for the first time in several years and for the last time ever. Lee was later to realize she was a very lucky woman. Though she did not know it then, Everett had by this time become involved with Nikolai Grishanovich, a former Red Army soldier and one of the most promiscuous men in London.

10

OUT

'We're the new Fab Four.'
Everett speaking about himself, Nikolai,
Pepe and Freddie Mercury

In February 1984 a lot of people were glad to be gay. The virus
that would stun the world and kill off some of its greatest artistic
talents was a year or more away from becoming front-page news.
Gay nightclubs were springing up. Gay culture was bubbling under.
The number-one hit in the charts was 'Relax', a gay sex song, banned
by the BBC, by the group Frankie Goes To Hollywood.

The lead singer, Holly Johnson, a working-class boy from
Liverpool, was excited to come down to London to celebrate
the record's success, and made straight for Heaven. The country's
best-known gay club, situated under the arches by London's Charing
Cross station, catered for a full range of party wishes from upmarket
drinking and disco dancing to a cellar bar and a locked room where
anything went. Lee knew eight people who had a key to that room.
All are now dead.

Johnson's memories of the scenes on party nights in Heaven are
full of images that could belong in Dante's *Inferno*. On one New
Year's Eve, he wrote in his autobiography *A Bone In My Flute*, 'ten
seconds before midnight, a 20 foot flaccid penis was revealed on
stage, and a countdown started: ten . . . nine . . . eight . . . The
huge cock rose in jerks, becoming more erect each second. At the
stroke of midnight, it ejaculated some kind of party snowstorm.
At the same moment the centre of the dance floor erupted with

champagne corks, streamers and party poppers wielded by young, body builder queens who had staked out the centre of the floor. A thousand gay men were going apeshit.'

This was one snapshot of the confident, extravagant, flamboyant yet still largely underground gay scene of the early eighties. Ten years later, when Holly Johnson himself was suffering from the Aids virus, he reminisced to me about one of his first visits to Heaven. One of the first people he saw there was Freddie Mercury, the lead singer of Queen. Mercury glared at him; 'Relax' had kept Queen's latest record 'Radio Ga Ga' off the top spot, and Mercury was none too happy about that.

Johnson's eye was then caught by a thin, bearded man dancing frantically and waving maniacally. Johnson immediately recognized him as Kenny Everett and asked him to dance.

'A lot of people were taking LSD or MDA,' remembers Johnson. (MDA, nicknamed 'Mary Don't Ask', was the precursor of Ecstasy.) 'Kenny Everett would be off his face, and dancing off the dance floor in Heaven. I made a couple of attempts to talk to him, both of which he deflected in a peculiar way. He didn't want to engage. I also saw him there a lot with his handsome and striking boyfriend Nikolai, an exotic Russian body-builder and ex-soldier, who I also saw at Coleherne's leather bar in Earls Court. Once I went back to their flat. Nikolai had some piece of trade in tow, and they disappeared into another room.'

As Holly Johnson's fragmented memories suggest, by the early eighties Everett was a leading and flamboyant part of London's gay scene. All his friends knew it; most of the broadcasting and music world knew it; his wife knew it, and anyone who frequented the trendiest gay clubs and gay bars knew it. But the great British public did not know it.

Mr and Mrs Cole learned their son was gay one Christmas Eve, in a scene that could have come out of a movie and once again did not qualify him for a place in the diplomatic corps.

By 1981 the extended family of Everett, Lee, John Alkin and John Pitt were enjoying a happy time. Lee was getting closer to Alkin; and Everett was with someone who was utterly comfortable with being homosexual, and with leading a quiet homely life as Everett's partner. For the public there was still the charade to act out. Lee had to leave Alkin at regular intervals to appear with her husband at premières and celebrity parties, and go on publicity tours. She even had to go with Everett on a tour to Australia, accompanied by his agent, Jo Gurnett, and John Pitt, who went along as his PA. When the evening's activities were over, Lee would have to creep out of her husband's room, and Pitt would take her place.

Back home, Everett and Pitt, Lee and Alkin would go out as a foursome. Sometimes they would visit Everett's sister Kate and his parents. For Alkin, new on this scene, it was a bizarre time. He marvelled at Lee's loyalty: 'There was still great love and affection in the air. She was nursing him through this coming out of the closet, staying by him so that he could explore his new self with her as a back-up and support system. Most wives would have been off like a shot – forget any family loyalties. But Lee always responded to family invitations, though at times it was all breaking her heart more than she let on.'

Alkin remembers the four of them going round for tea to Kate's house at Christmas 1981, when Mr and Mrs Cole were staying there. He and Lee sat on one sofa holding hands. Everett and John Pitt sat on another sofa, also holding hands.

'I couldn't get over the in-your-faceness of it all,' says Alkin. 'It was a totally bizarre situation. His mum and dad were presented with their son and his boyfriend, and their daughter-in-law and her boyfriend. After a glass of wine or two Ev would begin to extol the virtues of his boyfriend. "His eyes are limpid pools of love," he would say. "They are Gina Lollobrigida eyes." He would bring Pitt to his mum and dad and say, "Hasn't he got beautiful eyes, mother?" He would parade him, and she still didn't twig.'

It could be that Mrs Cole, who was and is a staunch believer in personal privacy, was just keeping her thoughts and suspicions to herself. But when Christmas Eve came, there was no room for doubting any longer.

Kate and Conor Horgan's three-storey house in Wimbledon was a nine-bedroom mansion with a fifty-foot hallway. That Christmas a lot of people were staying; in addition to Mr and Mrs Cole there was a French count married to Conor's cousin; the Horgans' good friend the opera singer Teresa Jennings, who is the daughter of actress Patricia Hayes, with her then husband, who looked rather like Sherlock Holmes; and a host of other friends and neighbours.

Kate, Conor and Mr and Mrs Cole were in the dining room,

sitting around a big fireplace. In the kitchen were the French count and his wife, in heated discussion about châteaux and inheritances. Further on, in the big drawing room, was Patricia Jennings, who had sung at Glyndebourne and was now giving a solo operatic recital. Three tableaux: the family gathering by the fire; the French count and his wife locked in an increasingly fierce argument; a soprano singing 'One Fine Day' from *Madam Butterfly* to a rapt audience, a Sherlock Holmes look-alike standing by her side.

Everett arrives with John Pitt. He comes in to the dining room and exchanges kisses with his mother. 'Where's Lee?' asks his mother. Everett replies: 'Lee's not here. This is my new wife.'

Conor remembers his brother-in-law's behaviour that night as being 'very immature'. Everett's announcement to his mother was certainly shock therapy, and she was duly shocked. Kate had more or less known for years, even before his marriage, that her brother was gay or at least bisexual. But their mother was now knocked sideways. 'My poor mother didn't know what to think or say,' recalls Kate. 'We had never told her. She looked a bit upset and rather confused. She turned to my father and said: "What do you think, Tom?" He said in his slow voice after thinking about it for some time and reflecting continually as he spoke with plenty of pauses: "Well . . . I suppose . . . if it makes him happy . . . why not?"'

Considering how Everett was to build up and seemingly believe the portrait of his father as the tough tugboat captain with whom he could never discuss his homosexuality, this quiet, gentle stoicism that was very much the real Tom Cole is particularly revealing.

Tom's answer, though, was probably not what his wife wanted to hear. Mrs Cole turned to her son-in-law: 'Conor, what do you think?' Conor excused himself, saying he had to go into the next room to sort out the French couple's problems. Applause rang out as Madam Butterfly concluded her performance. That night Mrs Cole could neither eat nor sleep. The next day was Christmas Day and Everett's birthday. The atmosphere was not conducive to celebrating either occasion; but no more was said about the revelation of the night before.

Everett and John Pitt lived together for more than a year; but Everett was beginning to get bored. As his good friend and bank manager, Eric Gear, noted: 'Ideally, he wanted the carpet-slippers life with someone who doted on him. But when he got it, he got bored. Then when he got the high life he wanted domesticity.' Pitt brought him a quiet life and an excess of domesticity. 'There was a gentleness and wholesomeness about that relationship,' says Alkin. But the quiet life, the gentleness and the wholesomeness were to change dramatically after he met Nikolai Grishanovich at a nightclub.

For the next five or six years the private life of Cuddly Ken was a series of out-takes from a Fellini movie. Kate remembers, wryly, giving him a book by the American psychologist Dr Wayne Dyer on *How to Eliminate Your Erroneous Zones*. It was about how not to feel guilty, and her brother, she knew, had a highly tuned sense of guilt. Everett was stunned by it. 'If there's something you're not happy about in yourself, fix it,' he preached to startled friends after reading the book, 'because you have all the potential to be the world's greatest human being.' Looking back, Kate has mixed feelings about helping her brother purge his guilt feelings. 'In retrospect maybe I didn't do him any favours,' she says, 'because he went off the rails a bit with Nikolai.'

Nikolai was dark, swarthy, doe-eyed and muscular, like nearly all of Everett's inamorati. Nikolai had an animal magnetism that attracted both men and women. And he was not shy of using it. Sensual and tactile, he was a funny and intelligent man, a former Red Army soldier who had indulged in the highly dangerous occupation of currency dealing on the black market in the Soviet Union during the Cold War.

When the authorities began to get close to him, he persuaded a female English tourist to marry him and he came to London, where he got a job as a computer programmer. But if he had humour, charm, sexuality and wit in abundance, he lacked any sense of morality. His conquests were legion and often nightly. Lee disliked him intensely. He occasionally behaved lewdly in public, which was something that, for all her own exotic past, she could not tolerate. And she saw her husband change markedly under his influence. She had wanted Everett to acknowledge his homosexuality, and to settle down contentedly with a partner, as many of her gay friends had done. But this amoral bisexual was not what she had in mind at all. 'He would mate anything,' she told friends. He continually brought 'low life' home. 'He'll be the death of Ev,' she said.

Everett's ideal was with psychological inevitability his opposite: six feet tall, dark and with bulging biceps. Nikolai fitted the bill supremely, and was funny and intelligent to boot. When he met Everett, Nikolai already had a boyfriend, a Spanish waiter, Pepe Flores. In fact Pepe was a university graduate and sculptor working temporarily as a waiter. But a waiter he remained in press stories for the next decade. Pepe moved in with the two of them in Everett's flat in what was to become the celebrated *ménage à trois* – the name, incidentally, of a nearby restaurant which Everett, no doubt with a delicious sense of irony, used to patronize.

In fact the Everett–Nikolai–Pepe scenario was not quite the *ménage à trois* it was later painted in the press, and indeed by Everett himself. Pepe was very much Nikolai's boyfriend. Nevertheless, the situation was undoubtedly out of the ordinary. Not content with his two partners in the flat, Nikolai would frequently go out to clubs and bars and bring pick-ups home.

Everett had a long and close friendship with Freddie Mercury of Queen which had been cemented when Mercury sent him a pre-release copy of 'Bohemian Rhapsody' and asked him if he thought it was too long. One day in 1988 Dave Cash was shopping in Kensington when he bumped into Everett, who said: 'You must come and meet Freddie.' He took him back to Mercury's flat and the three of them had tea together. Cash found Mercury charming and polite, though he and Everett were camping it up rather. 'Kenny,' Cash remembers, 'was the happiest I've ever seen him.' As he grew in confidence, Everett probably enjoyed being audaciously camp with Cash, who was never totally at ease with gayness, though he found Everett's increasing campness very funny. As Cash was leaving, Everett said of himself, Mercury, Nikolai and Pepe: 'We're the new Fab Four, dear. You should see us, darling. We're absolutely outrageous.'

Everett and Mercury did not have a sexual relationship but Nikolai and Mercury almost certainly did. Most who have come across the outlandish charms of Nikolai speak of him with a chuckling affection. But not everyone. When Dave Cash discussed him with me, he muttered: 'That bloody Russian, he infected them all.' It is indeed extremely likely that Everett, Pepe and Freddie Mercury all contracted Aids from Nikolai, who himself died from the disease in 1991, slowly and painfully.

Nikolai was a larger-than-life character, an outrageous joker who continued to have his salary paid by the multinational computer firm that employed him for a full year after he was sacked, by virtue of the fact that he hacked into the salaries department and kept himself on the payroll. He also had a little boy's plaintive charm and a childlike openness of expression which was breathtaking. He would tell you how good-looking he was and meant it. 'My mother found me so beautiful she would never let me do anything,' was his excuse for avoiding the chores.

Eric Gear, who knew Nikolai, says: 'He lived more than any ten people do. He was bisexual and would go after anything that moved, but in a most childlike way. He had a *naïveté* about him that was completely appealing. He never wilfully hurt anybody. But he would trample over people's feelings. He would enrage Ken because he would go off with somebody else and see nothing wrong in what he was doing. He still loved him. Kenny used to say he couldn't live with him, but couldn't live without him. When attacked about his alley-cat morals, Nikolai would roll his eyes and plead: "But what is wrong with loving people?" Yet sometimes he and Everett would spend the evening on the couch, a blanket wrapped around them drinking cocoa and watching television for all the world like Darby and Joan.'

Simon Booker, a good friend of Everett who produced him at Capital and co-wrote *The Custard Stops at Hatfield* with him, remembers: 'Nikolai was a barrel of laughs and, I believe, the great love of Kenny's life. Long after Nikolai had died Kenny had a picture of him in his studio. But Kenny was an incredibly generous person (he once just came round and gave me a new Bang and Olufsen television from Harrods) and some of us did think Nikolai was taking advantage of his generosity. The guy had come from Russia with nothing and suddenly was in this champagne set. You couldn't help but think sometimes: Well, is the Rolex absolutely essential?' Though Everett clearly adored Nikolai, the two of them and Pepe could have the fiercest arguments, which might continue for days. It was a volatile time.

This, it must be remembered, was a unique, short and never to be repeated period in Britain's social history. The gay liberation movement of the seventies had led to a new confidence among gay men, after centuries of denial and repression. This new confidence manifested itself among certain sections of the urban gay community in an outlandish promiscuity which was to be devastatingly punctured by Aids . For just under a decade many gay men lived life to the full, and very many of them were to suffer for it.

Everett would later remark ruefully that he belonged to a circle both in London and New York that was totally innocent about Aids and was now being wiped out. It is hard to think of another example in history of a particular grouping – and a grouping containing so many talented individuals – rushing headlong with such enjoyment and pleasure into a fatal trap that they never knew existed. Nikolai knew Everett. Nikolai also knew Freddie Mercury. Freddie Mercury knew Rudolf Nureyev. The list could go on and on, like a dark and devastating game of celebrity consequences, ending in illness, pain, secrecy, deception and death.

But in those few short years, those last carefree days of pre-Aids awareness, Everett's life did sometimes resemble a Bacchanalian romp, played out to a background of a still largely underground scene which never attracted the photographers of the style and showbiz pages and remained aloof from public attention.

'Ev was like that,' says Lee. 'It was bravado with him. Once he'd come out, he thought: Right, I'm going to be very outrageous. Basically, he was a little boy, and I used to say to him: "Little boys have to grow up. They have to be responsible."'

But these were not the responsible years.

Lee received a phone call from Everett, saying that if she and John were in town, he was throwing a party. As it happened, they were in London that night, so they popped in. Everett looked surprised to see them. 'Don't come upstairs yet, Lee,' he said. 'Sit there. Have a drink.' He came back with a huge drink and said: 'Drink it all down in one go.' She did. 'Then he took me upstairs,' Lee recalls. 'It was wall-to-wall queens On the stairs was this leather queen. In the middle of the room was Cleo Rocos dancing with them all. It was packed. They were all looking one another over. John said: "For the first time I know how a women feels. I feel I've been undressed in there." The party ended in fist fights. There were cigarette burns all over the carpets. Ev had to have the whole flat redecorated. After a few minutes I said: "Thank you for showing me in, Ev. Now can you show me out?" He said Claire Rayner had lasted ten minutes longer than me. I said: "You never invited Claire Rayner to this!" He bowed his head and said yes.

'I said: "Who are these awful creatures? Where do they come from?" He said: "I don't know." Ev had been in every bar, every club the night before, drunk, inviting everybody, and they all turned up. He went into the Coleherne, which is a pretty notorious pub, and invited the whole pub. But that was always Ev. His mouth worked before his brain.'

In fact, Everett was too popular and generous a figure ever to need to invite strangers to a party. At the pub the night before he had turned to Cleo and joked: 'We need dancing partners. Any dancing partners here?' Those who had heard came along and brought a seemingly endless stream of gatecrashers. He was often to gape wide-eyed at the results of his generosity and over-exuberance.

He was making up for his years of repression by exercising minimum discretion. Lee remembers his visits to her: 'A lot of the fellers he brought – and every time he came he brought someone – I felt I ought to nail my belongings down. A lot of people felt that.'

The *ménage à trois* led inevitably to dramas. Eric Gear threw a weekend party at his home in Kent, with a large bonfire in his garden. Everett, Nikolai and Pepe attended. Everett was railing at Nikolai for being drunk. Pepe had a white suit on and when it was time to go home Pepe said: 'I'm not getting in the car with you two.' He started to roll in the grass; his white suit turned green. 'They don't love me. Nobody loves me,' he wailed with Mediterranean melodrama in his thick Spanish accent.

Nikolai and Everett drove off. And Jane Gear drove Pepe to the local railway station. It was just after dawn and suddenly Pepe started wailing again as he ran wildly round the station: 'You don't luhve me, you don't luhve me.' The country stationmaster gaped at the unlikely couple: the upright convent teacher Mrs Gear with what looked for all the world like her secret but excitable toyboy.

Everett's own sexual experiments created dramas that he would turn into comedy. When they were married, he had behaved towards Lee with almost excessive respect, and treated her like a china doll when they were in bed. But Paul Gambaccini relates how one male partner tied Everett then left him. (In fact it was Nikolai and Pepe who had tied him.) Everett crawled to the phone, knocked off the receiver with his nose and dialled with his nose the number of a party that Nikolai was at so that he could come and rescue him. 'Do you know the lesson?' Everett asked Gambaccini. Was it never let a stranger tie you up? thought Gambaccini. 'No,' said Everett, reading his thoughts. 'The lesson is: Always get a push-button phone.' As Gambaccini says: 'It illustrates the way that whatever bad happened to him, he'd use it for humour.'

Everett never spoke publicly, and rarely privately, about this. But there is one reference in his own writings that might confound any psychologist. In his joke memoir *The Custard Stops at Hatfield* he wrote about his introduction to sex education as a small boy: 'I was eventually introduced to the wild and woolly world of sex by my father when I was about seven. He chucked this book on my bed called What Every Young Boy Should Know, and on the first page it said: "What every young boy should know, as transcribed from the cylinders." That confused me even more. The book was full of extraordinary things like: "Young boys who play with themselves should be strapped down to the bed." Can you imagine anything more designed to turn people into sado-masochistic freaks than reading that sort of advice while they're still in short trousers?'

Sado-masochistic freaks! Why should he choose, unprompted, so to describe private activities that harmed no one else? Another form of denial perhaps, or another expression of guilt in the complex psychological morass through which so many homosexuals waded as they were 'out' with their lovers, family and friends but 'respectably' heterosexual for acquaintances, employers and fans.

In 1985 Everett ended the public pretence, and 'came out'. The press had long pestered him about the state of his marriage, and occasional hints had appeared over the years that he might be gay. Press interest intensified sharply when Everett took Nikolai as his companion to the twenty-first birthday party of Princess Diana's brother, Viscount Charles Althorp. Everett had struck up a friendship with the Princess, who enjoyed his company and told him how Prince Charles used to shut himself away to watch his television show, 'his favourite programme', and would roar with laughter. Everett told her he had enjoyed watching her wedding on television. 'Oh, by the way, lovely wedding,' he would say

OUT

when he met her. 'Yes,' she would reply (somewhat ironically in retrospect), 'it was quite fun, wasn't it.'

Everett's appearance with Nikolai at the Althorp party hastened a decision he was already close to making. For years Lee had been trying to persuade him gently to come out. She had made him speak to Elton John, who advised him that you became more comfortable with life and with yourself after publicly acknowledging where your true emotions lay. And, Elton assured him, it could be done with dignity.

Elton John, too, had married but had long been known among his friends to be bisexual. As an international superstar, he had been particularly worried about threats of blackmail if he kept up the pretence. He told Lee and Everett that just after coming out he took his place in the Watford Football Club directors' box with his mother, Sheila. Some of the soccer fans took the opportunity to sing offensive songs about his sex life. He faced them and stood next to his mother and continued to face them week after week until the chanting died out. The football fans, not Elton, seemed dirty and degraded.

On St Valentine's Day in 1985, Lee and John Alkin were married at Pembridge Spiritualist Church in Notting Hill Gate. Everett was best man, and was slightly baffled that he wasn't allowed to give the bride away too. He was also slightly hurt that her new engagement ring had replaced the one he had given her. The wedding was attended by Elton John and his wife Renata, who were celebrating their first wedding anniversary and loved the fact that the reception was in a fish and chip shop – not exactly a usual haunt for Elton John. (One of Lee's circles of friends which meets at her home now is called the EXQWs – the ex-queens' wives' club. Renata is a prominent member.)

By October of that year the press interest in Everett had become so intense that he wisely decided to stem the flow of rumours. The advice of Elton John and other friends had impressed him. And he decided to tell the truth. Typically, over the next few weeks, he pulled few punches. He posed outside his flat with Nikolai and Pepe, thoughtfully giving the press a headline with his remark: 'Two husbands are better than one.' He forgot to tell his parents that he was going public. They discovered the fact only when their house was besieged by reporters.

Lee remembers: 'His parents heard from the press, which was very painful for them. To know Ev was to be in pain a lot, but also great joy. There he was chirping two husbands are better than one, the total over-the-top Everett. He just came out of his house one day, somebody collared him and he bloody well decided to talk. Then he rang me up and said: "Lee, I've just told the press I'm gay. What shall I do? I'm dreading tomorrow." I said: "You'd better come up and I'll give you a coming out party."'

The climate of the time was that any gay story was made into an Aids scare story. And the language used shows the fear and hostility that then surrounded the illness. Knowledge about the disease was small, and it was still being dubbed the 'gay plague' by the tabloids. When Everett came out in an interview with the *Sunday Mirror* on 6 October 1985, the story focused on what it called 'his amazing Aids pact with the two men who share his life'. Describing him as Mrs Thatcher's favourite comedian, it went on: 'Kenny, whose homosexuality is an open secret to showbiz friends, fears he could become a victim of the killer "gay plague". In an emotional interview he confessed: "I am devastated by the death of Rock Hudson. I felt ill when I saw pictures of what the disease had done to him."' He added that two years previously he had entered into an agreement with Nikolai and Pepe. 'We decided that if any one of us has got Aids, then we must assume that all three of us would have it. If that happens, and God forbid that it ever does, we would look after each other and care for each other . . . It would mean abandoning everything – selling our homes and everything we own, leaving our jobs and taking off around the world until we drop dead. We wouldn't give in to Aids – but go out in style with one last wild fling.'

In the event, it wasn't to happen quite like that. Asked if he thought he had Aids, Everett said no, as far as he was aware. 'If anyone thought I did I would be heartbroken. I don't want people to stop kissing me, hugging me, inviting me to parties . . . and I'd never be able to sell my flat.' What Everett did not reveal was that Nikolai already had Aids.

On the subject of his homosexuality, Everett said: 'In the past I have hinted in interviews that I am bisexual. I'm gay – but it's boring to make a big deal about it. It's not going to come as a huge surprise to people who have seen me dress up in women's clothing on TV. It's pretty widely known in show business, but it's not something I want to stand up and shout about. I would rather talk about my work than my private life.'

The following week Everett's friend Cleo Rocos wiped away the last part of the charade, speaking in the press about all the times they had been photographed arm in arm. 'I suppose I was living a lie, pretending that I was Kenny's girl,' she said. 'It was a bit of a charade to divert attention away from Kenny being gay. What else would anyone expect me to do? Kenny's my best mate and I love him.' She added, for no apparent reason: 'No matter what happens, I will never stop kissing him.'

Everett was by now rather enjoying his coming out. Posing with Nikolai and Pepe outside his flat a few weeks after his initial interview, he said: 'There's nothing worse than only having one husband.' Nikolai too joined in the revelations, telling reporters: 'Life is fun for the three of us because we all love each other. We all get on extremely well and there is plenty of room in the flat. No, I don't get jealous. I love Kenny but I don't want him exclusively for myself. I like my freedom.' That last sentence at least was true.

But Everett was rather more sensitive than he was letting on. Moving largely in showbiz circles, he received very little hostility about his coming out. But even that little affected him deeply. As he was walking near his home, a worker on a building site jumped down from the scaffolding, whipped out his penis and shouted: 'Get a load of that, yer poofter.' Everett was horrified, and talked about the incident long afterwards.

In all the excitement Everett never told his parents, sister or ex-wife that he was going to give an interview declaring his homosexuality publicly for the first time. Kate and her family had recently emigrated to Australia, so the publicity did not really touch her. But Tom and Lily Cole were not for the first or last time the focus of press harassment, and not for the first or last time refused to make any comment, but remained closeted in their private bewilderment.

Two years later Kate was picnicking in the Australian sun and, on an impulse, phoned her mother and said why didn't she and Tom come and join them out there. 'I thought you'd never ask,' said her mother, and the Coles got on virtually the next plane. There are still people close to the family who maintain that they 'fled' England because of their son's coming out, the pestering by reporters and the nudges they saw but never responded to at the local shops. And there may be an element of truth in that. Everett himself told the *Daily Mail* in August 1986, under the headline 'My sad mother', that Lily came close to committing suicide after he admitted to being homosexual. He was quoted as saying: 'I am heartbroken that my mother is so far away. She is the most important woman in my life . . . When it went public my mother felt a degree of shame. She was close to suicide. It was frightening and in the end she had to go to live in Perth with my sister. I'm desperately unhappy about the situation.'

Neither his parents nor his sister recognize that as being the case. Lily did indeed, as Kate acknowledges, 'go through agonies over his gayness', but they were agonies about the unhappiness her son was suffering, rather than any supposed public shame. His mother's shame and thoughts of suicide may have been more in Everett's head than in his mother's. And there was another, probably more pertinent reason, for his parents' being glad to go to Australia. Their son, Tom and Lily now knew for sure, was not going to give them grandchildren, whereas by emigrating they had their grandchildren less than a mile from their door. While they still loved their son deeply, emigrating was an easy decision to make.

By the following March, Everett was prepared to speak publicly, and without resort to one-liners, about how he had come to terms with his sexuality and how hard it had been to do so. He also gave an indication of why he may have had unhappy memories of his childhood: it was because of the isolation he felt inside over his gayness. 'When I lived in Liverpool,' he said in an interview, 'I thought I was totally alone in the world. I did not know any other gays. When I moved to London I discovered I was not the only one and that helped. It helps even more now that I am no longer pretending.

'But if I could push a button and make myself straight, I would. A man and a woman are two halves, and when they come together they become complete. That is something beautiful and it is what I always wanted. But for me it just is not possible.'

In subsequent interviews Everett began to wax rather less lyrical about the 'something beautiful' that is marriage. He thought it a good line that when he made love to Lee during their marriage he closed his eyes and thought of the Hollywood actor Burt Reynolds.

That making such a crack to several million readers could be hurtful to his wife simply never occurred to him.

A few months after Everett's coming out, Lee visited Elton John, who was staying at a hotel in Mayfair. She told Elton how her husband coming out of the closet had resulted in a lot of things being written and said about her which made her look very bad indeed. She was (and remains) particularly upset that newspapers were labelling their long relationship 'a sham marriage'. It hadn't been. They had both fought hard to make it work.

Everett arrived at the hotel, to join the fun, he thought. Listening to his ex-wife pour her heart out to Elton, he became embarrassed and began to realize for the first time the position he had put her in. 'He felt it was his fault,' says Lee now, 'and it was his fault.' So, in that hotel room, Everett said to her: 'The best thing you can do is write the whole thing down.' They continued to talk about it in Elton's hotel suite, agreeing that it could be beneficial to put down at least some of their story. 'Ev felt and I felt that our case would be helpful to other people who fell in love,' says Lee. 'It happens a lot. I get a lot of people who come to me with the problem. Homosexuals fall in love with a female or vice versa. And they think it's going to change them but it won't.'

With his blessing and the blessing of Elton John, Lee commenced her autobiography. Her marriage to Everett was only a part of a book which also chronicled the years with Billy Fury and concentrated in depth on spiritualism. Also, while she felt able to talk about Everett's homosexuality during their marriage, as he had come out, she omitted much, including all details of his sexual habits, and his relationship with Nikolai. Everett was allowed to approve or veto every page. And he even wrote the foreword to the book: 'Dear Viewers, When Lee asked me to read this book of her life and times, I was amazed at how much experience one small person could cram into a lifetime. Secondly, I was horrified at what she'd written about yours truly! All of it true, but oh my God, what a catalogue of goofs! Still, in between the disasters, Lee and I had loads of good times and the rafters rang with merry sounds of laughter. One's memory has a wonderful capacity for erasing the bad bits and enhancing the good moments, so when I eventually become a creaking OAP in my electric wheelchair with compact disc and built in colour TV, I'll have nothing but wonderful memories of our times together.

'It has long been my philosophy that we are here on Earth to continuously learn from our goofs (or is it gooves?) and only by doing so can we truly become perfect souls. I think I must have gone for the jackpot in life as, looking through the proofs (prooves?) of this book, my term on this planet seems to be strewn with award-winning errors. Still, ours not to winge and cry, and as dear old Oscar Wilde once said: "The aim of Life is self-development, to realise one's nature perfectly. A man should live out his Life fully and completely, give form to every feeling, expression to every thought, reality to every dream."

'It's to be hoped we are forgiven our sins along the way.'

Lee and John had a flat in Lanzarote and they went to stay there so that she could complete the book undisturbed. But one night shortly after Christmas 1985 they were disturbed. Sitting on the balcony writing, Lee said to John: 'I can hear someone calling my name.' He sighed. 'You're not going to start all that now,' he murmured, thinking it was a spiritualist allusion, 'we're on our holidays.' But she was right. As they peered out they saw Everett, Nikolai, Pepe and another friend, Brian, standing on the beach, their luggage by them. Everett was cupping his hands and shouting 'Lee!' The four had been on a winter holiday in the Sierra Nevada and had argued. So, with Everett's first instinct to 'return to mother', as Lee puts it, they had taken a plane to Lanzarote. She was obliged to put all four up in her flat for two weeks.

On the second day Lee and John saw something which stunned them. The street outside was lined with boys. Nikolai's charisma travelled well. The couple had not even known there was a gay set in Lanzarote. Suddenly it was on their doorstep, parading up and down the promenade. They noticed something else when Nikolai changed into his beachwear. His legs were completely covered in sores.

In 1986 the years of unfettered promiscuity ended suddenly and irreversibly. Nikolai had actually been HIV-positive since 1983. The others coped with it by joking about it mercilessly. If Nikolai spoke of something in the future, Everett would retort: 'No chance. You'll be dead by then.' Even Lee joined in, putting a black ribbon round the glass that Nikolai drank from.

Back in Britain, Everett remained unwilling to see a doctor to discover his own state of health. Once again, Lee lectured him and forced him to the doctor. 'But I'd rather not know,' he protested.

Lee retorted: 'But you must know. You've really got to grow up. You've got to change your way of living. You've got to be more healthy. You've got to stop going out all night.' He was HIV-positive. Lee, who was out for the day on the boat she and John had bought, phoned him from a riverside pub to discover the result of the test. 'He was very angry,' she recalls. 'And we were both devastated.'

Pepe later received the same diagnosis. Everett stated publicly in 1993 that he was HIV-positive and said he had known for 'about four years'. This fiction was faithfully repeated in all further coverage, including his obituaries. But it was wrong. At Lee's prompting he had learned he was HIV-positive as early as 1986. The last nine years of his life, including TV series, a radio career with Capital Gold and a part in a West End musical, were lived with that knowledge.

But while that knowledge caused 'the three fuckaneers', as Everett, Nikolai and Pepe were known by some of their circle, to moderate their lifestyles, 'moderate' is a relative term. Their continued audacity was to have one lasting and profound effect. In the spring of 1987, they were invited for a day out on the Thames with Lee and John on their boat. The trip was a disaster. By the time the boat moored in Henley, the three had drunk enough and were merry enough to be disporting themselves wildly, kissing and cavorting as a threesome, with lewd remarks being made to onlookers. Amazed bystanders began to murmur: 'Surely that's Kenny Everett.' That it never got in the papers was miraculous. But the reaction on the riverbank didn't seem to bother the trio as they grew bolder by the minute. Lee was embarrassed and angry. John was fuming. It was literally decades since Lee had been a drug-happy swinger. She and John were now model citizens of the riverside. And the Henley boating community did not take the outrageous public cavortings of three grown men lightly.

By the time the party got back to Lee and John's home, she could contain her anger no longer. 'Get off my property,' she yelled at Everett, who could not believe his ears. Then Nikolai started to cry. 'Oh Lee, I'm sorry,' he moaned. 'Get out!' she repeated. Everett shrank away with his two playmates, utterly humiliated, and never returned. The final break between Everett and Lee was to occur, ostensibly, over something quite different. But that day on the river convinced both that they had drifted too far apart. And Lee's contemptuous dismissal of him may well have brought home uncomfortably to him just where he was drifting. Certainly, it left him with a grudge against her which he was never to relinquish.

As it turned out, the days of the *ménage à trois* were coming to an end. Everett was beginning to confide in friends that he really desired a steady, quieter relationship with someone both steadier and quieter than Nikolai could ever be – and someone who wasn't having another relationship at the same time in the same flat, especially his flat. Eventually he gave the pair notice to quit. It was not solely for emotional reasons. Nikolai had no job, Pepe was a waiter. Basically, Everett had been supporting them both. They remained friends. Everett was a constant visitor at Nikolai's bedside as he wasted away in 1991, dying of Aids in the Lighthouse Hospice in West London, though the cause of death on his death certificate was given as bronchopneumonia. Pepe was present at the interment of Everett's ashes.

Though the wild years had devastating personal legacies, they did not affect Everett professionally one iota. Much, of course, never found its way into the papers. Even the act of coming out was a huge professional gamble for a light-entertainment star, yet Everett's ratings, popularity and fan base were unaffected by this declaration. Perhaps public tolerance was helped by the fact that his fans were young and had a natural affinity with a rock-music world view of rebellion and greater sexual liberation. But even that cannot detract from his unique triumph in making homosexuality utterly irrelevant to public acclaim for genuine talent.

It did not mean, however, that his internal suffering was over. It is significant that he rarely used the word 'gay'. Unusually among his generation he preferred to say homosexual. Asked why by Sue Lawley on *Desert Island Discs* in October 1993, he replied that he still thought of 'gay' in its original meaning of jolly or happy. The long process of coming out had been necessary; it had made him more at peace with himself; but it had not been a jolly or happy experience for him or his family.

However, he had set a precedent in public life. As BBC radio DJ and pop culture chronicler Paul Gambaccini put it a decade later on the Radio 4 tribute programme to Everett, *Radio Lives*: 'The public loved Kenny Everett so much that when these cesspool brains from Fleet Street and subsequently Wapping tried to print a sensational exposé about it, people would yawn and say oh that's interesting, and then they'd tune in their radio at nine o'clock the next morning and listen to the programme. One of the greatest contributions Kenny has made to this country has nothing to do with broadcasting; and that is, he was tabloid resistant.'

By the mid-eighties this was quite a feat. Kenny Everett had long since ceased to be a radio voice, familiar only to teenage pop music fans. His cheeky, mischievous face was now known throughout Britain and much of the rest of the world. He had become a TV star, gaining huge audience figures of fifteen million viewers, winning prestigious awards and making series that were sold to over twenty countries. He was also routinely described as one of the funniest men in Britain.

11

STAR

'We could do anything because he wasn't a comic who said: "This isn't me", as he had no sense of identity as a comic. One minute he was an insurance salesman; the next minute he was Queen Victoria.'

Barry Cryer, writer for Everett's TV shows

In 1978 Philip Jones, the legendary head of light entertainment at Thames Television, who had brought Benny Hill to the station, asked his teenage son if there was anyone he and his friends really liked but wasn't on the telly. Kenny Everett, the boy replied. It is to be hoped the lad got commission. Within a year *The Kenny Everett Video Show* was topping the ratings. And Thames had sold it to eighteen countries, including Australia, Canada, the USA, Ireland, Hong Kong, Yugoslavia, Zimbabwe and that little-known fan base for Sid Snot and Cupid Stunt – Swaziland. More sales were to follow, and Everett would later be grateful to French resistance to his humour. It was one of the few places he could go on holiday without being recognized.

Everett wasn't exactly a newcomer to television. From the magaziny hotch-potch of *Nice Time* in 1968 through the LWT comedy shows to guest appearances on chat shows and *Blankety Blank*, his face had been seen over the years. And his voice was even better known as it had been the one enthusing over the prizes in the game show first screened in the seventies, *Celebrity Squares*, sometimes indeed gurgling over the prizes when he would do the voice-overs live from a control booth as he got through the brandy.

150

Audiences loved him on chat shows as much as the presenters sweated over him on chat shows. Once his perennial forgetfulness and unpunctuality meant he ran on to the set just as the show was closing. Another time, on *The Russell Harty Show*, he suddenly bounded out of his seat and exclaimed: 'It's a live show! I can say "BUM"!' Harty went pale, wondering what was coming next. What came next was Everett singing 'Bum-tee bum-tee bum' quite innocently.

But none of these television outings had made him anything resembling a household name; and none had the coherence, spontaneity and innovation of *The Kenny Everett Video Show*, nor the essential team of director David Mallett and writers Barry Cryer and Ray Cameron, whose humour gelled with Everett's in the way that Spike Milligan's, Harry Secombe's, Michael Bentine's and Peter Sellers's had gelled together in *The Goon Show*. Their imaginations raced down a lateral path of surreal comic fantasy, but it was the same lateral path. And with the help of Mallett, later to become a top director of pop videos, they would actually, unlike most comedy shows then and even now, use the medium and its burgeoning technological possibilities as an intrinsic part of the humour.

There were two other essential ingredients for the show's instant success: a raunchy, lithe dance troupe of beautiful young men and women called Hot Gossip (with a future singing star, Sarah Brightman, in the line-up) whose mock-suggestive choreography by Flick Colby brought apoplexy to the second essential ingredient, Mary Whitehouse, officially the founder of the National Viewers' and Listeners' Association, unofficially the self-appointed upholder of morality in television, and even more unofficially a guarantor of ratings success when she complained.

Mrs Whitehouse did indeed complain by letter to Philip Jones about the show, or more specifically, about Hot Gossip's input. Thames's astute publicity man, Roy Addison, ensured that the letter found its way to the *Sun* newspaper, where it hit the front page; and a high profile for *The Kenny Everett Video Show* was ensured. When Barry Cryer met Mrs Whitehouse at a reception years later, he said: 'Thank you, thank you. I worked on the Kenny Everett show and you made us.' She walked away.

But even the *Sun* and Mrs Whitehouse couldn't have kept the ratings up for a poor series. As soon as viewers turned on they discovered the show was breaking new ground in comedy. The young, and indeed the very young (later research showed that twenty-seven per cent of Everett's viewers were aged between eight and twelve) delighted in his mischievousness and comic inventiveness. The show had its first outing in June 1978 in the old *Opportunity Knocks* spot at six forty-five on Monday evenings. It is a sign of how unready the public was for Everett the accomplished television comic that the press previews described it as a pop show.

Even Philip Jones may not have realized quite what a talent he had on his hands, as he too, in an interview, seemed to be half thinking of it as a music show. Jones, who had worked on *Thank Your Lucky Stars* in the sixties, said: 'I've wanted to do another pop show for years. But it had to have the right amount of humour. Kenny is perfect. He loves the music, but he doesn't take it too seriously.'

Yet right from the start it was clear that musical guests, however big – and they included Cliff Richard (hung up by the thumbs for a 'cliff-hanger'), Rod Stewart, David Bowie, Bryan Ferry and Sting – were only interludes between the sketches. Like Dick Emery's before him and Harry Enfield's after him, Everett's sketches revolved largely, though by no means entirely, round a series of caricatured characters. The difference with Everett's portrayals was that he deliberately did not attempt impersonations. A core part of the humour lay in the absurdity of seeing the Everett beard and unmistakable cheeky face as an integral part of virtually every character.

The Hollywood starlet Cupid Stunt (Cryer, who dreamt up that and most of the other names, is a lover of spoonerisms) had a wispy black beard to set off her enormous boobs and flowing blonde curls. The only one who didn't sport the beard was the Frenchman Marcel Wave; and on his last appearance he ripped off his plastic chin with a flourish to declare: 'You see, my little mange-touts, it was ME all the time.'

Michael Parkinson once interviewed Cupid on his chat show. 'I can't keep addressing her as Cupid,' he said to Cryer just before the programme. What's her surname?' 'Stunt,' replied Cryer. Parkinson glared at him. 'You bastard,' he hissed before going into a corner and rehearsing the name over and over again before interviewing the blonde-wigged Everett.

It was to Cupid that Everett gave his catchphrase. As she was being interviewed in sketch after sketch in his show (sometimes, to keep the budgets down, by a cardboard cut-out of Parkinson), she would extravagantly cross her wide-open legs, almost lifting herself out of her chair in the movement, to reveal a pair of bright-red knickers (some years before Sharon Stone made the uproarious gesture downright sexy) and drawl: 'And it's all in the best pahssible taste.' Unlike Sharon Stone, Cupid, with commendable dexterity, managed to scratch her breasts while crossing and uncrossing her legs. Cupid's interviews were a succession of double entendres told with wide-eyed Californian sincerity by the wannabe starlet: ' These directors, they don't really want to talk to you about films. They just want to get into you as a poissern.' Or of a famous Hollywood star, named with Everett's glorious disregard for libel, who had been on a long day's shoot with Cupid: 'He was so tired he couldn't stay awake for a second. Let's face it, he couldn't stay awake for a foist.'

Sid Snot, the nasal yob biker, was hugely popular, usually exacting laughs just from walking up to the camera and delivering a homily: ''Allo, Sid Snot 'ere. I come from a broken home. I broke it.' He was later joined by Gizzard Puke ('mugger to the gentry'), complete with chains and metal bits and Mohican haircut in a nod at topicality.

Everyone had their own favourites. The younger viewers loved the more outrageous creations, Snot, Puke and Stunt. But Cryer's own favourite, though not a favourite with viewers, was Quentin Pose, none too loosely modelled on the then art critic of London's *Evening Standard*, who would praise a picture's 'very nothingness'. Everett came on in a black sweater and, wringing his hands, exhaled with tortured passion: 'The room is empty, yet in a very strange way full, and yet . . .' Every Quentin Pose monologue ended 'and yet . . .'

Cryer and Everett also had an affection for the absurdity of Cough Man: Everett, dressed as Superman with a big 'C' on his chest, simply descended for the shot from a wire, coughed and flew off again. And Cryer loved the American general, Marvin D Bomb The Bastards. At Thames, Everett as Marvin D, entered in a jeep and his epaulettes would fly up, courtesy of a man with a wire just out of shot. But at the BBC he was told: 'We don't do it like that,' and they gave him radio-controlled flags. It went wrong every time. 'I pleaded: "Can't we have the man with the wire back,"' remembers Cryer. 'The technology was always letting us down.'

Cryer's attachment to Marvin D Bomb The Bastards lasted until 1982 and the Falklands War, when in a pub near his home he saw a group of teenagers with T-shirts declaring 'Bomb The Bastards'. 'It really upset me,' he remembers. 'The Ev catchphrase was current. But they didn't know or didn't want to know the irony of the point that was being made.'

Other characters came and went. To those who knew Everett, they must have carried double entendres that the mass audience would not have noticed. How he must have relished his long-delayed revenge on the American evangelist who interrupted his Radio London shows when he introduced his own Southern preacher man, Brother Lee. Spouting brother-lee love while delivering fire and brimstone from the pulpit, Everett used his inspired prop of enormous plastic hands to make the preacher look even more of a buffoon. 'The devil is going to breathe the fire of temptation on you. And it's a bad breath!' he glowered as the gospel choir banged their tambourines and chanted: 'Halitosis!' Everett himself must have had mixed feelings as one sketch had him going to the head of Religious Broadcasting at the BBC, whose door opened merely to reveal a grille through which Everett said: 'Forgive me, Father, for I have sinned.' 'I know,' an Irish voice responded, 'I've seen your show.'

So many sketches gave everyday phrases, events and gadgets a splendidly surreal turn. In one, Everett was at home watching a Western with 3D stereoscopic glasses which promised to 'let you experience the full effect'. Sure enough, as he put them on, a glass of whisky was thrown in his face and a cowboy went hurtling across the saloon bar, through the TV screen and into his living room.

The show won BAFTA and Royal Television Society awards and missed out on the top international television prize, The Golden Rose of Montreux, by only a couple of votes.

Ray Cameron, Barry Cryer's co-writer for Everett, died a few years ago. And sadly he and Everett were not on speaking terms for the last few years of Cameron's life, as the writer could not forgive Everett for siding with his wife, Coke Cameron, during their marriage split. But Cryer remembers the increasingly spontaneous development of the Everett shows. He remembers how not a single day was dull as the comic creativity came on the hoof, and he remembers the dichotomy of Everett, whom he describes as 'a gregarious recluse' – brilliantly funny, anarchic and inventive professionally, 'yet the most quiet, domesticated man. He was always talking about hoovering.'

(Everett indeed made cleanliness and tidiness a fetish. He used a loofah on himself every day, giving his skin a shiny effect. He wielded the vacuum cleaner with increasing affection and frequency, not only hoovering the plastic glass on his balcony, but even polishing the vacuum cleaner itself once that job was done. And he brought a feather duster into the Capital Radio studios to gather the dust the night cleaners had missed.)

Cryer also remembers the one time he argued with Everett. 'He came up with the name for this biker character, Sid Snot. I said: "Surely we can do better than that. Honestly! Sid Snot! Boy, was I proved wrong! Kids absolutely loved it."' Indeed Everett had a Top Ten hit, his only one, when he released 'Snot Rap' – Sid philosophizing to rap music. It reached number nine in the national charts in March 1983. (His previous best had been number thirty-two in November 1977 with 'Captain Kremmen – Retribution'. His other efforts on vinyl – 'Knees' (1966), 'The Edge' (1967), 'It's Been So Long' (1968), 'Train Number' and 'Happy Birthday From Cuddly Capital', failed to score).

Barry Cryer is one of the great English comedy writers and performers. His writing credits go back to *The Frost Report* in the sixties. And he was the warm-up man for the studio audience on *Monty Python's Flying Circus*. When he was working on *The Frost Report* with the likes of John Cleese, Ronnie Barker and Ronnie Corbett, he met Angela Bond, then Everett's producer on Radio 1. Bond introduced him to Everett and they became firm friends. In the mid-seventies Cryer had been working with Ray Cameron on the game show *Jokers Wild*. Cameron had largely been a game-show deviser. It was David Mallett, the director of *The Kenny Everett Video Show*, who very intuitively saw the zany possibilities of putting all three, Everett, Cryer and Cameron, together.

Then they were simply given their head. There was a script . . . sometimes. But often the three would think of ideas in the car going to the Thames studio. The show was recorded over two days. The first was taken up with Hot Gossip's dance routines and the musical guests. On the second day Everett would record all day without an audience. During that day he, Cryer and Cameron would go into a huddle in corners, adding to sketches as new thoughts occurred. That's what Everett loved: no audience. It was a natural studio sound. The laughter that could be heard on the programmes was the laughter of the crew.

It was a precious moment in television – *Monty Python* and Michael Bentine's *It's A Square World* are two other rare examples – where ideas for using the medium were dreamt up and explored during the filming, and thereafter were taken for granted. Everett and Mallett wanted to use a device called Quantec, in which the picture spun round. It was the first time it had been used for comedy in Britain. Then, at the end of part one of a show, Everett could hold up a card with a moving picture on, sit on it and say: 'So, what's in part two?'

Rarely did a sketch end without some quick-fire visual gag. The final shot was, for example, hurled back into a television set in a corner of the screen so that the next sketch could commence. The show was also among the first to use hand-held cameras, now taken for granted. And Everett, to the crew's initial amazement, would often end a sketch by simply walking out of the shot. At other times he would drag someone into the shot. Mallett also insisted on another precedent: a fade to white. It was unheard of before that to have a white background. It all meant that, in a rare departure for a comedy show – Terry Gilliam's graphics in *Monty Python* are one of the few other examples – the visual imagination rivalled the script. And more than with *Monty Python*, which kept Gilliam's animation apart from the other sketches, here verbal and visual anarchy became a unified whole.

The crew never knew what to expect. Everett's parody on Mary Whitehouse, 'Angry of Mayfair', would come on: a City gent with his pinstripe suit and umbrella, seething against lax standards on television, would turn round to reveal black bra, fishnet stockings and a suspender belt and bright-red silk panties as he left. That much they knew. Then, on an impulse, Angry of Mayfair tried walking right up to the camera and smashing the glass on the porto-prompt with his umbrella. It worked. They cost £70 each back in 1978. And he broke one every week.

The long-serving cameraman at Thames was Ray Gearing, who became a friend of Everett's. It was a small insight into the generosity that Everett constantly showed his friends that when Gearing did some broadcasting on a local hospital radio, Everett, unasked, spent a lot of time making jingles and links for him. Gearing found that, in the spontaneous and frenetic atmosphere of making the video show, the crew became involved in off-the-cuff scripting.

'When the show started,' says Gearing, 'all the crew thought: What the hell's all this? It was totally different from anything else. But after a short time everyone wanted to work on it. It was so off-the-cuff. The writers, Ray Cameron and Barry Cryer, would have the outline of a script and they used to ask us for gags for the characters. If we came up with a gag we would get a £9 fee. We used to put those payments into a fund for the Christmas party. They were wonderful parties. Hot Gossip would dance at them.

'I can still remember the odd Sid Snot joke we gave him. Sid comes on and says: "I went to Trafalgar Square today, right. I was feeding the pigeons . . . to my cat."

'Kenny hated yes men. He would much rather hear you say: "That was a bit weak" if something didn't work. He'd say: "That's what I thought" and go on to the next sketch. He wasn't the sort of person to ask for a retake. If Benny Hill said you could do that better, it was a cue to go again. If things went wrong with Kenny, he would just continue and turn the mistakes to his advantage. If you did do a retake, he would use both the original cock-up and the retake in the show.'

The atmosphere on the show was such that the professional cordiality spilled over into practical jokes before filming began. Cryer had masses of gay friends and Everett used to refer to him as an honorary gay, whispering to him conspiratorially: 'Married thirty years and four children. What a brilliant smokescreen.' One afternoon the two of them were discussing how there was a custom in the gay scene to wear a handkerchief just sticking out of one's pocket as a sign to other gays. The next morning Everett entered the studio to find every member of the crew had a handkerchief sticking out of a pocket: every conceivable pocket at every conceivable angle; some handkerchiefs came out of shirt collars, others out of trousers. He laughed fit to bust.

But generally, as Ray Gearing remembers, when the cameras stopped rolling, the zaniness would stop. Everett would be very quiet and go and sit down. 'The crew all loved him. I never heard him raise his voice to anyone. He was like Michael Barrymore in that respect, getting the crew on his side. Some of the new presenters who enjoy a reputation for zaniness, it's just a completely false act. Off screen they're shits.'

And off screen, Everett told Gearing that he never really liked being on screen that much. He loved the atmosphere of radio. If he was chatting to someone on radio, he said, and they were doing the ironing, then he was chatting just to that person, no one else in the whole world. TV was so much more general.

Despite his increasing success with the medium, it was Everett's essential dislike of television, Gearing said, that caused him to quit in 1988. It was the paraphernalia of make-up, costumes, wigs, lights, retakes, studio audiences and so on which contrasted so negatively for him with the fantasy freedom of a radio studio. He claimed to make the decision to quit during one sketch with Cleo Rocos. He was Quasimodo. She was Esmeralda. They were both wearing harnesses and were hoisted up into the air. Everett was dressed in less than comfortable sackcloth, had an eye blacked out, a glass eye stuck to his cheek, a woolly wig, and lashings of make-up. As he told the story later: 'With the harness around your parts doing the "O the bells, the bells" we were hoisted up into these four-million-kilowatt lights and a camera went wrong. And they decided it would be less expensive to leave us up there while they fixed the camera. So there we were slowly rotating in these frying lights dressed from head to foot in sackcloth and when we both came twirling round to each other I said to Cleo: "That's it!" When I came to sign the next contract Quasimodo came through from my subconscious and said: "Don't do it."'

It's a good story and, as often, only part of the truth. Certainly Everett was always happier in a radio studio than in a television studio. But Cryer remembers that they were prepared to do more series, if the offers had been there. Both Everett and the programme makers were realizing that after ten years of high-energy sketches and ten years at the top, it might be time to move on.

But for ten years TV did what radio could not. It gave Everett an international reputation. No one before him had ever made the cross-over from radio DJ to TV comic, let alone led the field in both spheres. Mallett, Cryer and Cameron recognized that spontaneity was Everett's great talent. They used to lie to him and say that they were only rehearsing; but the camera was always on to catch his *ad libs* and spur-of-the-moment ideas.

And then one morning Everett, Cryer and Cameron arrived at the Teddington studio to find it empty. The crew had been sent out. The three were utterly bemused. They had particularly been looking forward to that day as they had written a mini-series, *The Snots*, introducing Sid's similarly leather-clad, nose-running, sleeve-wiping family (and prefiguring Harry Enfield's Slobs). But a producer told Everett that the script had been leaked upstairs to Philip Jones, who had taken against the idea as too vulgar and wouldn't sanction its being filmed.

Everett went very quiet, then turned to Cryer and Cameron and said: 'I think we'll go upstairs and see Philip.' The three marched along the corridor, where they were halted by the tea lady. Everett chatted to her as normal, had a tea and a bun from her trolley, then turned again to his comrades and cried: 'Onward.' They went into Jones's office and discussed the matter with some rancour. Jones then tried to smooth it over. 'Let's continue the discussion over lunch,' he said. 'I've booked a table.'

'How unfortunate,' replied Everett, 'Ray, Barry and I are going into town.' Even then no one was entirely sure whether it was all an extended joke on Everett's part. But it was not.

They went into town. And then they went to the BBC for their next, and all subsequent, series. *The Snots* did indeed come to life at the BBC, though renamed *The Drains*. Diana Dors was keen to play Mummy Drain, but other commitments stopped her at the last moment.

Snots or Drains, it seemed a small business to cause such a breach, though Thames's decision to reschedule Everett's show against the all-conquering *Top of the Pops* on the BBC had also irked him. And just as Everett could be a generous and devoted friend, so he could take maximum offence when he felt he had been slighted, and did not forgive easily, if at all.

'Philip just didn't like these slobby people,' says Cryer of Jones's distaste for the Snots. 'He didn't think it was what Thames was all about.' Jones never forgave Everett for leaving Thames, and relations were not restored. Even today, he refuses to talk about him. The move to the BBC after Thames had originated and stood by the radical show was seen as gross treachery, though as Jones brought Morecambe and Wise the other way – from the BBC to independent television – he probably recognized, after the dust had settled, that such transfers of allegiance do happen. Nevertheless, it was a sad ending for all concerned, not least Everett, who was soon to come up against the familiar BBC bureaucracy. Studio audiences and completely prepared scripts were *de rigueur*, though he hated the idea of both. And to cap it all, the *Radio Times* wouldn't print Cupid's full name, which was rather to miss the point. But whether their refusal was a judgement on Everett's humour or reflected their lack of faith in their own typesetters, who knows?

Though he made numerous episodes of the slightly renamed *Kenny Everett Television Show* for the BBC between 1982 and 1988, Everett never found the satisfaction there that he had had at Thames, and was never allowed to display the same spontaneity. In one of his letters to Ray Gearing he wrote of the switch from Thames to the Beeb: 'Going to the BBC was like stepping out of a Rolls Royce into a heap of gorilla shit.'

Cryer found the BBC incredulous when they learned that sometimes he, Everett and Cameron dreamt up sketches in the car on the way to the studio. With the BBC everything had to be ready and scripted for the Friday night. And when Everett arrived there would be the studio audience seated. He found that an ordeal. His whole method of working was not a regimented BBC one. 'The BBC never understood him,' says Cryer, 'never knew what he was all about.'

Nevertheless, whatever pains the artists involved experienced, the programmes seemed just as funny. And it is unlikely that even the most hardened Kenny Everett fan, faced with two shows, would be able to tell which was from Thames and which was from the BBC. Viewing figures reached a peak of fifteen million.

Everett milked his antipathy to the BBC for full comic effect. In one of his first shows he cast himself as 'Head of Everything at the BBC', hearing that Everett had returned and demanding: 'Quick. Turn the television on. We must check to see there's nothing FUNNY going on.' He also satirized the BBC blockbusters. *Dallasty*, with Spam Stewing and her sister-in-law Juicy Stewing, had Miss Oily played by a different actress in every shot, as she almost was in the real thing. Though the skit's closing credits went by even more quickly than *Dallas's* own flashing credits, it was just about possible to identify the acronym for 'Creative Realisation Associates Productions'.

One of the many things that surprised the BBC was that Everett was incapable of learning lines before the day of filming. But on the day, he just absorbed them. It wasn't just the BBC that was surprised. When Spike Milligan appeared on a Christmas show, he was amazed to see all the autocues. 'Everett, haven't you learned your lines?' he spluttered. 'Remind me to send you an assassin for Christmas.' Geoffrey Palmer was another well-known actor who guested on the show and couldn't believe the unconventional approach. But part of the reason for the approach was that Everett, though the star of the show, remained utterly in awe of actors and actresses. They were the real professionals. They learned their lines. It would be presumptuous to put himself in that league.

It would have knocked him sideways if he had realized that most of the actors and actresses, singers and dancers, who came on the show were in similar awe of his comic talents. His show had taken over from Morecambe and Wise as the one celebrities most liked to guest on. And the one time there was an altercation it was with the pop star Adam Ant. Everett was doing a sketch about jeans that were so big the designer was in there with you. Adam Ant was cast as the designer to disappear in the jeans with Everett. Instead he disappeared into a corner with a coven of managers, who decided it wouldn't be seemly for Mr Ant. Another guest, Bob Geldof, who was leaning against the studio wall watching, took his chance and Mr Ant's place.

The formula changed little over the years, nor did the public's love of the show diminish. To publicize his new series in the autumn of 1986, Everett gave an interview to *Today* newspaper. He said, with no great conviction, that he was thinking of writing his autobiography. 'I shall probably call it Diary of a Slut,' he joked. 'It's going to be full of things that couldn't possibly be printed until after I'm dead. Its content will depend on how soon I'm likely to die. If I discover I have the dreadful Aida [his then public joke term for Aids] then it will definitely be the whole truth.'

That proposed autobiography was quickly forgotten. Besides, as he told *Today*, his ex-wife was about to publish her autobiography, in which he would clearly play a prominent part. What he said next was particularly pertinent, bearing in mind he was later to accuse

Lee of treachery and of outing him in her book (even though he had publicly come out in 1985) and was to cut her out of his life. He told the *Today* interviewer: 'She had the grace to send me a copy. Most of it is quite damning to me and she said she would take out anything that I didn't approve of. But there was only one thing in it I didn't remember doing. The time we were together was when I formed my character. Before I met Lee I was groping in the dark – after we met I was groping in the light.'

That 1986 series, one of his last, introduced new characters, including a comic undertaker, a country and western hillbilly and a rather sickly woman called Verity Treacle. 'For Verity I wear a wig, a pleated skirt and sit with my legs open – a sort of Thora Hird,' explained Everett in a less than flattering allusion to the veteran actress and presenter of religious programmes, though one she probably would have been tickled by.

The new series also featured the return, after a five-year absence, of the dynamic dance troupe Hot Gossip, complete with suspenders and fishnet stockings. They would ensure the luxury of controversy and publicity. But just in case anyone missed the point, their then choreographer, Arlene Phillips, gave what seemed like a well-rehearsed interview, saying: 'I understand the BBC have been quite staggered by some of our new routines. And they've actually told us not to do one of my favourites – a dance to the Prince song New Position.'

It worked. The BBC right-of-reply programme *Open Air* was dominated by viewers' concerns about *The Kenny Everett Television Show*. One viewer described an episode as pornographic; another described a dance scene as 'stylised sado masochism' – a criticism that must have made Everett swallow hard. The concern clearly stretched to the top. The BBC controller, Michael Grade – ironically, to be accused himself of sanctioning pornography ten years later, when he was chief executive of Channel 4 – reacted to the criticisms by joining the detractors.

'I think,' he said, 'that by and large the innuendo and smut quotient has grown a little bit and we've got to pull back. I think there are problems with Kenny Everett. It has run away with itself a little bit. But, on the other hand, it is a comic strip. There is nothing in Kenny Everett that the kids don't read in comics or see in cartoons.' He added that he was considering moving the show from its eight-thirty slot to some time after the nine o'clock watershed. To do so would, of course, have risked losing an adoring young audience who failed to discern either pornography or smut in the sketches.

The regular outrage at Everett's shows was all wonderful publicity, but it did show a most curious lack of understanding of the essential innocence of his humour. In June 1983 a report by a panel of teachers, 'Popular TV and Schoolchildren', commissioned by the then Secretary of State for Education, Sir Keith Joseph, attacked the show for its 'cheap smut' and for setting a bad example to children. The report, which also criticized the comedian Bob Monkhouse for sexual innuendo, said the casual linking of violence with sex in the Everett shows was 'unacceptable'. It added that the 'apparent obsession with women's bodies' was degrading and offensive, and the heavy reliance on sexual innuendo 'most worrying'. The teachers, who had also discussed the programmes with their own pupils, went on to admit that the children did not share their reservations.

The report conceded that many of the children thought that the show was wonderful. Apart from *Top of the Pops*, it was the most popular peak-hour viewing for children, with nearly one third of all four to fifteen-year-olds watching. It continued: 'It is clear from what young people say that his appeal is based on his versatility and his irreverence: he is naughty, and says and does rude things. Such qualities are hardly new (or reprehensible?) in children's entertainment and playground culture, but what is disconcerting is the delivery of cheap smut into the living room at a time when people of all ages are watching, often as a family group.'

The report was solemnly covered by education correspondents on the inside pages of the serious newspapers, but inevitably hit the front pages of the tabloids. One of the committee, Beverley Anderson, a head-teacher and future member of the Arts Council, was quoted as saying: 'Kenny Everett is sexist. I've heard girls complaining when he wears those big boobs. You never see the girls wear a big penis, do you?' That must have given Everett, Cryer and Cameron a moment's thought.

But Everett contented himself with responding: 'These teachers just don't credit children with the ability to recognize what's real on TV and what isn't . . . To say I can be responsible for encouraging sex and violence among schoolchildren is like saying

Vincent Price is encouraging people to go round sucking each other's blood.'

This was a period when views of comedy were becoming sadly polarized; a period of political correctness mixed with the emergence of a new wave of right-on comedians, who were not slow to borrow some of the zanier ideas from established comics, but not slow either to label them sexist. At around the same time as Everett was being lambasted by teachers, Benny Hill was stunned to find himself attacked in print by comedian Ben Elton, who criticized his skits of chasing girls round a park when the incidence of rape was on the increase. As it happens, it was usually Hill who was being chased.

But in the cases of both Hill and Everett accusations of sexism and setting a bad example were laughably inappropriate. Quite where the committee saw the casual links between sex and violence is unclear. Or perhaps not. On occasion Cleo Rocos would crack a whip at him, and he would suddenly be covered in cuts and sigh languorously: 'That's better.' The humour lay in its utter inappropriateness. It is hard to imagine children the length and breadth of the land going in for copycat encounters.

Like Hill, Everett on TV was one of the last links with the music-hall tradition in Britain: the mixture of song, dance, impersonation, topical satire and titillating vulgarity, the naughty but nice comedy, at which parents might get embarrassed lest their children find it rude, while the children, loving it, are embarrassed lest their parents find it rude. The reality was, the humour was always miles away from being shocking or pornographic, not just because dancers in suspender belts concentrating madly on a tortuous routine always look like dancers and never sex objects, but much more importantly because of the personality of the star.

Everett, like Benny Hill, the Two Ronnies, Morecambe and Wise and a host of turn-of-the-century vaudeville artists, used a language of mischievous suggestion and innuendo which, far from being pornographic, actually sanitized sex through the language of childlike innocence: naughty bits, bums and boobs; a comic mischief epitomized by the buxom Hollywood actress showing us her knickers while at the same time showing us her beard.

Those whose zealous search for it led them down the blind alley of seeing smut and sexism in the Everett shows, missed no end of cleverness visual and verbal. One sketch which managed to combine satire, audience involvement, slapstick and visual trickery was a Punk and Judy show with Everett's Gizzard Puke beating Cleo Rocos's Judy as miniature puppet figures, while Everett exacted revenge on the bane of his life, the studio audience, making them say all the 'Oh no, it isn't' lines like children. The sketch reached its climax with a puppet-size Margaret Thatcher impersonator thwacking Puke over the head as he yelled at her that he couldn't get a job, and an announcer's voice boomed out in best Party Political Broadcast style: 'Margaret Thatcher beating unemployment.'

Pop music and its leading personalities always played a part in the shows, though often in bizarre style. Everett himself, with the aid of a falsetto, a heavy fake tan and a set of buck teeth, managed to play all three Bee Gees and the interviewer questioning them. They probably would have come on themselves, though it would have been less funny. Bill Wyman of the Rolling Stones was interviewed by Everett with a life-size model of Mick Jagger behind Wyman and a set of questions that showed Everett thought he was interviewing Jagger. After demanding a camera close-up of Wyman's unremarkable lips, Everett said that the girls on the set had been preening themselves to meet the singer. Wyman swallowed his pride, got up and began to sing 'Satisfaction'. Rock stars queued up to get a spot on the show and be humiliated by the jester to the rock gentry.

Everett seemed to have a fairy godmother watching over him, or at least over his professional life. His television career was fantastically successful, like his radio career before it. Sackings and public rebukes served to enhance rather than detract from his prestige. Hints of his homosexuality, despite the best efforts of the tabloids, never bothered his legion of fans. His sexual excesses, depressions, suicide attempts and marital problems were unknown beyond a small circle. By 1983 this unpredictable and anarchic character had somehow almost reached his forties with his public profile as glittering as ever, and his street cred with the young as solid as it had been in 1965. He looked to be indestructible. And then Margaret Thatcher called a general election.

12

'LET'S BOMB RUSSIA'

'Now, do we need to worry about Kenny Everett?'
Cecil Parkinson, Conservative Party chairman,
opening election strategy meeting, June 1983

Kenny Everett's political career lasted less than three minutes. Within that brief time he earned more notoriety and national newspaper column inches than many a back-bench MP does in the life of a parliament. He had a political rally of party faithful cheering in ecstatic support; he offended and brought complaints from lobbies for the disabled, and from the Campaign for Nuclear Disarmament. Though appearing in support of the Prime Minister, Margaret Thatcher, he probably wreaked greater damage on her campaign than did the leader of the Labour opposition, Michael Foot. He saddened a number of his own friends. And he vowed the morning after he would never get involved in politics again.

It is the sort of journey from innocent zeal to world-weary resignation and cynicism that takes most people a lifetime. Everett did it in style, on national TV; and it was arguably the biggest mistake of his career. But as a piece of theatre it certainly packed a punch. His performance at the Wembley Conference Centre on Sunday 5 June 1983 is the only moment of that election campaign that most voters can remember.

He ran on to the stage, his head peering through an enormous blue rosette, his arms ending in two giant artificial hands. 'LET'S BOMB RUSSIA!' he began, to loud cheers. His eyes widened and he bounded across the stage. 'Let's kick Michael Foot's stick away,' he shouted, his voice rising manically to a climax on the last syllable, and referring, of course, to the leader of the Labour Party, who used a walking stick. The young Tory faithful had never heard anything like this. The cheers raised the roof. Then Everett gestured with a faint sideways nod of his head that he was going to take them into his confidence. A hush gripped the hall.

'Do you know, I was talking to Maggie the other day,' he said conspiratorially, in the fruity tones of the English shires. 'We were having one of our little teas together, and I said to her, I said: "Maggie," I said, "you're rolling that joint all wrong . . ."' High-pitched gasps of laughter from the audience mingled with the applause.

It was a performance, a rehearsed, scripted comedy act by a comedian who rather admired Margaret Thatcher, had been flattered to be asked to help out, but had little if any idea of Conservative policy and little interest in politics beyond admiring the perceived tenets of Thatcherism such as self-help and individual advancement. Nevertheless, it was appallingly ill-judged. And Mrs Thatcher spent much of the last week of that election campaign answering questions about Everett and whether the Tories really desired to bomb the Soviet Union.

On the BBC's *Election Call* programme she was questioned about whether people were losing their sense of humour. 'If you looked at the whole thing, you would see it was just plain fun,' she answered. 'Those youngsters were cheering because they were having tremendous fun there.' Everett's jokes had been shown on the news programmes 'wholly out of context, giving a wholly false impression', she went on. 'Of course people are going to cheer almost whatever is said under those circumstances by a person whom they all adore.' She later added: 'It's a pity you can't regard the remarks of a comedian as what they are – humorous.' That the Prime Minister herself had leapt to the defence of the embattled Everett seems even more ironic with hindsight, as only five months later he was to create a new broadcasting controversy by virtually calling her a four-letter word on air.

Though Everett told friends after the furore over Wembley that it was all just meant to be a joke, and he had hated the evening because it was like a Nuremberg rally, it is equally true that if there were base passions to be inflamed in that hall, he was certainly doing the inflaming. And though his friends and family still maintain that he was always totally apolitical, he was intelligent enough to know that appearing at a Conservative rally during an election campaign is a political act. Indeed he was unlikely to have accepted a similar invitation from Neil Kinnock.

Whatever his friends and family maintain, Everett was instinctively something of a Thatcherite, just as many of the pop and showbiz successes of the sixties were, however much their lyrics and protestations suggested otherwise. (Bob Monkhouse and Jimmy Tarbuck also appeared at that election rally.) Even so, Everett was not the avid right-winger that that manic performance caused him to be labelled by many for the rest of his life.

People rather liked the iconoclastic image of Mrs T smoking dope. But the 'Let's bomb Russia' remark was scarcely helpful to a party that had stressed that nuclear weapons would only ever be used in self-defence and in a climate where nuclear proliferation was an election issue. The reports of Everett's speech and Margaret Thatcher's defence of it are now in the Conservative Party archives at the Bodleian Library in Oxford, accompanied by a Jak cartoon that appeared in the *Evening Standard* the next week, showing a fur-hatted Russian in Moscow reading *Pravda* with a picture of Everett speaking from the platform under the headline: '"Bomb Russia!" – Tory Spokesman.'

The strongest reaction, however, was reserved for Everett's remark and accompanying gesture of kicking Michael Foot's stick away. One disabled group complained to the performers' union, Equity. And two letters to the *Daily Mirror* gave an indication of some of the public reaction. 'How strange,' said the first, 'that Kenny Everett who has always been so anti-Establishment, should be on a platform supporting Mrs Thatcher.' The second asked: 'Since when has elderly infirmity become the butt of a joke? I shall never watch another Kenny Everett show after his distasteful Tory propaganda stunt.' The Liberal Party leader, David Steel, joined in the outcry, saying: 'Although we can allow for Tory mistakes in having clowns on their platform, the reaction from the Young Conservatives was quite appalling.' Even a well-intentioned defence by Everett's Labour-supporting comedian chum Billy Connolly – that in show business you often acted like a bigot to expose bigotry – was less than convincing.

The man who was responsible for bringing Everett into the

Conservative campaign was the film director and Tory supporter Michael Winner. Everett rehearsed his jokes over lunch at Winner's house before going to the rally. He stood up in the dining room to scream out the 'Let's bomb Russia' line. 'You must do that gag in the rally,' a delirious Winner said. 'Do you really think I should?' asked Everett. 'Of course,' replied Winner, 'no one will care.' According to Winner, Everett had even toyed with the idea of 'coming out' at that rally, which would unquestionably have made it the focal point of the whole election campaign. 'I'm not sure, Kenny, I said, that a Tory rally with Margaret Thatcher is the best place to reveal to the world that you are gay.'

During that election campaign the BBC's flagship current affairs programme *Panorama* was filming some of the strategy meetings at Conservative Central Office held by the then chairman of the party, Cecil Parkinson. At the meeting on the morning after the rally he held up the morning papers and began the session on camera by asking his campaign committee whether they needed to worry about this Kenny Everett business. The consensus was that the world outside Wembley Conference Centre had no sense of humour.

Unquestionably, the reaction to his performance hurt Everett. It was not just the sight of fans writing to the papers. His own friends told him they disapproved of what he had done. Derek Taylor, the Beatles' publicist, and an admirer of Michael Foot, was one of many who informed Everett he was amazed by the sight of him joining the Thatcher camp and ridiculing a tireless and idealistic campaigner like Foot.

A year later, in September 1984, Everett gave an interview to the *News of the World* colour magazine, expressing his continuing bafflement as to why he had caused offence, and giving an insight into his fairly basic political principles. 'I'm still bewildered why people should take these political jokes seriously. Maybe I was a bit offensive about Michael Foot, but, fiddle-de-dee, I am sure he didn't mind.

'The only political feelings I have are that I'm doing quite well now, and I'd like to keep it that way, so I suppose I am a Conservative. If I wasn't doing well, I'd want to change things so then I'd probably vote Labour. It's as simple as that to me. The Labour Party keeps saying offensive things like, "We're going to squeeze the rich." And they dress so badly. I'm not the best dressed person in the world, but if I was after votes, I really would wear a decent frock.

'Margaret Thatcher is monstrously condescending, a really iron-clad person. I wouldn't like her to be involved directly in my life. But when you have horrors like Arthur Scargill ranting away, you need someone like her to neutralise him.'

In fact Everett and Margaret Thatcher barely knew each other, even though from 1983 onwards the press always referred to him as the Prime Minister's favourite comedian. There seems to be little evidence for this assertion apart from the fact that she was happy to have him appear at the notorious rally, and defended him against the onslaught afterwards. How much a compliment it was to be the favourite comedian of someone not exactly famous for her humour is a moot point. This was, remember, the woman who publicly praised her Cabinet minister Willie Whitelaw with the immortal line 'Every woman needs a Willie' and looked blank when people laughed. [1]

Certainly, after the Wembley fiasco Everett was careful in interviews not to give the impression that he and Mrs Thatcher were kindred spirits, and, not wanting to alienate his young audience again, went out of his way to distance himself publicly from her. In 1986 he told the *Daily Express*, with a typical concoction of fact and fiction: 'I met Margaret Thatcher once. She's a robot, you know. She actually shook hands with me while she was talking to somebody else.' He added that he later mistook her for a cocktail waitress and asked her to get him a gin and tonic. 'She gave me the filthiest of looks.'

As Everett approached his forties, his television shows continued to maintain their standards and fuel the BBC ratings just as they had the ratings at Thames. Everett may have been less content with the Beeb's more rigid production procedures, but the viewers didn't notice any difference.

Nevertheless, it was only a matter of time before he decided to return to where he was happiest: radio. His age put him at that awkward in-between stage, too old for Radio 1 but not quite comfortingly middle-aged enough for Radio 2. But, wisely, it was the latter he chose when he went back to BBC Radio in 1981. Contemporaries who stayed with Radio 1, such as Dave Lee Travis

1 No she didn't.

and Bob Harris, were to be slightingly discarded when the BBC's pop station attempted to renew itself at the start of the nineties.

Later, in the early nineties, Travis, Simon Bates and others were also perceived to be the target of send-ups by the new-wave comedian Harry Enfield with his Smashy and Nicey sketches, which played a surprisingly large part in persuading Radio 1's controller to go for a more youthful set-up. Everett was spared all of that, though his style remained so anarchic and individualist anyway that he would have been almost impossible to mock as clichéd.

Besides, he and the BBC had parted company long before that period. When he joined Radio 2 for a weekly two-hour live show on Saturday mornings in October 1981, the Radio 2 controller, David Hatch, announced: 'He is one of the most talented broadcasters in the last decade. And he's changed.' The last sentence was a clear reference to Everett's sacking from Radio 1 eleven years before. Everett agreed. 'Yes, I've changed. The Beeb is more tolerant. Look what Terry Wogan gets away with.' And a beaming Mr Hatch was moved to affirm: 'We trust him.'

Ah, well. On 19 November 1983 BBC Radio and Kenny Everett parted company for the second and final time. With an ironic symmetry, just as he had unintentionally insulted a member of the government's wife in 1970, so in 1983 he unintentionally insulted *the* member of the government, and Radio 2 did not renew his contract. Once again he could, with some justice, argue that he was more sinned against than sinning. As he was ending his show, his producer handed him a joke to read out. Everett did not even have time to read it through first to himself. He just delivered it, full frontal, to Radio 2's housewives, mothers and grandmothers listening in their homes. This is what Cuddly Ken told them: 'When England was an empire, we had an emperor. When it was a kingdom, we had a king. Now it's a country, we've got Margaret Thatcher.' Then he swallowed hard as the impact hit both him and them. 'Get out of that,' he said forlornly to the announcer who followed him.

Geoff Mullin, now head of music on Melody Radio, was that producer, and Everett's producer for his entire time on Radio 2. He used to accompany Everett on shopping trips after the Saturday show. When people began to surround them, Everett would whisper to him, 'Geoffrey, produce me out of here.'

Mullin admits liability for handing Everett the fateful joke. It was actually a piece of graffiti he had seen on his journey in to Broadcasting House. 'We always finished the show with a funny line, and, yes, I handed him that one.' But Mullin is adamant that, contrary to the story at the time, which has been repeated ever since, Everett was not sacked because of the insult to Mrs Thatcher. Indeed he was not sacked at all.

'He wasn't ever sacked from Radio 2,' he explains. 'He was actually at the end of his contract. That line was the last line on the final programme of his contract. There was a new contract on the table but he had a very busy TV schedule, so he didn't sign it.'

Whether that new contract would have still been on the table after the Thatcher joke we shall never know. Anyway, the sacking story did Everett's image no harm, and he never denied it in subsequent interviews. What Mullin also remembers is the dramatic change that Everett brought to Radio 2's music policy. 'It was very adventurous stuff for Radio 2, a completely different, almost avant-garde policy. We were the first people to play the Eurythmics anywhere in the UK and we kept on championing them. We played a lot of imported American bands and music from the British club scene. Kenny and I also used to raid the BBC archives for both music and comedy, and used a lot of comedy dialogue. And Kenny actually played a ten-minute stretch of Wagner on Radio 2. There has never been anyone like him and there never will be.'

Anyway, BBC departments are peculiarly autonomous, and any offence taken by Radio 2 was clearly not shared by BBC Television's Light Entertainment Department, which continued to employ Everett to make his television shows until 1988, when he quit while he was ahead, once more yearning for radio and returning to Capital, the one station which had always treasured him. Everett moved into a daily slot on Capital Gold, the oldies station, rejoining old sparring partners such as Tony Blackburn from Radio 1 and pirate days and Mike Ahern, upon whose skull he had inadvertently chucked a brick at St Edmund's Primary School.

Before that, though, there was some marital brick chucking to be done. By the end of 1986 Lee had finished her book. Everett and Nikolai took her out to the Hiroko Japanese restaurant in Shepherd's Bush and praised her to the skies. 'I'm going to go on tour with you,' he added, referring to a promotional tour for her book.

On 25 March 1987 Elton John celebrated his fortieth birthday, and his manager, John Reid, threw a celebration bash for him at Reid's home. Everett was there, as was Lee, whose book had just been printed and was to be serialized in the *Daily Star* a week later. Lee spent a long time that night talking happily with Everett. Later in the evening and after a lot of drink had been consumed, Everett and Nikolai had one of their usual dramas, a big argument, which this time involved the former Royal Ballet star Wayne Sleep, who was with them. A big row broke out. First Wayne Sleep came to Lee crying and complaining. Then Nikolai came up to Lee crying. Lee decided to separate them. 'Now, you sit there, Wayne, and you sit there, Ev. Nikolai, go and sit over there.'

'Don't you tell me what to do!' Sleep snapped at her.

'Don't you snap at me,' she shot back.

If the treatment of such major stars seems bizarre, Lee was unfazed. 'They were little boys,' is how she describes it now. Nikolai came up to her crying again and said Everett had disappeared. She went to look for him and found him fast asleep in his car.

She never saw him again, save one time in the Euston Road in London by the Capital Radio studios when her car pulled up alongside his. He waved madly at her, seemingly forgetting they were estranged – something which amazed her as much as when she turned on the radio one morning after three years of communication breakdown and heard him telling listeners about a recipe his wife made, and joking about something he said to her, as if they had been chinwagging the night before.

'After Elton's party, he suddenly turned,' said Lee. Part of the reason was the serialization in the *Daily Star* of her book, which unsurprisingly gave space to the more sensational aspects of their marriage. Everett's agent, Jo Gurnett, was not thrilled by this, nor were some of his other friends. And then there was the festering wound of that incident at Henley when Lee had ordered Everett, Nikolai and Pepe off her property. That wounded him. 'It wasn't the book,' she says now. 'When I saw him at Elton's fortieth, the book was printed, and he was quite happy with me. It was the serialization and me throwing Nikolai out. If you pin it down to what really did it I would say it was when I threw him and Nikolai out. But I just couldn't tolerate what was going on.'

She heard he was speaking ill of her book. She phoned him up.

'Excuse me,' she said, 'you read this book. You raved about this book. What's going on?' He refused to answer. Then she received a letter from him: 'You have compounded my agony,' it said. 'I will spend the rest of my life avoiding people like you.'

'It destroyed me,' says Lee. 'I got terribly low. I couldn't work. I didn't work for three or four years after that.' The book-promotion tour involving the former husband and wife did not happen. Invitations to appear on TV and radio dried up for Lee. Even her good friend Derek Jameson changed his mind about having her on his programme. 'He rang me up and said he was sorry but his producer had now told him the book was in effect banned by the BBC.' She heard rumours of a memo going round the BBC that she was to be avoided, that she had written an unseemly kiss-and-tell. She was flabbergasted. Her book had avoided the most controversial aspects of her ex-husband's lifestyle, and had not touched on his life with Nikolai at all. Besides he had approved it and written the foreword.

Then mutual friends began to tell her that he was speaking ill of her to them. 'I got accused of taking him for the money,' Lee recalls, 'and I didn't even seek alimony. My lawyer wanted to kill me. When I divorced Ev I didn't have any alimony, simply because Everett's always been paranoiac, and in my mind I felt that I was one of the people he trusted in – he totally trusted me – and I felt that if that trust in me is destroyed that would just about destroy him ever trusting anyone again. I literally just had my home when I split up with him. He turned very easily to paranoia, did Ev, and I knew if I went for alimony he would think I'd taken him like everybody else. So I didn't.'

The settlement included the garden flat in the trendy Notting Hill Gate area, all its contents and the Honda car. His sister Kate says simply now. 'There never seemed to be a period in his life when he managed to save a large amount of money.' The divorce agreement had also included a pledge by both partners not to talk to the press about their personal life. Some of Everett's closest friends maintain that his anger at Lee stemmed from his belief that parts of her book, and then its serialization, went against the spirit of the agreement. But his decision to write the foreword endorsing the book put him on shaky ground in maintaining this.

After the irreversible breakdown of relations between the couple,

Everett found that he had lost some of his starrier friends. Elton John and Freddie Mercury sided with Lee. Other mutual friends, including Dusty Springfield and Dave Clark of the Dave Clark Five, who was a good friend of Freddie Mercury, also decided to maintain their friendships with Lee. Elton John, though, did pay a warm tribute to Everett after his death.

Mercury and Everett had been much closer; and though they fell out, not only about Lee but because Everett accused him in a petulant row of taking his cocaine, it had been a very affectionate friendship, with great professional admiration on both sides. When Mercury went into tax exile, it was Everett and Lee who gave him a surprise farewell party at their Notting Hill Gate flat. In one of their last meetings, after they had both been diagnosed as having the Aids virus, Everett and Mercury discussed how they would handle the illness and the inevitable publicity. The conversation ended with Everett saying softly to Mercury: 'I will see you soon up there.'

Mercury's parties were camp and outrageous affairs. For the last one, not long before his death, he took over a hotel on the island of Ibiza. His estrangement from Mercury meant that Everett was not invited; but Lee went and ended up playing a pivotal role. Mercury's friends had filled the hotel with drag queens from clubs on the island. The drag was of the outlandish variety. One of the queens was dressed all in crinoline, and on his head was a big hat with two canaries in it. Lee was with Ken East, then head of EMI International, and his wife, Dolly. Lee and Dolly were both passionate animal lovers. There was about to be a fracas over the hat, but a slightly larger drama was already taking place.

One of the drag queens was doing a suggestive dance with a condom. Ken East, who found the vulgar humour offensive, and was also six feet four, ordered him successfully to stop, but then an even larger drama took place. Mercury had wrapped the whole party room in crinkly gift-wrapping paper. One of the drag queens was careless with a cigarette, and a fire broke out. It spread very quickly. Two of the drag queens screamed and threw their wine on to the fire, which made it spread even faster. Ken and Dolly East, Lee and John Alkin, who were at the table next to the blaze, managed to put it out. But the burning paper stuck to their arms. Lee still has burn marks on both arms by which to remember Freddie Mercury's last party.

175

Back home, Everett had one more professional surprise to spring. In 1991, at forty-six, the HIV-positive comic shocked himself as well as all his friends by announcing he was to star in a West End musical, *The Hunting of the Snark*. Jo Gurnett could not believe her ears when he informed her that he was going to do it. 'Do you realize you will have to learn a script, say the same lines and make the same moves night after night and twice on Thursdays and Saturdays?' she told the man who adored improvisation and spontaneity, and had a notoriously short concentration span.

But Everett was determined. One of the principal reasons was the knowledge that here was something of which his parents could be unreservedly proud. Typically, he managed to give them an uncomfortable jolt when they opened the programme and saw that he had described his origins as a Liverpool slum. But though that shocked them, they were still inordinately proud to see their son on the West End stage.

Describing how he got involved in the show on *Desert Island Discs* two years later, he said: 'I got rung up by Mike Batt, who is a musical genius, and he said: "I've got this wonderful West End thing I'm going to do – five and a half million pounds, a thirty-two- piece orchestra on stage. Would you come and sing and dance and juggle and do funny lines?" and I said: "No, absolutely not, I'd rather stay at home", because the bother and the nerves would be humungous. But he kept ringing and ringing and saying: "Well, you'll only have a few lines, you'll just have to come on, huge applause, wallop, line off." So I said: "Oh, all right," so the name went into the ads and he started giving me more and more lines, more and more steps; the whole play was two and a half hours and I was on stage for the whole two and a half hours, twirling and dancing, having to remember where I stand, having to remember lines. It was a nightmare, but I thought to myself, this is the most important thing you've ever done. If you forget your lines or you land in the wrong place or you fall over a dancer the orchestra will have to stop . . . you've got to get it right. You've got to concentrate. And I got it right. I remembered all my lines. I twirled in the right places.

'The opening night was such a success. I brought my mum and dad over from Australia, first class, Jumbo. There went my profits from *Hunting of the Snark*. And all my friends were there. It was a huge success. I really enjoyed the opening night. And that's the only thing I did it for, so I could say I'd done a West End musical spectacular.'

In fact, after the enjoyment of the opening night, there were not too many anticlimactic subsequent nights for Everett to endure: the show was a flop and closed within weeks. He didn't look completely comfortable on stage, and his reviews certainly didn't compare with those he had been used to on radio and TV, though reviewers seemed to agree that the thinness of the material gave him little scope to shine. The *Daily Telegraph's* critic wrote: 'You can almost see the panic in Kenny Everett's eyes, as he tries to make a zany comic character out of the billiard marker, with only a snooker cue and a desperately unfunny song to work with.'

It wasn't the only thing that was desperately unfunny. To promote the show Everett gave an interview to the *Mail on Sunday's* 'You' magazine on 20 October 1991. Asked about his marriage, he reminisced: 'It was a grave mistake to marry someone I wasn't physically or emotionally in love with. But at the time I didn't know what love was. The lady was a hoot, a huge character, whereas I was a lost child. We had massive rows.' He had got married despite his gayness, he said, because 'I did think that if I gave marriage a whirl, I would have a revelation in the sex department, that if she cavorted long and hard enough in front of me I would suddenly see what it was all about.'

He went on to talk about her book: 'She asked permission to write about me being gay, claiming that I could really help people, but I was shocked when the book actually came out and the public response was horrendous. One scaffolder took his trousers down in front of me and shouted: "Come on, you like this, don't you."'

Everett's memory was never his strongest point. But this was a travesty. He had been shown, and approved every page of, his ex-wife's book. He had written the foreword to it. The incident with the scaffolder had occurred not after publication of the book but two years earlier, when he had chosen to 'come out'. But now he was all but accusing her of having 'outed' him. This even led the journalist to ask him if the book had prompted his suicide attempt, though he did at least have the grace to deny the suggestion.

For the long-suffering Lee, this rewriting of history was the last straw. After years of protecting him, lying for him, loving him and mothering him, this public vilification drove her to distraction. It also, at Elton John's instigation, drove her to the law. Another paper from another newspaper group repeated Everett's claims. Elton John got straight on the phone to Lee, saying: 'If you don't sue, you must be out of your mind.' He recommended his own solicitor, famous for winning a multimillion-pound libel case against the *Sun*. Lee employed him, sued the newspaper and won. First, though, she wrote her last letter to her ex-husband, a heartfelt cry of years of pent-up anger and pain. She had never addressed him as Ken, and Ev now seemed too intimate for the circumstances. So she began baldly: 'Dear Everett'.

After pointing out the injurious inaccuracies in the magazine article, she went on: 'I'm so sick of your lies. You have been lying about me since we first met. But now I've decided enough is enough . . . What a convenient memory you have dear, geared as always for public sympathy, with not a care of who else may get hurt or tarnished . . . It saddens me that after 5 years apart you cannot recall any of the good times we shared. We also went through a lot together and I stuck by you every time. Most people's memories mellow with the passing of time and only the good remains. Not only have you erased all the good but are inventing the bad. When will you stop trying to blacken my name?'

She went on to remind him how he had written to her declaring he would spend the rest of his life avoiding people like her. 'In fact, that was the nicest thing you ever did for me, as the absence of you, though painful for ages has made my life much nicer and less seedy.

'If anyone should be full of hate, it really should be me − not you as you did things to me that were cruel and appalling and I always made excuses for you. As it is I feel not hate for you, I suppose the love I had for you is still there but now it's totally overshadowed by my distaste and dislike of you . . . So, the next time I hear by word of mouth or by written word, one more libellous remark, I shall slap a law suit on you.'

She received no reply. Communication between the two was never resumed. Perhaps, having come out, it may have been hard for Everett to reconcile himself to the years he spent attempting to be a happily married man. He may have grown to resent Lee for being a woman who had loved him and a woman whom he had loved, and one who thus made it harder for him to admit to himself that a heterosexual marriage was not a life he could sustain with any honesty.

13

REINVENTION

'I used to say to him: "Where does all this being poor come from?" He said: "Mum, the teenagers today don't want the Tony Blackburn public-school bit. They want some one who has come up from nothing."'

Lily Cole, speaking to the author,
March 1996

In September 1979 Everett was at the height of his earning and artistic powers. His Thames TV series *The Kenny Everett Video Show* was winning fifteen million viewers. He was still doing a Saturday radio show for Capital. And he was in constant demand for the lucrative voice-overs on TV and radio commercials. He was earning at least £1000 a day.

The *Daily Mirror* devoted almost a week of double spreads to 'Everett on Everett'. In the concluding one he mused on how his fortunes had changed. He, of course, kept mum about his marriage, which was in its death throes, and his interminable depressions, and concentrated on his material improvements. 'Sitting back, I can't help but smile at myself,' he wrote. 'Life's been pretty good to me so far. I've now got everything I want. I've got all the gadgets I need at home, including a £350 telephone which tells the time, takes its own messages and has all kinds of contraptions on it. And I've got a fridge which produces crushed ice at the push of a button.

'That's the great thing about being born in Liverpool, in a little terraced house, vaguely poverty stricken, and being hit a lot at school. Everything nice that happens, it's all a bonus.'

If he was vaguely poverty-stricken then it was very vaguely. He could just as truthfully have said that his parents sent him to a fee-paying school in a stately home in Yorkshire for two years, or that well into his twenties he used to forsake the bright lights of London and his flat with fellow DJs to spend his week-long shore leaves from pirate radio in that terraced house with his parents – the place where secretly he felt most comfortable.

'He reinvented himself when he left home,' says Kate. 'He took on a new persona. He wanted to break free of the discipline. We were very well brought up. We had to be polite. I think we had a normal, happy childhood, and the normality of it didn't sit well with Ev. He wanted his childhood to be full of drama.'

Everett made up for the lack of external drama. In interview after interview he painted a picture of being badly bullied at school, of living in poverty and of being unable to converse with his parents. A multitude of celebrities fictionalize their childhoods. The remarkable thing about Everett was that he seemed to grow to believe his own fiction. Small and intelligent, he may well have been a target for bullies at St Bede's, though any bullying that did occur was not severe enough for his family or friends in Liverpool to be able to recall.

His mother once said to him in exasperation: 'Where does all this being poor come from?' He replied that it was an act for his fans. They didn't want the Tony Blackburn public-school bit, he said. They wanted you to have come from nothing. That his fictions could be hurting his fiercely proud parents who had struggled to give him a comfortable childhood, simply did not occur to him.

As he began to realize he was gay, he may well have suffered internal torments as a teenager about how he would broach the subject with his parents. And he was probably right in thinking that few parents in working-class Liverpool in the fifties would have been over the moon at the prospect. But no one who knew his quiet, caring, stoical father Tom or his adoring mother Lily would recognize the tough, inflexible portraits he painted publicly of them, just as they would not recognize his portrait of himself as frightened, uncommunicative and awkward. 'He was a happy, gorgeous child,' says Lily.

He told Sue Lawley on *Desert Island Discs* in October 1993 that he was frightened, even as an adult, about what his mum and dad would think of his homosexuality. 'My parents didn't know how to handle gayness,' he said. 'Gayness in those days was something very odd and if your son was gay you didn't talk about it. Plus my father was a tugboat captain. You can't waltz up to your father and say: "Dad, I know you're a great chunk. But I want to be in show business and do silly things, and by the way, I'm gay." I think he might have killed me.' And yet when he did tell his parents he was gay, his father was the first to accept it.

Perhaps he never really knew how proud his parents were of him. Tom and Lily told me how their hearts leapt when they were on a train and heard a couple of young people discussing how good *The Kenny Everett Show* had been the night before. Yet Everett himself never rated his own enormous talent nor thought what he did was really a proper job. He would tell friends how he wanted to move on from 'doing silly sketches' to write and direct films. (He did star in one spoof horror film, *Bloodbath at the House of Death*, which was not a success.) Kate recalls: 'Dad once said: "When are you going to stop being a DJ and get a proper job?" He never forgot that. He would often talk about how insufficient it was to be a DJ.' Indeed, an airport customs officer looking at his passport once asked him what qualifications you needed to be a disc jockey. Everett replied: 'You need to have your brain removed.'

And yet, when I met Tommy Cole in Australia, he beamed with pride as he recalled his son reminding him of how he had bought him his first tape recorder and saying: 'I couldn't have got on radio without you, Pop.' Remembering that, he added: 'He was a wonderful boy and everybody loved him. We never had a row in our lives in our house.'

For the fiercely private Lily Cole, any public scrutiny of her family was an affront. Over many years she had to endure reporters phoning in the night, or talking to her neighbours. She was devoted to Everett just as he actually was to his parents, though he never admitted it in print and possibly not always to himself. I sat in their retirement cottage with them in Australia and watched a video-letter he had sent them, a guided tour of his flat, in which he joked and chatted with great affection. Mrs Cole told me that her son's gayness was no great surprise: 'A mother always has an instinct about her children. I always knew it was there. I had a feeling that he might have been, but he didn't say anything, so I didn't say anything. I never interfered with Maurice's or Kate's life. His private life has nothing to do with anybody as long as he's happy.'

But it does seem that it caused her some pain, though never – again contrary to interviews Everett gave – was there a breakdown in communication between them. According to Kate: 'There was never any sort of estrangement. There was never an argument. My mother adored him. She worried about him all his life. She went through agonies over his gayness but never criticized him. She adored him and would have given up her life for him.'

Nearly every press cutting that exists on Kenny Everett contains inaccuracies. But in most cases this was his own fault. 'I would say to him why do you tell the press all these things,' says Barry Cryer. 'He said: "So they'll go away!" I said: "Yes, but they'll go away and write it down."'

In 1982 Everett published his supposed memoir *The Custard Stops at Hatfield*. Immensely funny, it was written at a time when he was living with John Pitt, the Australian waiter, and yet painted a picture of a continuing happily married life and did not mention homosexuality or any of his male partners at all. He had grown up, he wrote, in a street that 'was a bit like a battery farm for humans', and in a house where 'all that broke through the plasterboard was the sound of the people next door having rows and opening tins of soup'. He went on: 'We didn't talk a lot, my parents and I. Not past a basic "How are you, what's for dinner?" level anyway. But I suppose there wasn't a lot to talk about, me being all shy and confused.'

It all came as a great surprise to his parents and sister, and to his wife. Lee confronted him: 'If you're going to write a book, why not tell the truth?'

In fact, the book was largely written by Everett's good friend and producer at Capital, Simon Booker. The two of them took off to a country hotel for a few days and Booker interviewed Everett at length and then wrote the book. As far as Booker remembers, Everett never even read the result. 'It wasn't the whole truth,' agrees Booker. 'It was a piece of jolly memorabilia. Kenny contributed the awful title. I don't think he contributed much else to the writing. The gayness wasn't in the public domain then, so at that stage it wasn't an issue. He told me his life story, but the problem with Kenny, bless him, was that he never could remember anything very much.'

The irony was that Everett wanted to invent drama and conflict where there had been none, and was desperate to portray normality where there had been no end of drama, conflict and torment. A number of those who rose to fame in the sixties reinvented their childhoods. John Lennon forgot his middle-class upbringing in Liverpool so that he could be a working-class hero. Everett also needed a past of inverted glamour.

Of course, the fact that his memory played false when judged on external evidence and the memories of others, does not mean he was being false to his own feelings. It may have been the truth as he saw it, when he told the now-defunct tabloid *Today* in September 1986: 'When I was young I always felt there was nobody I could talk to. My parents weren't the kind of people I could communicate with. I would have liked their help and understanding.' If he felt unable to talk of his fears and his feelings to his parents, it is no matter that they might have been utterly receptive and sympathetic, the truth for him, inside, was that he couldn't properly talk to them. That some of his neuroses were self-inflicted, even imagined, did not make them any less real to him.

On occasion, though, reality did take a back seat. His continuing reinvention of his own life story meant that his fourteen-year marriage was in effect written out of the script. The grudge he bore against Lee ensured that not only did he convince himself that she had revealed to the world that he was gay, but he also publicly forgot the years they spent together. On *Desert Island Discs* he managed to summarize his life without once mentioning his ex-wife's name. And he referred to the marriage in slighting terms (which hurt his ex-wife enormously when she heard the broadcast) as merely part of the process of determining his own sexuality.

He said: 'I thought if I married this jolly lady, with whom I was great friends, I thought maybe one day I'd wake up and look at her and snap, and I'd think: Oh, I get it, you know, the shape and the lumps and the softness and everything, and suddenly it would fall into place. But I realized a lot later that you are what you're born and if you're born gay, you're gay for ever.'

Ironically, once Everett had found himself and at least begun to accept himself for what he was, it may well have had an effect on his talent. His show on Capital Gold in his last years was never less than entertaining, and boldly introduced the listeners to more classical music than they would have anticipated, but it lacked the sparkle, innovation and sense of the unexpected that had characterized much of his previous radio work. Perhaps the fact that the format of the station meant that he played only old records prevented him from becoming excited by the discovery of the new, which he had always enjoyed. But others saw a deeper psychological factor.

'I think coming out took a lot away from him in the artistic side,' Lee says. 'I heard him a few times at the end and it wasn't the same driven Everett. I do think that when he started getting sexually satisfied, in a way he lost his art, he lost his talent. His hunger went. It was so sad. With him the drive was this unrequited thing. His tragedy turned into his talent.'

Part of the great invention was, of course, the persona of Kenny Everett. With a new name, the shy and confused Maurice Cole was able to go into a radio studio and later a television studio and act out his fantasies. The person who thought himself ill endowed and unattractive, and toyed with suicide, could be a wild-eyed comic fantasist, a heroic space captain saving the world. Not for nothing was Everett's favourite movie Frank Capra's 1946 weepie *It's a Wonderful Life*, in which a suicidal James Stewart is dissuaded from ending it all by his guardian angel and shown what his home town would have been like if he had never been born. It turns out he had changed so many lives for the better. Everett virtually knew the film by heart.

Tony Blackburn, who had observed many times how introverted people could come into their own in a radio studio, comes closest to articulating it: 'He was one of those strange people that preferred keeping people, certainly listeners, at microphone length. He was a shy person, that was all it was, he was very, very shy. You can go into a studio and that microphone is the person you are talking to and it doesn't answer back so therefore you can be a giant-sized version of what you really possibly want to be – or dread being.'

Everett the inspired talent never really translated into Everett the millionaire businessman, especially when compared with many of his contemporaries, and nearly all of the late-eighties and nineties comics, who made a priority of marketing and exploiting their talent. Every WH Smith, every Woolworth has videos of Harry Enfield, Rik Mayall, John Cleese, Ben Elton and so many others. Look for packaged videos of Kenny Everett shows and you look in vain. The ideas flowed from him in torrents. But financial planning bored him, both for his personal security and for the long-term marketing of his talent. It was a frustration to his bank manager, Eric Gear: 'Ken should have been a very wealthy man, in the Noel Edmonds league,' he says. 'His pension fund could have been worth £3 million. But he let people reinvest it.'

Gear once begged him to invest for the day when the TV and radio offers dried up. 'What will you do when it all ends,' he asked him. 'Oh, look at Jimmy Young,' replied Everett. 'He keeps going.' Everett simply could not get interested in building up wealth, nor in envying those who had it. Only once did Gear see him bitter, or at any rate introspective and thoughtful, about how he had not cashed in on his celebrity status. He had come round to Gear's house after visiting his old friend Lulu, the pop singer, for lunch. Everett sat for a while in thought then looked at Gear to say: 'That girl has everything. Gold-plated toilet rolls. I should have had all that.'

He did not always help himself, of course. His shyness in public meant that he refused to do any club discos after those very first Radio London outings with Dave Cash. That was a frustration for his agent, Jo Gurnett, who, back in the mid-seventies, was being offered £5000 for Everett to officiate at a single disco. There would have been many more such offers if he had accepted.

One fascinating example of his lack of focused ambition and his boredom with the very thought of the business scene can be found buried deep in an interview with Ray Connolly of the *Evening Standard* dating from June 1978. The piece was ostensibly about the success of *Captain Kremmen*, which was just about to become a cartoon strip in the London newspaper. But towards the end of the interview, Everett stopped talking about Kremmen and mentioned another wheeze he had thought up.

He wanted to arrange for Michael Aspel to use the Everett studio at his and Lee's home in the Cotswolds 'to record some of the classic books on to tape for people to listen to in their cars'. Connolly suggested quickly that he shouldn't make this idea public in case someone did it before he and Aspel got round to it. Everett just shrugged. 'It doesn't matter,' he said. 'As long as someone does it. That's all that's important.'

Years before they started in earnest, Everett had dreamt up the 'talking books' idea, now a multimillion-pound business. He just forgot to pursue it.

The most bewildering, perhaps most endearing, aspect of Everett's complex persona was the innocent little boy lost, born into the wrong age, yet who could at the same time be manipulative and inhabit a world far removed from the stylized cinematic romance that he wanted life to be. Often he seemed unable to come to grips with the realities of everyday life.

The Little Boy Lost character sometimes seemed so marked that even his closest friends wondered if it was an act. He turned up for events a day late. He once drove to have dinner with Tony Blackburn and forgot to turn off the M4 just out of London and drove in a dream almost to Wales. Some months before his death Everett went round to Jo Gurnett's flat for dinner. He had been going there for years. She was one of his closest friends; they spoke most days and she even accompanied him on shopping trips as well as all his professional outings. But Everett never arrived. It later emerged that he had gone to the flat above. 'You never knew whether he was doing it for effect,' she said, 'or whether he was genuinely confused.'

On Sunday 4 April 1993 the *People* printed a snatched picture of Everett standing in the street, looking upset, tired and drawn. He had, it is true, just made one of his regular visits to the clinic; but in fact the reason for his appearance was that it was raining, and he was annoyed. However, HIV rumours had been circulating Fleet Street for a long time, certainly since 1991, when Nikolai had died. Whenever Everett had been asked if he was worried about catching it, he could and would always reply with absolute honesty: 'No' — because he already had it. But equally he knew it was only a matter of time before a newspaper published a front-page picture alongside the inevitable coded story.

The *People's* story was headlined 'Friends Concerned Over Health Of Kenny Everett'. With the customary cloying insincerity and sledgehammer hints about Nikolai, the Sunday tabloid's piece, which dominated the front page, was a model of the type of writing that characterized intrusive stories about celebrities with suspected HIV or Aids. It said: 'The comic who became a national favourite on TV and radio looks pale and drawn as he walks from his London home to keep a nearby hospital appointment.

'Few fans would recognise the gaunt figure as Kenny Everett. He has swapped his trademark beard for a moustache – and beneath the giant umbrella he wears a cloth cap, muffler and glasses.

'DJ Kenny, 48, who was devastated when his gay lover Nikolai Grishanovich died from Aids two years ago, was keeping an appointment on Wednesday at the exclusive Cromwell Hospital. Kenny, often absent from his Golden Oldies show on London's Capital Radio, has visited the private Kensington hospital several times in the past two years.

'And the man who has always lived on the edge is clearly suffering again.'

There was little sign in the story of the friends who were concerned for his health; but the point had been forcefully made. Gaunt was the key codeword. It had been used of Freddie Mercury too in the months before it was confirmed that he had Aids.

Everett, who was returning from a weekend break in Italy when the story broke, arrived at his flat to find reporters waiting for him on the pavement. Asked by a *Sun* reporter if it was true that he was HIV-positive, he immediately said yes. It took only a split second for him to work out that had he said no, the denial story would still have fuelled the rumours. He then gave what amounted to an impromptu press conference in the street, complete with gags. Questioned as to whether he might have infected Nikolai, he answered with mock anger: 'No, he probably infected me, the bastard. I'll get him back for this.'

He also made it clear that he would not be turning maudlin, an emotion it would in any case be hard to associate with him. 'My sense of humour will be the last thing to go . . . I've been wondering what to put on my tombstone, and I think it will be: "No punchline – ring Barry Cryer."' He added that he saw death in his own philosophical way. 'I can't imagine I was nowhere before this. I'd like to come back living in Spain or Italy or somewhere. As long as I don't come back bald or in Bosnia, I don't mind.' Asked if his health problems might curtail his broadcasting with Capital Gold, he responded: 'It's not affecting my work. How healthy do you have to be to play "Da Doo Ron Ron"?'

The experienced *News of the World* reporter Sharon Ring said of that street press conference: 'He handled it brilliantly. I don't think you can point to a story which was handled so brilliantly, so wittily, so cleverly.'

The next day there were more jokes when Everett reported for work at Capital Gold. He thoroughly enjoyed dropping down in front of aghast DJs Kid Jensen and David Hamilton, contorting his face, wrapping his hands round his neck, sliding slowly down his chair and moaning in fake pain: 'Haven't you heard, I'm dying. I can hardly breathe. I'm going. I'm fading.' After he had done his show, he walked into the Capital foyer and saw there were TV cameras there. He grabbed a bunch of flowers from the reception desk, lay down in the middle of the foyer and crossed his hands over his chest like a corpse with the flowers on his stomach. In a theatrical whisper, he panted: 'Ooo, it's very close . . . any minute now.'

In the same week that the story broke about Everett, Holly Johnson of Frankie Goes To Hollywood gave an interview to *The Times* announcing that he had Aids. This interview was seized on by the *Sun*, and Johnson was attacked for his lifestyle. It caused the leader writer of the *Independent on Sunday* to examine the cases of both Everett and Johnson, and to congratulate them for their dignity in their suffering.

The piece concluded: 'The experiences of Kenny Everett and Holly Johnson in the past week have been different. Everett was outed in speculative press reports which he was ultimately obliged to confirm, while Johnson chose to volunteer the state of his health in a formal interview. Both men deserve credit for their dignified behaviour. At a time of great difficulty and pain, when they might reasonably expect some privacy, they have gone some way to meet the demands of the media (and the public) for personal disclosure. What they do not deserve is to be put in the stocks erected by those who say they have only themselves to blame.'

As it happens, this was a comment that never seemed to be made publicly about Everett. Just as when he came out in 1985, the public affection for him appeared to safeguard him from the sort of tabloid attack that was visited on others, including Johnson and Freddie Mercury.

The winter of 1993 saw Everett in the Australian summer, taking part in the Gay Mardi Gras in Sydney, dancing and skipping in the street procession beneath a banner reading 'Boys On Tour'. It was, in fact, the American banner, which Everett held at the American contingent's request.

To be with Everett was to expect the unexpected and find laughter in the least likely places. Once Kate took him to a black-tie dinner after the Perth Cup, the highlight of the local social calendar. As Everett's skin was allergic to wool, he wore his striped pyjamas underneath his evening suit. Perth's two leading gossip columnists failed to recognize him, even though his shows had been widely broadcast in Australia. One rejoiced in the name Holly Wood. 'More like Milton Keynes,' sighed Everett in a classic put-down when they were eventually introduced, and raised a trouser leg to display his pyjamas as he departed.

He continued to broadcast for Capital for more than a year, until July 1994. Shortly before that Richard Park had taken him aside and told him he thought his show needed 'some more fireworks'. Perhaps both knew it was nearing time to call it a day. By now Everett's health was experiencing those unpredictable and extreme variations that Aids sufferers know all too well. His sense of humour still did not desert him. He became deaf in one ear but told fellow DJ Paul Gambaccini: 'It's a good job Capital Gold is only broadcast in mono.'

His radio career could not have ended on a higher note. In June of that year the Sony Radio Awards, the most prestigious in the industry, presented him with a Gold Award to honour his achievements in radio broadcasting, paying tribute to the way he had 'consistently bewitched audiences'. To a rousing ovation at the Grosvenor House Hotel in London's Park Lane, it was presented to him by one of his heroes, George Martin, the Beatles' producer.

There was an added stress to the health swings that Everett was by now experiencing. In one of the few interviews he gave in that last year, he spoke for many other Aids sufferers when he gave public vent to his irritation with his insurance company, PPP, which would not pay medical expenses of Aids sufferers. A letter to him from PPP in late 1994 said: 'PPP will not pay benefit for treatment of any medical condition which arises in any way from HIV infection, except for the initial diagnosis and the immediate treatment.' The company went on to explain that 'covering people for every conceivable eventuality or need that might arise would make the price for such coverage unrealistically high. For instance we do not pay for non-surgical treatment of medical conditions which are likely to continue or to keep recurring, and this is the basis for excluding from benefit payment for treatment of medical conditions arising from HIV infection. However, we do pay for the cost of making the initial diagnosis of HIV infection and its immediate treatment; our members are entitled to in-patient benefits for one stay of up to 28 days in this regard.'

Everett voiced his disgust, saying: 'I have been with PPP for more than twenty years, and now it is saying it won't pay for anything that arises from my being HIV. I signed up with PPP to be taken care of for the whole of my life, and well before Aids was known about. I think it should look after me. It just isn't fair.'

However, the paper he spoke to about it overplayed its hand and made out that he was financially bereft, causing, to his acute embarrassment, members of the public to send cheques, and even his friend Michael Winner left a message on his answerphone saying: 'Anything you need, Kenny, money, anything – just ask and I'll send it over.' Everett rang him back to assure him that he did not need financial assistance. When Winner asked how he felt, he said: 'Bits are falling off, it's awful.' Everett also wrote him a letter, saying: 'Dear Mikey poohs, Thanks for your note. Very sweet. Didn't know you were a sweetie pie. I thought you were a tyrant! Must be a gimmick. I'm feeling grotesque at the moment. Tea if I recover? Ken.'

In fact Everett was far from depressed or self-pitying. His attitude to life and the death that was inevitable ranged from his father's stoicism to an upbeat bravado. An indication of this came in an interview which he gave to *Hello* in July 1993, posing for their pages like a film star, with his niece Joanna, on whom he doted, supplying the female glamour ingredient the magazine's readers expected. In all the scores and scores of interviews he gave over the years it was probably the only one where he came close to telling the truth about himself and how he felt – choosing to do so, perhaps, with deliberate irony, in a magazine famed for unprobing, artificially upbeat interviews.

Asked if he'd thought about the way he'd like to die, he said: 'Yes. I want to be on a dance floor, and in the middle of a great tune. I'd do an unexpected movement with arms and legs in all directions so that people would part like the Red Sea. Then I'd just slump to the sound of wild applause as I die.'

Interestingly, Everett was asked if he would change anything in his life. He voiced two regrets: 'I don't think I would have said "Let's bomb Russia" at the Tory Party Conference. It was only a joke but it caused an awful furore.' He added: 'I was a very uptight, nervous child and I think I would try to cultivate friendships a lot faster than I did. I was very shy . . . I just wish I'd been more relaxed earlier in life.'

That much certainly seemed to be true, but quickly he once again began to paint a picture of his unhappiness as a child that neither his parents nor sister would recognize; an unhappiness that may have indeed existed in his head or an unhappiness that over four decades since childhood he had convinced himself existed. He said: 'The worst thing that ever happened to me was being a child because I was in a constant state of neurosis about sinning and getting run over before I could confess. I was told that if that happened I would go to hell for ever. My fun only started when I grew up . . . Because I was born in such a down state, and was so neurotic as a child, I've spent a large amount of my life persuading myself to be the opposite – jolly and carefree and frivolous. I know the horrors of Aids, but what's the point of looking ahead to death when you can be getting on with something jolly in the meantime. I haven't made a will or planned a funeral. Spike Milligan has thought of the best inscription for his tombstone: "I told you I was ill . . ." so I can't really beat that.'

Finally he was asked how he would like to be remembered. He answered: 'Oh, as someone who made people laugh a bit. That's probably the best you can do in life. If you can't be a classical composer who leaves behind delightful music, then leave them with a giggle on their lips.

'You should always leave a room with a funny line. Even if you're not thinking of leaving, but you accidentally say a funny line, you should leave anyway. I love to laugh. I love that moment when you're on the floor grasping your sides and you can't breathe. That's my favourite feeling in the world.'

In November 1994 he had what was to be the last of his twice-yearly lunches with Dave Cash. The two chatted merrily, avoiding touching on their respective attitudes to sexuality, as they had done since that heart-to-heart talk nine years before. As they were drinking their coffee a young couple walked by, boy and girl, very trendy, very attractive. Cash's eyes followed the girl. 'Great arse!' he said admiringly. 'Yes,' agreed Everett also lost in admiration, 'hasn't he!' Kenny and Cash burst out laughing together. They were not to meet again.

As well as the love and care of his family in those last years, Everett was sustained by a small number of very close friendships, which in their turn revealed in him a character almost unrecognizable to his fans and acquaintances. His central relationship would be belittled if it were described as just a friendship. It was a five-year relationship which, were it between heterosexuals, would unquestionably be described as a marriage. After some of the excesses of the eighties and the years with Nikolai, Everett found what he had long, very long, been seeking: a life of calm and contentment based around a mutually loving relationship.

Freddie Baldini was an Italian businessman from a wealthy family. To listen to him speak now about Everett, shaking and close to tears, and still devastated by his death, is to realize the inadequacy of terms such as 'boyfriend' and 'partner', which are all that a heterosexual vocabulary, and indeed legal system, allow.

Everett met Freddie in the gay nightclub Heaven in 1989. He was inevitably Everett's opposite: well-built, immaculately dressed, very dark, confident and strikingly handsome. He was sitting with a mutual friend, Simon. 'Who is this good-looking guy, Simon,' said Everett, 'making you look even more drab than you usually do?' Meanwhile Freddie, who had never heard of Everett, was gazing at the stranger with the big eyes and clever conversation. They arranged to meet again. 'We started dancing together,' remembers Freddie, 'and giggling, and from friends we became lovers.'

They lived together in Everett's flat for three years, until Freddie's job took him abroad, after which they would spend weekends and holidays together. They went clubbing; they visited the cinema; they played Lego with Coke Cameron's children; best of all, they went for long walks in the English countryside. Though Everett was 'out', Freddie was not, so their relationship, while known about among their friends, was never public property.

Again, the lack of a proper vocabulary for gay relationships leaves Freddie with a sadness that people may not realize that Everett was effectively married for the last few years of his life. 'Kenny had a relationship and was happy,' he says now. 'It's important that people know we were happy together. Certainly we were like a married couple. There was maximum respect, love and affection; and that will never change and people have to know this. All people talk about with gays together is drugs and sex, but there's something more real, which is life. Kenny was the main reason I stayed in London. I came out with Kenny. Before, everything was touching and running.

'He was very attractive, witty and smart, but also very moody, very easy to have a fight with, because I'm Italian and I'm very moody too. Kenny's main problem was that he would feel uncomfortable everywhere after about two days. If we went on holiday he was ready to leave after two days. At restaurants and in public he would become very uncomfortable. But every day with him was a show. Every day was fun. And we were a family for five years, a family with friends. Kenny had a family until the end. He had me and Kate and Joanna. He was never left alone.'

All who knew the couple said they adored each other. But complete contentment was not in Everett's personality. 'He could be very depressed,' says Freddie. 'Kenny was not easy to deal with. He was a very difficult personality. When he was depressed he didn't speak much, and never told me he was depressed. He never said it was because he was HIV-positive, but he did become very depressed towards the end. He became very moody, got upset easily and would then apologize. A lot of times he was like a frightened child. I felt I wanted to protect him and take care of him, and I could see in his eyes he was frightened of the world. Yes, he had the funny lines at the right times, but I could always see when he was depressed or frightened.'

Towards the end Everett told Freddie he did not want them to be together at his death. 'I don't want you in all this,' he said. 'I don't want to be anywhere else,' Freddie replied. 'I want to be with you. I will miss you a lot and I will never be as comfortable with anyone else.'

A friendship which continued for over ten years or so was with Cleo Rocos, the striking, dark-eyed actress who came as an eighteen-year-old fresh from drama school to audition for *The Kenny Everett Video Show* and ended up playing Miss Whiplash and various similar concoctions on his shows, her screen-filling embonpoint and electric-shock hair often subsuming the diminutive Everett. Once, indeed, he used trick photography to announce the show as a Lilliputian puppet peeking out of her cleavage. 'The difference between men and women,' mused Everett aloud when he saw her rehearsing, 'is that men have testicles and women have chesticles.'

Their friendship became an extraordinary, lengthy, stylized, unconsummated romance. As Cleo told Radio 4 in a tribute programme to Everett: 'Every Friday we would get together, and he would line up all the tunes and I'd wear an evening gown and he'd dress up and he'd draw all the curtains. He used to call it Club 91 because he used to live at number 91. And we'd dance all night until the next afternoon and he wouldn't open the curtains because he'd say the night would last longer and it did and we'd dance and dance and laugh and fall on the floor and laugh and go outside and climb on to his roof and look at all the stars and he never got tired of the good things. He'd give you his soul virtually, and when someone does that you have to treasure it.'

On midsummer night in 1989, Everett even asked her to marry him, waking his friends at two in the morning to share his proposal with them. He took her by the hand and led her on to his balcony, and said: 'I never want to spend any time without you. Would you marry me?' He looked up for the moon and saw instead his satellite dish, but would not be deterred from the romantic gesture. Pointing at it, he exclaimed: 'Marry me and you can half of this.' Eric Gear was one of those woken at two a.m. to be told the news. 'What we want is to get married in an old country church,' said Everett. 'How about your one?' By morning he and Cleo had thought better of the idea. Cleo often likened their relationship to that of the couple in the romantic comedy film *When Harry Met Sally*, because they, like the couple in the film, used to watch television together over the phone and clink their glasses down the line, if they were in different places. Indeed, it was when he invited her round to watch a video of that film for the first time, that he told her he was HIV-positive. Everett stood up, glass in hand, and said: 'Oh, there's just something I want to tell you. I'm HIV-positive. Does that matter to you?'

'I said: "Matter?"' recalls Cleo, '"of course not, don't be stupid." But inside I felt like all my furniture had collapsed . . .' It didn't matter. The two would continue their stylized romance and go on holidays with friends. And Cleo accompanied him when he went to see his parents and sister in Australia.

REINVENTION

She was, everyone who observed them agrees, completely obsessed and besotted with him. When they were away together, staying in separate bedrooms, she would have her alarm wake her at five a.m. so that she could put on her make-up (she never appeared before him without it on) and bring him in his breakfast as he awoke. Whole sections of the day could be spent dancing to the Gypsy Kings on the CD player. At other times they would go into a private, quick-fire repartee which fascinated onlookers. It was a vivid, enormously affectionate relationship surrounded by laughter, criss-crossing between platonic friendship and a love affair, and ending up in a no man's land in between. Certainly, it does not easily lend itself to description or understanding by anyone other than the two people involved. She now has a shrine to him in her home.

But Everett's closest friends did not come from the world of show business at all. Eric Gear worked at a bank in Bond Street when Everett came in for a loan in 1979. He had already been a star on Radio 1, on Capital Radio and on TV. 'What arrangements do you have for a pension?' Gear asked him. 'Don't the government look after that?' asked Everett. Gear swallowed. Could successful people really be that unworldly? He gave Everett advice and a piece of his mind in equal measure, saying at one point: 'Look, I'm just a bloke from an ordinary working-class family myself.' Everett was amazed. Bankers surely, like the one the Beatles sang about in 'Penny Lane', were born rich, with motor cars. But this one was a working-class boy made good, just like him. 'Do you fancy lunch?' he asked Gear.

This stolid banker and his wife Jane, a teacher, both several years older than Everett, became his closest friends and second family. He would go on walking holidays at least once a year with them and with Eric's brother George and his wife Betty, who also became close friends. He stayed with them at their home in Kent, went to their children's weddings and phoned them regularly.

Though Everett would refer to himself playfully as 'the star', he loved the fact that they never treated him as one. They were, he would sometimes say, so cosy. He was one of the family. Once Gear said to him: 'Ken, in bed at night, do you think you're famous because you're so great?' 'Don't be daft,' Everett replied. 'I'm still that frightened little boy from Liverpool.'

When Eric spent ten days in hospital, Everett visited him every day – more visits than even his wife made. When Jane was in hospital, she turned on the *Kenny Everett Show* on Radio 2 and blushed to hear Everett telling the listeners who she was and which hospital she was in, adding: 'If you're passing, you'll recognize her. She's flat on her back with her legs in the air, her usual position.' When she came home to convalesce, he rang her every single day for two months.

Eric Gear became Everett's bank manager, but that was incidental to their friendship. Everett loved being around the couple, loved the domesticity and contentment he found there. He went there some years for Christmas. They had a very traditional celebration with their children and later grandchildren; and Everett, who up till then had not liked Christmas very much, even though it coincided with his birthday, began to love it. He would put the kettle on and make himself a cup of Oxo, as he used to do when he was a boy. 'You're the only ones I really feel at home with,' he told them. And he made them one of his needlepoint tapestries, depicting a teapot. 'You remind me of a comfortable old teapot,' he said.

But with the Gears, as with everyone close to him, he did suffer depression, sitting in their living room for hours and discussing the meaning of life. He was also, Eric and Jane quickly noticed, 'obsessed with religion'. Eric told him frequently: 'Ken, you're so obsessed, one day you will go back to the Church.' Jane is herself a Catholic, originally from a small village in the West of Ireland. Everett would talk and talk to her about aspects of the Roman Catholic service. And then one day in 1986 a very strange thing happened.

Jane helped out at a convent where they rehabilitated alcoholics and drug addicts. In that year she received two medals for her work, medals which had been blessed by the Pope. She showed them to Everett. To her amazement he demanded to have one. 'He almost fought me for one,' she recalls. 'He took it and wouldn't let it go.' At first she thought it was a joke, but he made it clear it wasn't. He needed to have one of those medals, one of those medals blessed by the Pope. Eventually, she let him have one 'and his pleasure knew no bounds'.

Yet at other times he would round on her, storming: 'It's all hypocrisy. The Catholic Church is big business. How can you really believe in God?' Eric recalls: 'He wouldn't let the subject go. Deep down he was deeply worried. I used to quote that Jesuit maxim: "Give me a child for the first seven years and you may do what you like with him afterwards."' Everett often asked Eric and Jane to pray for him.

The Gears knew all of Everett's serious boyfriends, and had no problems with his homosexuality. Yet it became evident to them that he did. 'You don't know how lucky you are to have a conventional family,' he would say to them quietly and often. He would sit and play cards with them, eat fish and chips and go to the local pub. And he would rage against God for making him like he was. 'Next time I come back,' he said to them with a classic backhanded compliment, 'I'm coming back just like you, really ordinary.'

He would talk too about Liverpool, though perhaps it was the Liverpool that had taken root in his head rather than the Liverpool he had actually lived in. He and Jane would have *Monty Python*-style arguments over who had been brought up the poorer. As Jane had had no shoes until the age of fifteen, there was really no contest. But Everett persisted. 'We had a lavatory down the back garden,' he said and sat back triumphantly, until Jane put an end to the conversation. 'We had no lavatory at all,' she said in her soft but firm Irish lilt.

Another obsession Everett would discuss endlessly with the Gears was life after death. He said: 'When the first one of us dies, shall we come back to let the others know?' It was not something they felt an equal interest in, and thought no more about it. But both Eric and Jane will attest and be unable to explain that when, in a small private ceremony, they interred part of their friend's ashes in his former garden in the Cotswolds, the church bells suddenly started to ring.

Everett played long and often with the Gear children. Only once did he turn to Eric and Jane and muse aloud: 'It must be wonderful to have a child of your own, to be able to say they have your blood in their veins.' Eric says now: 'My belief is that if he had ever fathered a child of his own he would have been very good with it. He was very sensitive, very kind and gentle.'

Eric could be gruff with him, and Everett accepted it from him. He would sometimes bring him down to earth when he rhapsodized over a boyfriend. 'But he's got such lovely, big, brown eyes,' Everett pleaded. 'So has a rabbit,' barked Gear. Once Eric talked to him about the dangers of the gay scene in the eighties. 'It's all right for you,' said Everett. Gear had no answer.

In the summer of 1994 they went on their last walking holiday together. Standing on a bluff in Dovedale in the Derbyshire Peak District, Everett turned to Eric and said: 'It wouldn't be as beautiful as this in heaven. Wouldn't you like to be here for eternity?' Eric would ensure that some of his ashes were interred on that very spot.

Another time Everett came up to Jane and pointed to a church. 'What do you think of that church, Jane?' he asked. Jane had stopped attending church. Everett said to her quietly: 'How do you think your parents feel now that you don't go to church?'

It came as no surprise to Eric when, a few weeks before Everett's death, he received a phone call from Kate. 'You won't believe this,' Everett's sister said, 'but he has just asked me if he could go to Mass next Sunday.'

14

LETTING GO

'You're going straight to heaven, kid. Have a good trip, baby.'
                    Kate's last words to her younger brother

In January 1995 Kate Horgan put her own life on hold. She left her husband, grown-up children, friends and career in Australia and returned to England to be with her brother. For the next three months, the last three months of his life, she spent virtually every waking hour with him. She fed him, she mopped his brow, she made him laugh. She would wrap him up warm and take him for walks and drives. She stayed in London for a further six months after his death to put his affairs in order. Several months were spent re-recording eighty hours of his tapes to give to the National Sound Archive. She organized his funeral. She held his hand as he died.

Journalists who wrote inaccuracies about Everett found a Mrs Horgan on the phone giving them a calm, scrupulously polite but not easily forgotten reprimand. She had slipped back more than forty years. Her brother was once again little Maurice Cole in Liverpool. And any problems he might have were also her problems. Any school bullies who thought they could push this skinny, sensitive lad around would have to answer to his big sister, Cathy.

Everett, too, was going back. The years of reinvention were slipping away. To the surprise of his parents, they began to receive faxes from him in Australia signed 'Mo'.

Kate had been with him in London the previous November. They had gone with Eric and Jane Gear to the Cotswolds for a picnic – he wanted to do it one last time – and had made a bizarre sight, picnicking at a folly near the village of Broadway in the freezing-cold weather. Shortly afterwards she returned to Australia and he went with her, as he was in relatively good health. They jogged on the beach together even when the temperature reached forty degrees Centigrade. They ate out at restaurants and he talked of moving to Australia for six months of the year. When he began to get stomach pains, she thought it might be the food, but it wasn't.

'He was beginning to be not well,' remembers Kate. 'And he was going back to London and a wild fiftieth-birthday party, and I knew that was not going to do any good at all. And I was fearful for him. But we tried to make light of it together. I said: "What do you want for Christmas?" He said: "Psychedelic flowers." But the little brat was so out of it he didn't even remember getting my flowers. He had a wild time and his health suffered. At this point we had been faxing every few days. Suddenly the faxes stopped coming. And he wasn't answering the phone. I was a bit panic-stricken. Eventually I got him, and said: "I've got a suitcase packed and I'm ready to come." He said: "Oh? Really?" I could feel him light up. And I said I'd be delighted to come over to London for a month. He said: "My days of wielding a Hoover are over."'

Initially Kate moved her belongings into her son's London flat, which was round the corner from Everett's fifth-floor Kensington home. When she first went into Everett's flat he was lying on his yellow sofa eating a bowl of corn flakes. His face was the same colour as the sofa. She set about like Mary Poppins, cooking and cleaning. But the first night, as she was leaving to return to her son's flat, Everett begged her not to go. She stayed, sleeping in her clothes in the spare bedroom. There was no lift in the block of flats, and the next day she lugged her suitcases up the six storeys to her bedroom in her brother's apartment and did not leave him. The one month she had intended to stay was to turn into ten.

She listened to music with Everett. Together they watched his favourite television programmes, the American comedies *Ellen* and *Roseanne* and the British comedienne Jo Brand. She accompanied him on the hospital visits, which he dreaded, for endoscopies and colonoscopies, or for painful injections into his thin veins, and she got to know the fantastic team of doctors, nurses and helpers at the Chelsea and Westminster hospital; and when they did discover that one nun had upset Everett – he awoke once to find her making the sign of the cross over him and saying: 'May your sins be forgiven' – Kate had her removed from the case.

Everett hated hospitals and made it clear he did not want to die, or even stay, in one. She arranged for specialist nurses to attend him at home, where a saline drip and morphine pump were attached to him. His bedroom became a miniature medical centre, and he was able to take advantage of the unsung but brilliant structure that now exists of home help, shopping and other services for Aids patients who want to stay at home, though it all had to be approached tactfully as this patient cherished his independence.

The strain told on them both. Kate's husband came over from Australia at the end of March to spend some time with them. Conor recalls: 'When I got to London, Kate was a shadow, she was skin and bones. She had lost her voice and she had lost weight. There was a point in that summer where I thought we were going to have a second funeral.'

Brother and sister talked long and intensely over those last three months. 'It was a condensed time,' says Kate. One evening, sitting by the fire, Everett said to her: 'You're so lucky. You have three fabulous children. I wish I had a family. I haven't achieved anything with my life.' She replied: 'But you have. You are unique. You have brought so much pleasure to millions of people. You're a genius.' He denied this, then leapt up. 'OK, let's look it up in the dictionary,' he said. He went to the bookshelf and took down his battered old dictionary and looked up 'genius'. He read aloud the definition, which stressed an aptitude for creative activity. And he pondered. 'It described him perfectly,' says Kate. 'And it seemed to dawn on him for the first time what his talent was. Ev's whole problem was he didn't really like himself. He lacked a lot of confidence in a way, which was a tragedy.'

For Everett, some days were better than others. One afternoon Kate phoned Barry Cryer and invited him over. As he arrived, Everett brightened. Cryer was taken aback at first to see his friend horizontal on the sofa, but instantly laughed and said: 'I don't want to hear how you are. It's very boring. You're a melodramatic old queen.' Everett returned the banter, and the two spent the afternoon joking and reminiscing. Kate was able to leave them alone for a couple of hours.

Once, brother and sister went for a walk in Richmond Park. He loved being in the open, and this was a real treat. He still lay in the sun on his balcony whenever he could. It was a favoured place, the balcony with its artificial grass which he had even hoovered regularly, so fastidious was he. Only now he was too weak to do even that.

On another day they walked down Kensington High Street until Everett became too breathless, when they repaired to the Britannia pub, the old haunt of Richard Burton, Peter O'Toole and Richard Harris. Everett had been teetotal for some time now, but, perhaps inspired by the actors' famous binges, he announced to his sister: 'I'll have morphine and a lager chaser.'

Tentatively, they began to discuss the funeral. Dr Gazzard, the Aids specialist who attended Everett, had said he should have another six months to live, but Everett knew enough about it to realize that it was an unpredictable affliction. He told Kate that when he had attended the funeral of his friend Edward Duke, acclaimed for his one-man Jeeves and Wooster show, he had been much moved by the funeral and requiem mass at the Church of the Immaculate Conception in Mayfair. 'It was the most moving funeral I've ever been at. I would adore that, but I guess it won't be possible,' he said sadly. Kate replied: 'If that's what you want, that's what you shall have, I promise you.'

Some days the tragedy turned into comedy. On one occasion Freddie arrived back, after a weekend away, with a touch of flu. Everett had been sleeping, motionless for some time. Freddie came in and turned for sympathy to Kate and Conor. 'I'm a-fucking dying here,' he moaned in a stronger than usual Italian accent. Everett emerged from his deep sleep. His body seemed to gather strength and sat itself up. He glared at his lover and relatives. 'Ex-CUSE ME!' he said in his campest tones. 'I'm the one who's fucking dying around here.' That point established, he swooned back on to his pillow and left the world to sort itself out as the others burst into a rare fit of laughter.

But sometimes there was no comedy to alleviate the tragedy. For Freddie, who left his job to stay in the flat for the last three months of his lover's life, watching his partner die was an agony which he still finds hard to describe without breaking down. 'He had blisters inside him. He was literally falling apart. It was a nightmare for me watching it. I wouldn't wish this experience on my worst enemy, if I had one. I remember Kenny in bed staring at the ceiling. He wouldn't speak to me. He wouldn't speak to anybody. I said: "Please speak to me. It will make me feel useful." One day he said to me: "I feel so useless. I cannot go to work. I cannot do anything." I said: "Well, Kenny, you exist, you are here for me. You will have nice days again."

Some days were worse than others. He had already contracted and recovered from TB and pneumonia. And his skin was very tender. It was painful for him to be touched. Some nights were especially bad. A week before his death, Kate and Conor came into his room in the middle of the night. He was very agitated and removing the morphine pump. 'I'm going,' he said. 'I want to go.' His face was swollen up. He had been vomiting, which, as a cleanliness fanatic, he particularly loathed. His eardrum had recently burst and caused him enormous pain.

'Don't,' pleaded Kate. 'Taking the morphine away won't kill you. It will only put you in more pain. Don't do anything till the morning. You'll feel better then.' She and Conor sat on the bed and began to cheer him up a little. When they talked about the Beatles, he became almost animated. 'Did you ever meet Yoko Ono?' Kate asked. Suddenly Everett transformed his face. To their astonishment he looked Japanese. He started speaking in a voice that was pure Yoko Ono: every nuance, every inflection. They were convulsed with laughter. They were getting the last, private Kenny Everett show.

The laughter subsided. 'Ev,' said Kate, 'would you like to see a priest?' He nodded.

Conor rang the local Catholic church, Our Lady of Victories, in Kensington. It was just before midnight. Father William Hofton, the priest on duty, answered and sounded weary. People had a habit of ringing at unearthly hours just to find out the time of the next day's mass. Conor explained the situation, and Father William said he would come the following day. In fact, he arrived within minutes. He sat down at Everett's bedside, clasped his hand, and said: 'Let go, Kenny, let go.'

Kate and Conor left them alone. After half an hour the priest went. The change in Everett was marked. 'Suddenly he looked at peace,' Kate remembers. 'His skin looked better. Even the swelling on his face had gone down. A new light had come into him.'

Father William recalls now: 'I said: "Let go" because he was dying, and there's an element in people that we all hold on to life because it's precious. I think he had fought as long as he could. So when I gave him the sacraments, I said: "Come on Kenny, let go, you're at peace with God. Your relationship with God is well."'

Father William was a regular visitor over the next week, Everett's last. As it happens, he was one of the very few visitors. When Everett died, the number of people claiming close friendship with him suggested there had been queues of celebrities on the streets of Kensington to come and see him in those last weeks. The startling truth is that in the three months before he died, not half a dozen people came to visit. Only slightly more telephoned the flat. The fulsome avowals of friendship expressed in the public prints are not always translated into action.

As luck would have it, if luck it was, there could have been no better priest for Kenny Everett than the one who answered the phone that night. Father William, still a young man, with an infectious, open enthusiasm and utterly lacking in pomposity, had been a professional musician before entering the priesthood and knew a number of people in the theatre. Many of his parishioners in Kensington were gay, many had Aids. He had little time for clergy or indeed non-clergy who passed judgement on people in such a situation. His role was clear. 'The priest is not there to be judgemental,' he says. 'They want to be loved and to be assured. If I can bring some peace, that is God working through the priesthood. Many Christians can be judgemental, but certainly Christ wasn't.' And the icing on the cake was that Father William was a Kenny Everett fan.

There was an instant chemistry between the two. Father William described to me with striking honesty and self-deprecation a situation that is rarely spoken about, a time in which he feels he received help as well as giving help. 'There was a very nervous, frightened man, obviously in some pain and I was very nervous. What can you say to someone who is dying? How can you help them? The fact that we were both quite natural in what we were trying to do for each other just cemented the relationship. Kenny helped me tremendously as a priest. I am very squeamish with people who are sick and one of my closest friends had died of Aids. For a priest it's wonderful to help someone in that very intimate part of their lives, going from one world to the next.'

As Everett's confessor, Father William is prohibited from revealing any details of what Everett said to him in their talks over those last days, but he says he was very moved by the dying man's honesty and integrity. Homosexuality, though, was not mentioned. What was clear to Father William was that Everett had been thinking about his life and his faith for a long time. He had been treated badly by the church in the past and he felt cast out. So for thirty years he had shunned it. Being HIV-positive had concentrated his mind, and he wanted to put his life into perspective. He did, Father William agrees, 'ask if he could come back' to the church. And his conversations with the priest brought him tremendous relief. Father William, who, like all visitors to Everett's flat, could not help but notice the meticulous tidiness that Everett insisted on, saw his spiritual return as in some ways an extension of this fastidiousness.

'It's true what they say about once a Catholic,' says Father William. 'There's this in-built fear that if you die outside the church you go to hell. That fear was there with him . . . When someone is dying, it takes a lot of courage and trust, especially when you've had such a bad time with the church . . . But he wanted to put everything in order. He was an extremely tidy, fastidious person. He was a very simple man. He realized he had to put his spiritual life in order and be right with God. After the sacraments and our talks, that side of his life was put at peace. He wasn't frightened at all. That calm and that peace was wonderful to see.'

Each day the priest would come. Sometimes they would converse; sometimes when Everett was too weak to talk, Father William would talk and he would just listen. Sometimes Father William lay on the bed next to him to talk with him. They prayed together each day. Over those last days, Everett received from him all the sacraments, communion, and was anointed with holy oil several times.

Everett, typically, had not made a will. It was not so much that it was a reminder of mortality – more that it was a reminder of reality. Making a will would have involved thinking about finances, solicitors, estates, executors. Death he could handle. The bureaucracy of life bored him silly.

Nevertheless, by April Eric Gear had convinced him that he must make a will. If he did not make one, then his parents, as next of kin, would automatically inherit everything and be saddled with the legal business and traumas that that could involve. Everett agreed this must not happen. He was asked what he wanted to bequeath and to whom. He said he wanted to leave everything to Kate, and that she should look after his parents and make bequests to his closest friends. At this point he burst out crying and said to Eric: 'I've got so few friends.' He was wrong. Just as he underestimated his charm and attractiveness throughout his life, so now he underestimated the number of people who liked him. It was the only time in his illness that he had cried, apart from when he asked Dr Gazzard how long he had to live and learned that his life was to be played out in months not years.

On Monday morning he signed the will, which had already been drawn up, with Father William and his doctor present. The doctor climbed on to the bed and helped him to sit up. Everett asked for his glasses, read the will and signed it. By this stage his hand was so unsure that the signature went almost vertically down the page, but all present attest that he was perfectly lucid, alert and clear in his mind.

He had not worked for some time, and he had never saved nor capitalized, in terms of financial investment, on his worldwide popularity. So there was not a huge amount of cash to leave. The estate came to £350,000, but this was almost totally accounted for by his two-storey Kensington flat and his BMW car. Kate also gave a number of personal items to her brother's closest friends. Lee, who was not named in the will, was presented with a tapestry of a cockerel that she and Everett had once worked on together.

Making the will was not actually thought of as a last-minute gesture. It was still believed that he had at least several months, possibly considerably more, to live, and would enjoy the spring and summer. His niece, Joanna, was getting married later that year. In her uncle's bedroom she gave a little fashion parade of her wedding outfits. He became sad and said how much he wished he could be at the wedding. Joanna decided to bring the wedding forward to June and to relocate it from Australia to Tuscany. That way Everett could be at the wedding of his only niece, to whom he had become exceptionally close over the preceding few years. He also talked quite seriously of emigrating to live in Perth, Western Australia, and so be near his sister and parents, niece and nephews.

*　　　*　　　*

On Sunday 2 April Freddie went away on a business trip, telling Everett he would see him in a few days. He never saw him again.

The health of Aids sufferers can veer dramatically and rapidly from one extreme to another. Everett signed his will on that same Sunday. On Monday night his health deteriorated, and by the following morning it was clear that the end was very near. His breathing was very heavy and he could not talk at all.

Father William came to visit early that morning. 'I talked with him for an hour and a half. I just talked about God, about Heaven. We can't describe it, but we can comfort people. I read the Psalms to him, and held his hand. He received the last rites, which includes a general confession. I anointed him that morning. The sacraments were celebrated every day, and he seemed to draw great strength from that. In his face you could see the great relief the sacraments would bring.' Father William spoke the prayer beginning: 'Go Christian soul to the God who created you, to the Son who redeemed you and the Holy Spirit who breathed life into you.' One of the nurses remarked: 'That was powerful stuff.'

'It brought dignity to his death,' says Kate. 'He was incredibly peaceful and strong.' When the priest left, Kate came and sat with her brother. 'You're going straight to heaven, kid. Have a good trip, baby,' she said softly. He looked at her and nodded. Shortly before ten a.m. Eric Gear arrived at the Kensington flat and sat with Everett for a while.

'Ken was propped up in bed and breathing roughly,' he remembers. 'There was fruit by the bed. It was a lovely, sunny day. I said: "Don't try to talk to me, Ken. I'll talk to you."' Gear remembered a scene from a film he had seen, and put Everett's hand in his. He said he would ask questions and Everett should squeeze once for yes and twice for no. He said Everett should eat some fruit. Didn't he want to get fit again? Everett squeezed once. 'It's a lovely day. Don't you wish you were out walking with us?' Everett squeezed once, very hard. Then Gear said: 'I've got to go and have a pee now. Shall I send Kate in?' Everett squeezed once.

Kate came in and held his hand. Jo Gurnett also arrived and sat with her. Gear went to the lavatory. When he returned, Kenny Everett was dead. 'He was breathing with great difficulty,' says Kate. 'And then, he wasn't breathing any more.'

Jo Gurnett knew how strong the press interest would be, and advised that the body be taken to the undertakers very quickly as photographers would soon be arriving in the street outside. Kate would have liked her brother to lie where he was for rather longer, but agreed. Jo Gurnett prepared a press release. The doctor from the Aids clinic urged her strongly to state that he had died of an Aids-related illness. It would encourage other sufferers, he explained, to know that Aids was acknowledged and not disguised as something else.

The next day the death of Kenny Everett was front-page news in all the national papers, both tabloid and broadsheet. The tributes were heartfelt, emotional and lavish, mainly concentrating on his radio career, where, it was widely agreed, he had no equal. So effusive was the praise that the punning pocket cartoon on the front page of the *Independent* showed Everett entering Heaven, the nightclub, as an angel with a halo above his head, something of an irony considering his long and tortured ambivalence over Catholicism, let alone his lifestyle. But in the welter of public affection that was being expressed for the man, such unconscious ironies were overlooked.

His friends were at first angry that he wasn't going to see the spring and summer after all, and had died well in advance of the doctors' predictions. But soon they came to realize that he had died with dignity and remained lucid until very near the end. Some of the awful symptoms, including the severe skin lesions and premature ageing that can afflict Aids sufferers, had been spared him. In Australia, poor Mr and Mrs Cole barely had time to grieve. Reporters scurried over their retirement village trying to trap them into giving a quote. One even phoned from London to ask: 'How do you feel about your son's death?'

Father William, who had become touchingly close to Everett over that last week, realized with regret that he had not thanked him for the fun and pleasure he had given so many people, a point he made at the funeral. A number of people connected with Everett have claimed extrasensory experiences relating to him since his death. It is odd to hear of one from a Roman Catholic priest. And yet Father William likewise claims such an experience. He says: 'I was shocked and surprised, when two days after he died, I was in my bedroom at night cleaning my teeth and getting ready for bed. I wasn't thinking about Kenny at all. Suddenly in the room there was this very strong smell — it was the smell of Kenny's flat. I turned round to the door and said: Thank you for all the fun. It's the only experience of that kind I have ever had.'

For Lee, the unexpectedly early death was a shattering blow. The reconciliation she confidently believed would happen had not occurred. And Everett had died while she still felt anger towards him — something she found difficult to cope with. However, she now thinks of him with great affection, and says his spirit has been in contact with her on many occasions and with good will.

His sister Kate looks back on a brother she adored and a talent to amuse and outrage that she still delights in. 'But he was never comfortable with himself,' she says now, 'never happy with the way he was. He craved a simple normality, and from the age of nineteen he never had it.'

The funeral was on Monday 10 April. Kate had dressed her brother in his favourite clothes, his blue and white houndstooth-check jacket, cream drill trousers, white socks and white sneakers. A misunderstanding over a typically flamboyant gesture by Cleo Rocos resulted in her absence from the ceremony. She and Everett had a long-running private joke concerning bananas, and would present each other with gifts based around a banana motif. After he died, Cleo, who had already surprised the family by giving a lengthy interview to the *Sun*, sent 150 bananas in a four-foot-long red toy sports car to the undertakers with the wish that it be placed on top of one of the hearses and transported to the funeral. The family appreciated that it was intended as a loving gesture but vetoed the idea when advised that it would need a separate hearse to transport the car full of bananas, and that the press would most certainly take it out of context. The undertaker conveyed to Cleo the family's veto, but did so a little bluntly. She assumed wrongly that meant she was not invited and made her farewells in the funeral parlour, giving Everett a final manicure as she did so.

Everett's last request was honoured. After the cremation, half his ashes were interred under the willow tree in the garden in the Cotswolds. Half were interred on a bluff at Dovedale in the Peak District, the scene of so many walking holidays.

The funeral, held at the Church of the Immaculate Conception in Farm Street, managed to be both a starry and a dignified affair. It included a requiem mass, as Everett had so dearly hoped,. and Puccini's Symphonic Prelude, which he had chosen on *Desert Island Discs* as the most beautiful record he had ever heard and the one which he would like 'to be on the gramophone as I am hoiked aloft in a ray of God's lovely sunbeam'. (It had so entranced listeners to that programme that it was later released as a single.) The sun streamed in through the stained glass. Father William had chosen Fauré's *Requiem*, and 'Strawberry Fields Forever', Everett's favourite pop record, was played at the cremation. There were Bible readings from his niece Joanna and from Barry Cryer and Jo Gurnett. Terry Wogan had wanted to give one of the readings, but there was not space in the programme. Father William knew that whatever he said would be in the press, so he wanted to be sure to say something that would be helpful to the family and to people with Aids. He said: 'All of you are asking: "Where is Kenny now?" I'm going to tell you. Kenny is with God, because that is where I sent him.' He added: 'The one thing I forgot to say to Kenny was thank you for the joy and fun and pleasure he brought to millions of people.' He also said that Kenny had a great sense of humour, which is a gift of God. He would have a very welcome place in Heaven because God has a sense of humour.

Father William understates it now by saying that that little speech got him into 'a lot of trouble'. He received hate mail and abuse. He wrote back to his accusers saying they did not know of the true God, who has compassion.

Among the wreaths was one from Ringo Starr and another from the rock group Queen, with the late Freddie Mercury's cousin adding that it was also from 'Freddie in spirit'. The wreath from Cleo had the message: 'Muchachito, for your journey to the land of the smiling fruit and bongeley glee-filled cherubs. Don't cha cha without me. I will love you and miss you forever. All my love always, Cleo.' Another wreath had the more simple message: 'Goodbye son, love you, mum and dad', and another 'Goodbye baby, I shall miss you always until we meet again, Kate.'

Barry Cryer still expected the coffin to open and the cheeky face to peek out with a grin and a Goon-style 'Hulloo'. As Cryer was leaving with Jo Gurnett, a helicopter flew above them. They both said simultaneously, referring to Everett's notorious unpunctuality and forgetfulness: 'It's Ev. Late again.'

The service was packed with the stars of Everett's profession. Only a very small number of them had really been close friends. But colleagues and friends alike were visibly moved as they paid tribute. Jo Gurnett looked round at one point and whispered to herself, as if infected by his self-doubt: 'There you are, he *was* loved.'

Paul Gambaccini said afterwards: 'The entire A team of the profession turned out with the exception of the very youngest. In other words there they were — Wogan, Edmonds, Freeman, Blackburn, Tarrant, Dave Cash. This was a case where no one imposed their ego on the proceedings. Everyone was solemn, because everyone knew this was the master. And everyone knew they owed so much to him because he'd helped make the profession popular.'

But it was an A team that lacked some key players. His parents were far away in Australia. Some of his male lovers were either dead, seriously ill or long vanished. Cleo Rocos's banana gift meant she stayed at home. Some who had been important in his career — Angela Bond for one — could not face the anguish of being present.

Dave Cash did attend, but it quickly proved too painful. He may never have fully come to terms with Everett's lifestyle or his politics. But he had loved him as a friend, and their careers had been intertwined since they first sat on a converted minesweeper listening to tapes of American radio shows.

On the morning of the funeral, Cash was telephoned by his old chum Peter Sarstedt, the singer who had a massive hit in the sixties with 'Where Do You Go To My Lovely?' 'I'm not letting you go there alone,' said Sarstedt. He picked Cash up and drove him to the church. Cash avoided his old Radio 1 colleagues, Wogan, Blackburn, Gambaccini and the rest, knowing he couldn't face up to a showbiz funeral. He picked a pew at the back with Sarstedt. But before long he had broken out in tears, and Sarstedt took him out well before the end of the service.

They went to a nearby pub, where Sarstedt ordered four double Jack Daniels and poured three of them into Cash's glass. A few hours later he poured Cash into bed.

The next morning Dave Cash returned to the church. This time it was empty and silent. He lit a candle for Everett and then went to sit alone in the tiny cloistered garden belonging to the church; an incongruous, solitary patch of peaceful greenery in the middle of Mayfair. He sat silently, thinking back over the years he had watched his infant radio partner grow into stardom. But from all those years one image kept coming into his mind.

It was back on the Radio London ship in the disc jockeys' mess. There they all were, cult heroes, pirates, studs, swigging their cans of lager, feeling adventurous, rebellious, mould-breaking and, above all, illegal. Suddenly a little elfin face peeked round the galley doorway, and said in a camp Northern accent: 'Who'd like a nice cup of tea? I've just got pot brewing.'

Cash looked at the church where the day before he had wept uncontrollably. But this time his eyes filled with tears of laughter.